Let's Go Camping

CAMP FACILITIES

WATER

Almost every campground has a water supply (and all the ones in this book do). The majority will have water on tap — sourced from the town mains, tanks or springs — but sometimes you will have to fetch it from a nearby river or stream. You will often see notices advising you to boil or treat water before drinking, but in the absence of official signage, it's up to you to determine the quality of your water supply. If you are unsure, treat it — giardiasis (a nasty intestinal upset caused by the minuscule parasite *Giardia lamblia*) is a high price to pay for bravado, impatience or a lack of suitable equipment.

Here are three methods for ensuring your water is fit to drink:

1. **Boiling**
   Three minutes on a rolling boil is sufficient. This is the most effective method.
2. **Chemical treatment**
   Usually iodine or chlorine tablets — they take about 30 minutes to work.
2. **Filtering**
   Water filters are widely available from outdoors shops.

Be considerate in your water use. Many regions experience water shortages during the summer months and camps in these places may have a limited supply. Use water sparingly and take short showers.

ABLUTION FACILITIES

All commercial campgrounds have bathroom facilities, usually communal showers, toilets and sinks. However, the showers are likely to be very busy first thing in the morning and around early evening — life will be easier if you avoid these times.

Basic campsites (such as those managed by DOC) will probably only have toilets, and a sink if you're lucky. If you choose to bathe in a nearby lake, river or stream instead, don't use soap. Alternatively, draw water from the spigot or other source and use it to wash well away from waterways. Once you've finished, tip the grey water into the ground where the soil will filter it before it returns to the water table.

DOC is upgrading many of its campsites' facilities to include comparatively pleasant composting and even flush toilets. However, expect to encounter a good number of old-fashioned long-drops. We recommend that you always carry a supply of toilet paper and don't peer too closely into dark corners (especially at night).

Use toilets whenever you get the chance. Should you get caught short on a walk, it's perfectly okay to go au naturel: just make sure you choose a spot at least 100 m away from tracks, picnic areas or water sources, dig a hole at least 15 cm deep and, when you're done, cover your waste and paper well.

COOKING FACILITIES

Holidays are an opportunity to indulge yourself and try something new, and a camping trip ought to be no exception. While you might be eating similar fare to what you do at home, everything tastes better when it's eaten outside or earned by a day's adventures.

And while you're on the road, besides the usual holiday treats of ice cream and fish and chips, you might like to splurge on some local specialities. Who can resist a Gisborne chardonnay, Kapiti cheeses, Marlborough cherries, West Coast whitebait or Central Otago stone fruit? The more intrepid may even want to catch their dinner — by packing a fishing rod and acquiring a licence where required.

Camp kitchens range from the most basic of shelters, which may not even have a tap or sink, to fully equipped facilities with many of the appliances you have at home. Your average camp kitchen will have bench space, sinks (with hot water), at least one fridge, hot plates and maybe microwaves and toasters. Many will also have a water-boiler and perhaps an oven. Some commercial campgrounds have barbecues and the most generous will supply gas free of charge. The majority of camp kitchens don't provide pots, pans and utensils, however. We recommend you always carry your own equipment.

Almost all commercial campgrounds have fridges and freezers. However, during peak times, especially around Christmas–New Year, they will probably be full to bursting. Be considerate of others: refrigerate only what you need and use your chillybin for overflow.

In basic campgrounds with little or no kitchen facilities, you will need to bring all your own cooking equipment, including a portable barbecue or gas stove. See Cooking Out of the Kitchen for more tips on cooking in the outdoors.

If cooking with gas, always check the connection between the gas cylinder and grill, stove or fuel line before lighting. Ensure that gas cylinders are secured safely in a well-ventilated area when in storage.

Never cook with gas in enclosed areas. Carbon monoxide poisoning — the silent killer — is a real possibility. There is also a serious fire risk.

LAUNDRY

Most commercial campgrounds will, at least, have a washing machine, and many will have a dryer. Washing lines are almost always provided, but you'll need to bring your own pegs. If there isn't a washing line, an elasticated line stretched between two trees will do nicely. If you're desperate to launder in a DOC campsite, use biodegradable detergent and wash well away from waterways.

COOKING OUT OF THE KITCHEN

If you're cooking at a commercial campground with ample facilities, your camp cuisine is limited only by your own imagination and taste. However, meal times at DOC campgrounds or those with little or no facilities are a trifle more challenging. Here a few things to consider:

- Plan your meals in advance and make sure you have all the ingredients. You may be more than an hour away from the nearest shop.

- Know your equipment. If you haven't used your stove before, test it before you leave home.

- Take more than enough fuel. Stone-cold saveloys are no meal for the hungry.

- Use your perishables first. Eat your fresh foods while they're fresh — save dried and canned goods till last.

- Many great meals can be made with long-life products such as risotto,

packet pasta and tinned fish. A supply of UHT milk will mean you can always have a bowl of cereal and a cuppa.

- Keep it simple. One-pot wonders are the way to go — less cooking time, less fuel and less washing up.

- Spice it up. You can't take your whole pantry away with you, but there's no reason why you can't take small quantities or sachets of ready-mixed herbs and spices. Our favourites are hot chilli, curry pastes and Mediterranean herbs. Plenty of garlic helps, too.

- Avoid getting detergent into our waterways. Wash dishes in a bucket or bowl well away from streams, rivers and lakes, use detergent sparingly and tip your grey water into the ground so it can be filtered before returning to the water table.

- Food scraps attract vermin and should be disposed of properly. Wrap them and place in bins provided, or take them away with you.

RUBBISH

Take nothing but photos, leave nothing but footprints. Many of the places you visit will have rubbish and recycling bins, but as you move deeper into our wild places these facilities become sparse — as is evident by the litter which lies around our road-end campgrounds, parks and reserves. This rubbish is not only unsightly, it's also harmful to humans and wildlife and attracts vermin.

You and you alone are responsible for your rubbish. Here are some guidelines:

• Reduce the amount of rubbish you produce. Buy products with minimal packaging and dispose of it responsibly.

• Re-use what you can, for example plastic shopping bags. Refill your water bottles where you can — most of New Zealand's tap water is perfectly drinkable.

• Recycle. An increasing number of commercial campgrounds have a recycling centre: use them when you can. Where no recycling facilities are available, pack your recyclables and dispose of them when you next pass a recycling station. Local i-SITE offices will be able to tell you where the nearest one is.

• Always use the rubbish bins provided, and be prepared for places where there may be no bins by bringing your own rubbish bags (re-using those shopping bags, perhaps?). Take every skerrick of refuse away with you when you go.

• If you come across other people's rubbish, be the better person: remove their rubbish as well as your own. Leave the place tidier than when you arrived.

• Don't burn plastics — they release noxious fumes, including dioxins, into the atmosphere.

• Use only designated dump stations (see page 14).

• Follow the New Zealand Environmental Care Code (see pages 17–18).

OTHER FACILITIES

Most commercial campgrounds offer an array of additional facilities, including internet access, television lounges and playgrounds, as indicated by the symbols on page 19. Any other useful facilities are mentioned within the campground descriptions.

VISIT OAMARU

A boat on the shore of Lake Benmore, North Otago

TENTING TIPS

A tent is your ticket to adventure, allowing you the flexibility to roam far and wide, at low cost, with the benefits of fresh air, fun and amazing views right outside your bedroom. You may even discover (or rediscover) a little romance. Many New Zealanders are skilful at tenting, demonstrated by unfailingly competent pitchings and — quite hilariously at times — the most ingenious rig-ups creating sprawling, multi-tent communes complete with beer fridge, fairy-light gazebos and the family standard flying high overhead. Talk about a home away from home!

Set off unprepared or ill-equipped, though, and there could be tears. The cornerstone of any happy camping trip is a dependable tent, particularly as New Zealand's changeable weather means you're likely to experience a wide range of conditions.

If you don't already own a tent, or are looking to buy a new one, it's worth doing your homework. There are hundreds of tents to choose from, and most will look fantastic fresh out of the box. But not all are created equal. While price is generally a good indicator of quality, it's not always the case and is not the only factor to consider.

Tents vary greatly in size and weight. If you'll always be camping out of the back of the car, you can (within reason) disregard the matter of weight and bulk. A large, multi-room tent may be challenging to pitch but will be comfortable — especially for families,

and particularly on rainy days when you may be cooped up inside (heaven forbid) and be glad of that extra space. If you're a tramper, however, you'll be carrying your tent at some stage, so unless you want to buy two tents, you'll be restricted to one that weighs less than about 5 kg (preferably less than 3 kg).

Beyond the tent itself, there are other factors which will dictate your happiness once you've arrived at the campground. Here are just a few:

Seek out the shade
In the middle of summer you'll be glad of respite from the sun, especially in the early mornings when you're trying to have a lie-in.

Head for shelter
If the wind whips up, you'll be better off in the lee of trees, a hedgerow or shrubbery (although be wary of branches that could fall on you). In exposed situations, a strategically parked car can make a good windbreak.

Stay high and dry
Pitch your tent on the high ground, and never camp too close to rivers and streams.

Make the most of your site
Although car-camping allows you to bring as much gear as you can cram into your vehicle, most campgrounds will allocate you a space little bigger

than your living room. To make the most of every inch of it, pitch your tent in one corner then put up an awning, shade sail, gazebo or sun umbrella. Combined with a groundsheet and outdoor furniture and hey presto — you've got an alfresco lounge. Those with limited car space would be wise to at least pack a rubber-backed picnic blanket: it will allow you to lounge around outside or lie under the stars at night.

Be prepared for adverse weather
The camper's nemeses — rain, storms and the cold — are unfortunately common features of every New Zealand summer. The first line of defence for tenters is a high-quality, modern tent in good condition. That said, even the best tent can spring a leak or snap a pole, so don't forget your repair kit. Make sure you pack a roll of high-quality duct tape — you'll be amazed at what it will fix. (Turn to page 16 for more tips for keeping warm and dry.)

Organise that car boot
If you're camping in a small tent with little room for storage, you'll find life much easier with an organised boot. Plastic crates are great for the job — one each for food, cooking equipment, footwear, etc.

Keep the insects at bay
Keep your tent zipped up when the

sandflies and mozzies are around, and don't switch on the torch at night when the tent is unzipped — unless of course you like sleeping with hundreds of flying insects and creepy-crawlies . . .

trampers), self-inflating roll mats are surprisingly comfortable. Proper pillows will make a big difference to your comfort, too, so throw them in the car if you've got room.

Be ready for bedtime

A comfortable night's sleep is paramount. Enduring a cold, fitful night on a thin foam mat is not conducive to happy holidaying. Your best bet is a rubberised, cotton-covered airbed. However, if space and weight are an issue (as they will be for

Keep your stuff safe

Keep your valuables locked in the car, preferably out of sight. Keep wallets, purses and passports with you as much as you can.

A checklist of camping essentials can be found at back of this book (page 228).

KATHMANDU

Why is campervanning so popular? Well, for starters, it's warmer, more comfortable and offers greater personal security.

Campers used to fall into two main camps: the tenters and the caravanners. However, the latter have evolved into the burgeoning and diverse world of campervanning — motorhomes, four-wheel-drive campers, and all sorts of small vans.

Many are available to buy as well as hire from numerous rental companies, and the tourist trails are teeming with them.

So why is campervanning so popular? Well, for starters, it's warmer, more comfortable and offers greater personal security than tenting. It's also very convenient: you arrive, you park and you're ready to relax. Here are a few tips to make things run smoothly:

Check your vehicle thoroughly before you set off
Test the brakes, check the oil and water and the tyres and make sure the spare wheel is in good order.

Secure everything inside
You don't want your pots and pans crashing about in the back as you round every bend.

Wear your seat belt
That means everyone — whenever the vehicle is moving. It's the law.

Be considerate of other road users
Generally, you will be moving more slowly than other traffic. Pull over and let people pass when it is safe to do so.

Take plenty of rest stops
Driving a campervan is tiring. You should plan to drive no more than 250 km in one day. Ideally, you should be travelling a lot less so you have time to stop and smell the roses.

Make sure you have enough fuel
Most campervans use more fuel than cars, and petrol stations — especially on the South Island — can be few and far between.

Always use a designated dump station
These are marked on your road atlas, but you can also obtain a list from i-SITES or download it from www.camping.org.nz/content/library/Finding_a_Dump_Station.pdf

Conserve power
When you're not plugged into a powered site, the appliance battery system won't last forever and will recharge only when the engine is running. Switch off your electrical equipment when you're not using it.

Note that vehicles with solar panels are available, with several hire companies already offering them.

Ensure adequate ventilation when using gas appliances
Check that all vents are clear and open. Don't use your gas stove for heating. Never leave gas appliances running when you are resting or asleep.

Pack your belongings in soft bags
They will take up less room and fit more easily into storage cupboards.

Bring some outdoor furniture
When the sun is shining, the best place for lounging and dining is outside. Don't forget some form of shade (at least a wide-brimmed hat) and sunscreen too.

Keep your valuables locked in your campervan, preferably out of sight
Keep wallets, purses and passports with you as much as you can.

Consider joining the New Zealand Motor Caravan Association
Benefits include discounts at holiday parks and on the Cook Strait ferry, custom insurance schemes, a bi-monthly magazine and their useful travel directory.

The term 'freedom camping' refers to staying overnight in an area that is not a designated campsite, such as reserves on the beachfront or in the bush or the mountains. Freedom campers sleep in their tent, caravan, campervan, bus or even car. This type of camping is largely free, and there are generally no facilities.

You can't, however, just camp anywhere you like. Some freedom campers leave a large and particularly unpleasant environmental footprint in the form of abandoned rubbish and piles of human waste. To address this, concerned parties (largely central and local government) have been imposing greater restrictions upon the range of the places you can camp and the length of time you can stay there.

So, where is freedom camping allowed? The rule is: assume nothing — always ask a local. The best places to check are the local i-SITE, DOC office or regional council.

Once you've established where you can camp, be sure to follow the rules and regulations. These vary slightly from place to place, but are generally along these lines:

• Campers must provide their own chemical toilet, which must be emptied only in official dump stations.

• Leave the area clean and tidy. Take your rubbish away with you and dispose of it responsibly, recycling as much as possible. Around the East Cape there is a rubbish-collection service available at freedom-camping sites — paid for as part of your freedom-camping permit, issued by the Gisborne District Council. (Visit www.gdc.govt.nz for more details.)

• You need to provide all your own water. Potable water is not available at freedom campsites.

• No semi-permanent structures are allowed. No post-holes are allowed — awnings must be self-supported.

• Your camp mustn't interfere with or damage dunes, trees and other vegetation. Structures shall not be attached to any tree or shrub.

• Leave 3 m between each tent / caravan / campervan, in case of fire.

• No open fires are allowed; gas cooking only.

• Act responsibly and respect the access and enjoyment rights of other public-space users.

• All dogs must be restrained.

• All motorised vehicles must be roadworthy.

• Beaches are public places — all road rules apply.

• No motorised vehicles are allowed on dunes.

• A freedom-camping permit may be required in certain areas, such as around the East Cape. Check with the local i-SITE.

• Freedom camping is restricted to two days in any one place unless otherwise indicated.

• Follow the New Zealand Environmental Care Code (see pages 17–18).

• Don't camp where you see a 'No Camping' sign. This is an official Land Transport sign, and as such is legally enforceable under national regulations and bylaws. That means, not only will you get turfed off your site, you'll most likely be liable to a fine, too.

For more information on freedom camping, visit the New Zealand Freedom Camping Forum website at www.camping.org.nz.

The nature of camping means that you will spend a lot more time outdoors and have fewer facilities than you're used to. Staying warm and comfortable in this scenario requires just a few extra items of clothing and equipment, and a little bit of forward thinking.

Take appropriate clothing
New Zealand's weather is highly changeble and conditions vary greatly around the country even during the summer season. It may be boiling hot, but it may also be freezing cold — and there may well be mad dashes through the rain to the toilet block. Make sure you have clothing and footwear for all conditions.

Slip, slap, slop
With any luck you'll enjoy your fair share of bright, sunny days. However, the intense New Zealand sun can burn in minutes. Don't forget to bring a hat and sunscreen, and cover up when you can.

Prepare to be bitten
Sandflies and mosquitoes can be a pain in the neck, arm, leg and bum (if left exposed). See Bites and Stings for advice on these annoying little buggers.

BITES AND STINGS

Unfortunately, sandflies and mosquitoes are an integral part of the New Zealand camping experience, although some places are worse than others — Fiordland and the West Coast of the South Island lay claim to the largest and most voracious sandfly populations. They like to hang around water and bush, and are often found at beaches and at the edges of lakes or wetlands. Sandflies are most active at dawn and dusk, while mosquitoes love nothing better than a hot summer night.

It pays to be prepared for their attentions. At the time of day when they are most active, make sure your tent is zipped up or your van windows closed. Tenters should also avoid camping too close to water. If you're outdoors, your best protection is to cover up as much bare skin as possible, avoiding the need for vast quantities of insect repellent.

There are many repellents available, most containing the active ingredient DEET. However, a cheap, natural alternative can be made by mixing eight parts of a carrier oil (olive or vegetable oil, for example) with one part citronella oil, which you can buy from your pharmacy (not to be confused with the large bottles of citronella oil you can buy from hardware stores — this is for burning only).

Wasps are common in the New Zealand bush, particularly in beech forest in summer. They give a nasty sting and can be very dangerous for those who are allergic to them. If you do get stung, cool the affected area in water if possible and prepare to suffer from pain, swelling and a fair bit of itchiness. Antihistamine tablets or cream will help alleviate these symptoms.

THE NEW ZEALAND ENVIRONMENTAL CARE CODE

More people than ever are visiting New Zealand's natural places. With this increase comes a greater impact on the environment, including damaged plants, unsightly rubbish, polluted water and deteriorating facilities. You can do your bit to help protect the environment by following these simple guidelines.

TOITU TE WHENUA: LEAVE THE LAND UNDISTURBED

Protect plants and animals

Treat New Zealand's flora and fauna with care and respect. It is unique and often rare.

Remove rubbish

Litter is unattractive, harmful to wildlife and can increase vermin and disease. Plan your visits to reduce rubbish, and dispose of it properly (see pages 10–11).

Use toilets provided

In areas without toilet facilities, bury your toilet waste in a shallow hole well away from waterways, tracks, campsites and huts.

Keep streams and lakes clean

When washing dishes, clothes or yourself, wash well away from the water source. Soaps and detergents are harmful to water life; drain used water into the soil so it is filtered before returning to the water table.

Take care with fires

Portable fuel stoves are less harmful to the environment and more efficient than open fires. If you light a fire, keep it small, use only dead wood and make sure it is extinguished by dousing it with water and checking the ashes before leaving (see page 18).

Keep to the track when walking in the bush or in undisturbed areas

This will lessen the chance of damaging fragile plants and disturbing animals. Resist the temptation to shortcut corners — you can see the damage it does.

Consider others

People visit rural areas for many reasons. Be considerate of other visitors who also have a right to enjoy the natural environment.

Respect our cultural heritage

Many places in New Zealand have a spiritual and historical significance. Treat these places with consideration and respect. Learning about the places you visit will help you understand and acknowledge the value they have for others.

Enjoy your outdoor experience but camp carefully

Take a last look before leaving an area: will the next visitor know that you have been there? Protect the environment for your own sake,

DIDYMO – HELP PREVENT ITS SPREAD

Didymo (*Didymosphenia germinata*), also known as 'rock snot', is an invasive alga that threatens our waterways. It can form massive blooms that not only spoil the aesthetics of rivers it infests but also affects fish, plants and insects, opportunities for boating, fishing and swimming, and irrigation schemes. No one knows exactly how didymo got here or how we're going to get rid of it, but what we do know is that it is very easily spread from one waterway to the next — by as little as a single cell in a tiny drop of water. Please do your bit to help stop its spread.

Check

As you leave the river, check for and remove all visible plant matter from your clothing, and fishing and boating equipment.

Clean

Clean all equipment with a detergent solution.

Dry

If cleaning is not practicable, allow all equipment to dry for at least 48 hours before you visit another river or lake. For more information, visit www.biosecurity.co.nz.

for the sake of those who come after you, and for the sake of the environment itself.

FIRE

A campfire is one of life's great pleasures, and a practical one at that. Not only does it warm the body, it will bring the billy to a boil and toast a marshmallow, too. The fire is also the heart of the camp, a glowing, crackling hub around which folk will gather to have a yarn, sing a song, tell a ghost story or simply sit, hypnotised by the dancing flames.

Out of control, however, those flames are one of the greatest threats to our natural environment. Many campgrounds do not allow open fires at any time, or there may be fire bans in place. Check around the campground for signs, ask your camp host or contact DOC or the local council. If in doubt, don't light one. If you do light a fire in a fire-ban area, you may be liable for any damage caused.

Fire safety should be taken seriously. Here are a few reminders:

- Use fire pits or fireplaces where provided to contain your fire.

- Don't light fires in windy conditions.

- Keep fires, camp stoves and barbecues at least 3 m away from dry vegetation and anything flammable.

- Never start a fire or use a cooker or barbecue underneath low-hanging branches or shrubbery.

- Make sure your tent or van is upwind of the fire.

- Keep it small. Use only dead wood and burnable rubbish. It is an offence to cut any living vegetation in conservation areas.

- Don't burn plastics — they release noxious fumes, including dioxins, into the atmosphere.

- Never leave a fire unattended.

- Always keep handy something to kill the fire — plenty of water, sand or a fire extinguisher.

- Make sure you extinguish your fire properly. Check that the ashes are cold before you go to bed or move on.

- If things get out of hand, dial 111 and ask for the fire service.

KEY TO SYMBOLS

 potable tap water

 laundry facilities

 water, may need treatment

 full recycling facilities and rubbish disposal

 no tap water

 rubbish disposal service

 hot showers available (may be coin- or token-operated)

 no rubbish disposal service

 cold shower only

 internet (terminal or Wi-Fi)

 basic shelter, few facilities (eg DOC shelter)

 television lounge

 kitchen shelter (electrified, with sinks and fridges as a minimum)

 playground

NORTH ISLAND CAMPGROUNDS

1   Tapotupotu and Kapowairua
2   Maitai Bay
3   Bay of Islands Holiday Park
4   Puriri Bay
5   Kauri Coast Top 10 Holiday Park
6   Pakiri Beach Holiday Park
7   Long Bay Motor Camp
8   Waikawau Bay
9   Hahei Holiday Resort
10 Kauaeranga Valley campgrounds
11 McLaren Falls Park
12 Ohiwa Family Holiday Park
13 Maraehako Bay
14 Tolaga Bay Holiday Park
15 Lake Waikaremoana Motor Camp
16 Te Tapahoro Bay
17 Blue Lake Top 10 Holiday Park
18 Reid's Farm Recreation Reserve
19 Whakapapa Holiday Park
20 Raglan Kopua Holiday Park
21 Onaero Bay Holiday Park
22 Oakura Beach Holiday Park
23 Kaupokonui
24 Tutira Country Park
25 Waipatiki Beach Farm Park
26 Kuripapango, Kaweka Forest Park
27 Castlepoint Holiday Park
28 Martinborough Village Camping
29 Holdsworth, Tararua Forest Park
30 Otaki Forks, Tararua Forest Park
31 Paekakariki Holiday Park

GeoSmart

SOUTH ISLAND CAMPGROUNDS

32 Whites Bay
33 Mistletoe Bay
34 Kahikatea Flat, Pelorus Bridge
35 Totaranui
36 Golden Bay Holiday Park,
    Tukurua Beach
37 Kerr Bay, Lake Rotoiti
38 Kohaihai
39 Punakaiki Beach Camp
40 Marble Hill, Lewis Pass National Reserve
41 Lake Mahinapua Recreation Reserve
42 Okarito Community Campground
43 Gillespies Beach
44 Alpine Adventure Holiday Park,
    Hanmer Springs
45 Molesworth Station
46 Arthur's Pass Road campgrounds
47 Rakaia Gorge Camping Ground
48 Akaroa Top 10 Holiday Park
49 Clarke Flat, Peel Forest Park
50 Lake Alexandrina and Lake McGregor
    Camping Reserve
51 White Horse Hill, Mount Cook
52 Temple Valley, Ruataniwha
    Conservation Park

53 Portobello Village Tourist Park
54 Moeraki Village Holiday Park
55 Cameron Flat, Mount Aspiring
    National Park
56 Kidds Bush, Hawea Recreation Reserve
57 Alexandra Holiday Park
58 Skippers Canyon, Mount Aurum
    Recreation Reserve
59 Kinloch
60 Mavora Lakes
61 Milford Road campgrounds, Fiordland
    National Park
62 Te Anau Lakeview Holiday Park
63 Monkey Island, Te Puka o Takitimu
64 Curio Bay Holiday Park
65 Purakaunui Bay
66 Pounawea Motor Camp

→ LET'S GO CAMPING IN

NORTHLAND AND AUCKLAND

**Off Cape Reinga Road,
5 km east of Cape Reinga,
36 km east of Cape Reinga**

Contact
DOC Kaitaia
09 408 6014
www.doc.govt.nz

Capacity
Tapotupotu:
45 unpowered

Kapowairua:
200 unpowered

Open
Tapotupotu all year;
Kapowairua summer only

Bookings
not required

Price
$7.50 adult / $3.50 child

Just 2 km south of
the Cape Reinga car
park is the turn-off to
Tapotupotu, a beautiful
sandy bay popular with
daytrippers who dip
down the 3 km gravel
road before or after
visiting the cape.

Wouldn't it be convenient if the first campsite in this book could be at Cape Reinga, the northernmost point of the mainland? Unfortunately it can't be, but that's because the northernmost point of the North Island is in fact the Surville Cliffs, further east on North Cape. We can, however, very nearly oblige, because there are two particularly splendid DOC campsites at the northern end of the Aupouri Peninsula — that sandy extremity bounded in the west by Ninety Mile Beach.

It is, of course, a pilgrimage of sorts, this long car journey (108 km, about two hours) from Awanui at the base of the peninsula to Te Rerenga Wairua, the tip of Cape Reinga where a lonely pohutukawa reaches out to the sea. This accounts for the surprisingly busy road (up to 1300 vehicles a day during summer), one that is bound to get even busier now that sealing of the road is almost complete.

Te Paki Recreation Reserve covers the north of the peninsula. Formerly a farm (sold to the government in 1966), its unusual geography and unique habitats can be explored via a network of tracks. Both these campsites, administered by DOC, lie within the reserve's boundary.

Just 2 km south of the Cape Reinga car park is the turn-off to Tapotupotu, a beautiful sandy bay popular with daytrippers who dip down the 3 km gravel road before or after visiting the cape. A very attractive area — complete with pohutukawa-shaded picnic tables — is set aside for their use. Further along the beach, we lucky lingerers can avail ourselves of a picturesque and spacious camping area, with terrific waterside pitching set along the dunes and skirting the inlet. This is a classic example of cove camping.

Dedicated rangers keep the grounds well manicured, the lush grass nicely mown. There's drinking water, cold-water showers, flush toilets and rubbish collection in peak season. And that, fellow campers, is your lot . . . but you will desire little more, so content will you be to swim, fish, surf and snorkel, or just relax in this magical place.

As the crow flies east, Kapowairua (Spirits Bay) is a little under 15 km from Tapotupotu. This campsite, however, is much less visited, being at the end of a bone-shaking 16 km of winding gravel road once you've turned off the Cape Reinga Road. It's a different kettle of fish for other reasons, too. More open in aspect, the bay has a wild beauty, marked by rocky bluffs and peculiar stones which stand in dramatic contrast to the rural setting on the flat. Over the fence from the camping area is a paddock, home — when last we visited — to a dozen or so proud piebald horses which gambolled across the hillside. Beyond the dunes, the ocean is met on Te Horo Beach, a vast arc of white sand. The waves crash hard against its steeply pitched shore — do be very careful if you intend to swim.

Kapowairua camp sprawls over a large area, set well back from the beach behind the dunes. It's a couple of minutes' walk to the sea. There is plenty of room for everyone; privacy and shade can be found among small stands of trees and there are some welcoming nooks scattered about. While the facilities aren't quite as flash as those at Tapotupotu, they pretty much fit the same bill: drinking water, long-drop toilets and cold-water showers. Rubbish is collected in peak season only (for a small fee); a ranger may be in residence at this time.

Offering a truly back-to-basics experience in a place of outstanding beauty and solitude, Kapowairua is one of the great road-end camps of New Zealand.

The bay has a wild beauty, marked by rocky bluffs and peculiar stones which stand in dramatic contrast to the rural setting on the flat.

PREVIOUS PAGE:
Waipu, near Whangarei
LEFT: **Tapotupotu**

VISIT NINETY MILE BEACH AND THE FAMOUS TE PAKI SAND DUNES

You can do both from Te Paki Stream Road (turn-off 17 km south of Cape Reinga). From the car park at the end of the road it's an hour's walk to the beach. Follow the coast north for an hour or so and you'll reach the southern end of Scott Point, where you'll get a model view back along Ninety Mile Beach, stretching 103 km into the haze. Spread over this area are the Te Paki dunes. They are a sight to behold, some over 150 m high. Energetic types will want to scale them for sure, while adrenalin junkies will leap — or surf — from their peaks. (If that sounds like you, look out for signs along the Far North Road: 'Sandboards for hire'.)

FOLLOW THE CAPE REINGA COASTAL WALKWAY

This walk stretches 53 km (three–four days) from Kapowairua, past Cape Reinga and Cape Maria Van Diemen, on to Te Paki Stream on the west coast of the peninsula. The coastal views will amaze as you pass tranquil beaches, spectacular headlands, mountainous dunes and swamplands full of birds. You can access the track by car at four points, giving you the option of picking up the path for a day walk. Two great options from our two campsites are Tapotupotu Bay to Cape Reinga (four hours return) and Kapowairua to Pandora (seven hours return).

JOIN THE PILGRIMAGE TO NEW ZEALAND'S FAR NORTH

Said to have been named Te Rerenga Wairua ('the leaping place of the spirits') by the legendary explorer Kupe, Maori believe that the souls of the dead depart from this point on their journey from Aotearoa to their homeland, Hawaiki. This and other stories are well told in flash new interpretive displays along the path from the rather stunning gateway to the lighthouse, as neat as a new pin. There are various other ambles around the promontory, taking in expansive views over the flaxy, sandy landscape and the seemingly boundless waters where the Tasman Sea meets the Pacific Ocean. This *does* feel like the end of the line. Gaze in wonder at the wild blue yonder. Wouldn't you want your spirit to fly this way too?

LEFT: **The Cape Reinga lighthouse at dusk**
RIGHT: **The headland at Cape Reinga, Te Rerenga Wairua**

DESINATION NORTHLAND

Maitai Bay Recreation Reserve, Karikari Peninsula, 42 km northeast of Kaitaia

Contact
DOC Kaitaia
09 408 6014
www.doc.govt.nz

Capacity
110 unpowered

Open
all year

Bookings
not required

Price
$8 adult / $4 child

ISTOCKPHOTO

If you're seeking New Zealand's 'tropical paradise' beaches — those dressed in bright sand and basking in sunshine, facing the Pacific Ocean — you have to be prepared to share them with the masses, particularly in the irresistibly warm north where much of the coast has been subdivided and added to the outskirts of Auckland. Happily, though, a few prime bits of Northland and the Coromandel have been set aside in the conservation estate to be enjoyed by one and all. Beautiful Maitai Bay is one of these places.

Situated on the northeastern side of the Karikari Peninsula, the bay is reached via gravel road through cow-patty pastures. Press on through the campground — we'll get to that later — and the bay lies beyond like a glittering surprise. Below grassy dunes sporting the odd clutch of trees, a crescent of golden sand slopes gently to the sea. The coastline follows a tight arc — from certain perspectives the bay seems completely enclosed. And on a blessed day the waters sit like a limpid pool. Out on the wings fly low hills adorned with remnant forest, craggy rocks at their feet.

The camp sits up high behind the dunes, with only the luckiest spots affording ocean views. It is divided into two areas — top and bottom camp — which are similar, offering bushy nooks and hedgerowed alcoves spread through spacious, undulating grounds, with plenty of possibilities for privacy and shade. There are flush toilets, cold showers and water spigots dotted around (the water should be treated before drinking). In keeping with the rural surroundings there are carpets of lush grass the cows next door must surely covet.

This is a very popular family camping spot in the summer holidays, so you're likely to be neighboured by big, cheerful groups. There'll be boats (yes, there's a boat ramp), toboggans, salty children and wet towels strung on the tent ropes. An on-site ranger (peak season only) will check on toilet paper supplies and adjudicate scraps over the beachball. Rubbish bags will also be collected for a small fee. The rest of the year, you'll have this little paradise nearly all to yourself, and the fact that you have to take your own rubbish out will seem a very small price to pay.

The nearest shop is Bayview Services on the main road at Whatuwhiwhi, 6 km away. Open daily, it sells fuel, groceries, ice cream and cold beer — so now you're all set.

ENJOY A FEED
OF FISH 'N' CHIPS

In the tiny seaside town of Mangonui, about 40 km (40 minutes) southeast of Maitai Bay, just off State Highway 10, the Mangonui Fish Shop serves up freshly landed catch fried in a crisp, clean batter along with terrific chips and a lemon wedge. No fancy extras here (unless you count the lemon wedge?) — just a good honest dinner, eaten straight from the paper, of course. We advise against a takeaway; you can't beat eating it on the shop's deck overlooking the harbour — with fishing boats swinging at their buoys — washed down with a cold bevvy from the bar. It'll taste a million dollars. The village itself is a lovely place to linger. Once a thriving port, today you'll find it home to a handful of galleries, cafés, shops and holiday getaways. Explore the streets on the heritage trail (one and a half hours) starting at the old courthouse on Waterfront Road.

DESTINATION NORTHLAND

TAKE A WALK TO
WHANGATUPERE BAY

This walk is about three and a half hours return, starting along Merita Beach then up Poroa Stream before a 15-minute grind up the steep hill to the Paraawanui Trig (142 m). On a good day you'll be rewarded with striking views of Maitai Bay's crescent beach and brilliant blue waters. Did you know that American and New Zealand scientists launched rockets from Maitai Bay as part of a space experiment during the solar eclipse of 1965? Nor did we!

SWIM IN THE WARM(ISH),
CLEAR OCEAN WATERS

This is about as gorgeous as New Zealand beach swimming gets, especially when there's nobody else around. (And with the camp largely obscured by the dunes, it may feel that way even if up on the hill there are 500 people barbecuing their sausages.) This is a very friendly beach, perfect for newcomers, the young and the infirm. Snorkelling and the chance to spot one of the regularly visiting dolphins are on the cards too.

LEFT: **The tropical paradise of Maitai Bay**
ABOVE: **The Mangonui fish 'n' chip shop: a highlight of Doubtless Bay**

Puketona Road,
5 km west of Paihia

Contact
09 402 7646
www.bayofislandsholidaypark.co.nz

Capacity
250 unpowered / 100 powered

Open
all year

Bookings
essential peak season

Price
$16 adult / $8 child

*The grounds boast a
veritable arboretum
of tall trees, forming
a sheltering canopy
. . . We'd go so far as
to say they make this
one of New Zealand's
best 'park' campsites.*

An area of often astounding natural beauty, the Bay of Islands is most famous for its multitudinous islands, gorgeous beaches and clement climate which warms its shores for most of the year. However, this area is no cultural desert either. Densely populated by Maori very soon after their arrival in Aotearoa, it also proved popular with early European settlers. And it was here, of course — at Waitangi — where representatives of those two peoples came together to negotiate and put the first signatures to the Treaty, our founding document.

All this makes for bustling summers, particularly in the tourist hubs of Kerikeri, Paihia and Russell. Catering to the roving masses are numerous campsites — only Rotorua boasts more per square kilometre. They run the gamut from back-to-basics conservation camps in bushy corners to fully serviced holiday parks with every bell and whistle. The standard is high across the board. However, at the serviced end of the spectrum it is the Bay of Islands Holiday Park, on the main road out of Paihia, where we choose to pitch our tent.

And here's a surprise: it's not on the beach, but rather on the Waitangi River, which flows over the Haruru Falls a little downstream. The busy main road runs right by, which ordinarily would put us off, but in this case most sites are barely affected, being largely out of earshot of the zooms.

The grounds boast a veritable arboretum of tall trees, forming a sheltering canopy. Mature and mostly exotic — such as gum and magnolia — these handsome specimens are the defining feature of this 3.6 ha park. We'd go so far as to say they make this one of New Zealand's best 'park' campsites. A serious contender for the green thumb award, the ground-level gardening is also impressive. Thoughtfully landscaped with lovely lawns, there are interesting beds of flowers and foliage, alive with the twitter of birds.

Individual sites are delineated along non-negotiable lines, but are spacious and intelligently arranged — there's hardly a bad spot. The park's riverside terrace, with a gently sloping hill behind, make for particularly pleasant camping, the waters babbling by in a soothing fashion. This is also the area farthest away from the road. Picnic tables are dotted around.

The facilities blocks are ship shape. The huge bathrooms have ample amenities and are amongst the most cheerful we've ever clapped eyes on. The kitchens have refrigerated lockers and outside is a barbecue patio. The lounge / games room is comfortable, sporting a pool table, television and internet terminal (with Wi-Fi). For outside fun, there's a playground and trampoline, a swimming pool, and hire-kayaks for paddling the river. The office shop has newspapers, ice and a few edibles, and a tour-booking service. Should it rain, some very cute cabins are available.

VISIT THE BIRTHPLACE OF THE TREATY

The Waitangi Treaty Grounds (Tau Henare Drive, www.waitangi.net.nz) are the local highlight for many a visitor. Featuring the restored colonial-era Treaty House, the former home of James Busby where the Treaty was drafted and now a museum, there are many other attractions to be enjoyed. See a fully carved whare runanga (meeting house), the large ceremonial waka known as Ngatokimatawhaorua and the naval flagstaff that marks the place where the Treaty was signed. The gardens are beautiful, too. Local Maori guides host excellent one-hour guided tours on the hour 9.30am–2.30pm in summer ($12 adult / $5 child; New Zealand residents enter free). The on-site Waikokopu café and its 'homemade incredible edibles' is well worth a visit.

Te Whare Runanga, built in 1940 to celebrate the 100th anniversary of the Treaty of Waitangi

DESTINATION NORTHLAND

SAIL THROUGH THE HOLE IN THE ROCK

To get a real sense of the Bay of Islands, you have to get out onto the water. Besides squeezing through the gap at Piercy Island, you can indulge in a bit of island hopping — with around 150 mainly undeveloped islands within the Maritime Park, there are plenty to choose from. Go for a swim or a snorkel, try your hand at kayaking or swim with dolphins. It's all possible, weather permitting. Salty types can help crew yachts and even a tall ship. Most, however, just choose to cruise. There are innumerable options and operators on hand — almost as many as there are islands. There are booking offices in Paihia, Opua and Russell, or seek help from the experts via www.northlandnz.com.

WATCH HARURU FALLS

Sometimes a gentle, pretty cascade and at others a thunderous torrent, these falls are a mesmerising sight. Access them from the car park clearly signposted off Puketona Road, a couple of minutes' drive from the campsite. From the falls you can walk to Waitangi (four hours return) on a well-graded track that snakes along the riverbank before crossing the estuary on a boardwalk, cutting through dense mangrove swamp. These hardy plants play host to a wide variety of marine life and several species of wading bird, so keep your eyes peeled and ears open.

Whangaruru North Road, 30 km southeast of Russell (turn off Russell Road onto Rawhiti Road, then into Whangaruru North Road at Ngaiotonga)

Contact

DOC camp manager
09 433 6160
www.doc.govt.nz

Capacity

75 unpowered

Open

all year (no vehicle access in the wettest months, July–Oct)

Bookings

recommended peak season — if you want a beachfront site

Price

$9 adult / $4.50 child (peak)
$7 adult / $3.50 child (off-peak)

The bay is named after the handsome trees endemic to this area, specimens of which can be seen among its forest remnants.

Most of the truly spectacular campsites in Northland (come to think of it, pretty much nationwide) are those at the end of a gravel road. Particularly typical of Northland is that the road-end will bring you to a coastal reserve. Take a look at an atlas or road map: see how all those extremities are coloured green? These are set aside for us — every single one of us — to visit, enjoy and take care of for generations to come. Treasure them. Rejoice in them. Even when it rains non-stop and your tent has sprung a leak.

It never rains in Northland, making the shelterless Puriri Bay a winner. (Okay, that first part was a lie.) The bay is named after the handsome trees endemic to this area, specimens of which can be seen among its forest remnants. One old dear stands sentry on the foreshore, the wizened focal point of what is a fairly small bay, room enough for only 30 beachfront sites, plus some more up the back and a smattering on the terraces above. The bay faces out into Whangaruru Harbour, an aspect affording shelter from the easterly winds that buffet the shores of Bland Bay over the hill.

Previously a farm, the land here was reputedly passed to the government by an admiral whose name is attached to the bay to the east. Cattle still graze there to this day, muddying the lush paddocks, while over the fences tracts of regenerating bush patchwork the landscape, providing refuge to birds including brown kiwi and kereru (or kukupa, as they're known in Northland).

This is a pretty campsite, with plenty of interest for those inclined towards simple contentment. The sheltered beach is good for swimming and boating (ramp available), and there is good fishing to be had (so they say) off the rocks. There are plenty of tracks to walk, including a short hop to Picnic Bay, popular with daytrippers for . . . you guessed it, picnics!

Rubbish skips are available during peak season; the rest of the year you'll need to take any refuse with you when you leave. There are eco-loos and cold-water showers. Rangers (quite likely to be Gordon and Colleen) can be found in their bus on site from Labour Weekend to Easter. They handle bookings and keep an eye on things. For security purposes, a barrier arm is in operation between 9pm and 7am.

Should this campsite be full, you could try Otamure, just down the coast at Whananaki (26 km east of Hikurangi). It's a similar set-up (DOC-operated, with toilets, cold-water showers, spigots, rubbish collection and rangers-in-residence), with very nearly beachfront camping. The beach is gorgeous, and the gnarly old pohutukawa as pretty as a picture.

Waterfront camping at Puriri Bay

VISIT HISTORIC RUSSELL

With the cursing, fighting and whoring antics of the region's whalers long over, Russell has had to come up with some new attractions. The three heritage walks (ranging from 30 minutes to two hours; map available from the museum) are a great way to learn about Russell's tempestuous past and snoop around some beautiful old buildings. The walk up to Flagstaff Hill (made famous by the rebellious chief Hone Heke) is a must, as is a dip in the ocean at Long Beach over the hill from the centre of town. It'll take around 45 minutes on windy roads to get to Russell from the campground but it's well worth the trip.

WATCH THE WAVES CRASH IN AT DRAMATIC OCEAN BEACH

Enclosed by lofty and precipitous cliffs, this two-hour loop walk, starting (or finishing, if you prefer) at the southern end of the campground, takes you to one of the most spectacular beaches in the area. A steep climb out of Admirals Bay rewards walkers with expansive views across the harbour and south to the curving peninsula of Mimiwhangata. Inland is a mixture of farmland and old pasture reclaimed by regenerating native forest. Although large tracts of manuka dominate the scene, the bush is actually quite diverse, with more than 350 species recorded.

**Trounson Park Road, Kaihu,
32 km north of Dargaville**

Contact
09 439 0621
www.kauricoasttop10.co.nz

Capacity
60 unpowered / 32 powered

Open
all year

Bookings
recommended peak season

Price
$18 adult / $12 child

KAURI COAST TOP 10 HOLIDAY PARK

The name of this holiday park gives some indication of its appeal — handy proximity to the justly famous and now sadly diminished tree. There are several other campgrounds within the shadow of the remnant Northland west-coast kauri forest, but this corker Top 10 wins hands down for its beauty, comfort and convenience.

This peaceful 2 ha park has a beautiful natural setting, ranging over riverside terraces almost totally encircled by healthy bush. The most handsome feature, however, is the Kaihu River, born here where two smaller rivers meet. These waters flow almost right around the park in an ever-changing combination of babbling brook and serene holes. A dip is definitely on the cards, and there's a jumping board for the larrikins to leap off.

A keen gardener is hard at work round here (could that be Herb or Heather, the owners?), evident by manicured lawns and lots of pretty bedding plants and shrubby corners. The largest tenting area — a riverside idyll with three young willows for shade — is used only in peak season. The rest of the time it's left for ball games (although sometimes the river invades the pitch). Alongside is a finely crafted open-air kitchen, with nice stonework and a wooden roof, complete with all the standard kitchen facilities including water boiler and gas hobs — an irresistible alternative to cooking indoors, especially on a balmy evening. There are plenty of picnic tables throughout the grounds too, and ample room for laying down a blanket on the grass.

The central facilities block is fairly modern, and features an open-plan kitchen and dining area with indoor / outdoor flow to a covered deck (with barbecues) overlooking the playground and river beyond. All amenities are ample and in excellent condition — the Top 10 network certainly keeps the bar raised in this regard.

This is a particularly social campground, and families will love it here. There's lots of room for running around, and the river shallows are good for a paddle. A terrific adventure-style playground should provide a few hours' distraction, as will the trampoline. Tubing trips are also run during the summer season, and who can resist that super-soggy fun? However, the not-to-be-missed activity is the guided night walk (see page 35) which is run by your kindly hosts. This can be booked at the office where you will also find basic grocery supplies and some cute kiwi t-shirts.

VISIT WAIPOUA FOREST AND HAVE AN EXCUSE TO USE THE WORD 'AWESOME' IN ITS PROPER CONTEXT

Botanist Leonard Cockayne, surveying this ancient kauri forest in 1908, described it as 'one of the most rare, beautiful and at the same time significantly interesting to be met with, not only in New Zealand, but in the world at large'. That it's still here is something of a miracle, most of it having been ravaged by early European settlers.

The kauri of Waipoua — up to 2000 years old and 16 m in girth — can easily be ogled from the 18 km stretch of road that passes through the forest, and via the various walking tracks leading off it. The visitor centre near the southern end of the road (now run by the local iwi, Te Roroa), has a tired but interesting photographic display; towards the northern end is the paramount chief of Aotearoa's tree tribe: Tane Mahuta. If you somehow remain unmoved by the sheer size and mana of this mighty tree, remember: this sprouted from a single seed, around the time the calendar clicked over from BC to AD. *Awesome!*

Waipoua Forest is 25 km from Kauri Coast Top 10 Holiday Park, and you can plug the gaps in your kauri knowledge at The Kauri Museum at Matakohe (www.kaurimuseum.com), 45 km south of Dargaville on State Highway 12.

DESTINATION NORTHLAND

LEFT: Kauri Coast Top 10 Holiday Park with a view of the Kaihu River
ABOVE: The boardwalk through magical Trounson Kauri Park

EXPERIENCE THE SIGHTS AND SOUNDS OF THE FOREST AT NIGHT

This guided night tour is run by Herb and Heather (of the holiday park) every night, weather permitting. The two-hour walk takes in a loop on easy terrain and boardwalk through Trounson Kauri Park, a 5 km mini-bus ride away. You will almost certainly hear the call of the kiwi. You can also visit Trounson in daylight, where you will find it equally illuminating with its excellent nature trail and highly educational information display that tells the story of this precious 450 ha reserve, gifted to the government by James Trounson in 1921 — well done, good fellow.

Pakiri River Road, 17 km northwest of Leigh

Contact

09 422 6199

www.pakiriholidaypark.co.nz

Capacity

100 unpowered / 30 powered

Open

all year

Bookings

recommended peak season

Price

$20 adult / $8 child unpowered;
$22 adult / $8 child powered

The tiny settlement of Leigh has remained inexplicably low-key and sleepy considering its proximity to the uber-village of Warkworth and the boutique vinopolis of Matakana.

Being so handy to New Zealand's largest city, it's hardly surprising that the near-end of Northland is so popular with Aucklanders popping off for holidays or weekends away. The closer you keep to the highway, the less likely you are to find happy-camper heaven, however. Stray off the beaten path and your chances will increase.

The tiny settlement of Leigh has remained inexplicably low-key and sleepy considering its proximity to the uber-village of Warkworth and the boutique vinopolis of Matakana. Perhaps this says something about the appeal of eating and drinking versus the popularity of donning a wetsuit and snorkel — for Leigh-on-Sea is next to the amazing Goat Island Marine Reserve. And just on from there, down an unbeaten path, is our pick of the near-north: Pakiri Beach.

It's a big old beach, Pakiri, made of fine, white sand that squeaks when you walk on it. From the shore, Hauturu (Little Barrier Island) can be seen 30 km out to sea, and Mangawhai 20 km northwest along the sands. Behind handsome dunes, the land remains largely houseless. The campsite, in fact, is the major man-made feature of the bay, spread over a large area and surrounded by farmland, with the Pakiri River running along one side. Seabirds mill about, including bold black-backed gulls and bad-tempered oystercatchers (well, they sound like they're in a bad mood).

Once you get beyond the high security gates, you will find this a welcoming camp — an 'oldie but a goodie' — catering to all sorts of people, from schools and big family groups through campervan tourists to solo travellers in pup tents.

The powered grid at the centre of the park is largely plugged into by permanent caravans. We are delighted to tell you that the best spots are reserved for casual campers — particularly the handful of prime sites sitting perched above the river mouth: these are the ones you should go for.

That said, the unpowered paddock — through a gate and well away from the electricals — has some good riverside spots, too. The paddock has lush grass and plenty of water spigots, although it's a little bit further to the amenities block. Pine and pohutukawa provide shade.

In the middle of the park, the main facilities block is old but in good nick. The kitchen is a stainless-steel workhorse, complete with gas hobs and all other vital equipment. There's a covered alfresco dining area out front, complete with coin-op barbecues. A separate block next door has a games room with ping-pong and a television lounge with a very small screen.

There's a fish-cleaning sink for the anglers, and cabins and flats for non-campers. The office shop has basic groceries, chippies and sweets, and kayaks are available for hire.

SADDLE UP WITH PAKIRI BEACH HORSE RIDES

Trot along deserted Pakiri Beach, over unspoilt white dunes, through lush pohutukawa groves or up into the hills for impressive views along the coast and out to the islands of the gulf. Expect friendly, experienced guides and around 60 happy horses, chosen for their 'kind temperaments and unflappable attitudes' — that's the horses we're talking about. A variety of rides are available from one hour through to an all-day trek or overnight safari. Tel 09 422 6275, www.horseride-nz.co.nz

TOURISM AUCKLAND

PHOTONEWZEALAND / ARNO GASTEIGER

Pakiri Beach Holiday Park sits in a enviable spot at the mouth of the Pakiri River

SWIM WITH GOOGLY-EYED SNAPPER AT THE SEA ZOO

Goat Island Marine Reserve is known as the best place in New Zealand for snorkelling — not quite the Great Barrier Reef, but a fascinating marine world nevertheless. You can hire snorkels and wetsuits from Seafriends at the top of the hill (tel 09 422 6212, www.seafriends.org.nz). The usually calm, clear waters make it excellent for learners — you can't fail to see a fish. And they will certainly see you — they may even follow you. There is something very, very strange about turning around to find a school of googly-eyed snapper watching your every move — like *you're* the one in the zoo!

TRY TO AVOID GETTING HALF-CUT AT THE LEIGH SAWMILL CAFÉ

Is this the best pub north of Auckland? Probably. It certainly has all the right ingredients: seriously good beers, handcrafted on site; tasty, wholesome food; and a warm, inviting environment largely made out of wood. Outside is a homely garden bar (with roaring brazier on cold evenings), plus a sizeable playground complete with a brick yacht. If this isn't enough to tempt you, it's also a great music venue and regularly hosts some of Aotearoa's hippest bands and musicians. Tel 09 422 6019, www.sawmillcafe.co.nz.

FAR NORTH AND BAY OF ISLANDS

AHIPARA HOLIDAY PARK
164–170 Takahe Street, Ahipara

Contact: 09 409 4864
camp@ahipara.co.nz
www.ahiparaholidaypark.co.nz

Tariff: $45–150

BAY OF ISLANDS RV PARK
251 Puketona Road, Paihia

Contact: 09 402 5686

Tariff: $15

BEACHSIDE HOLIDAY PARK
Opua–Paihia Road, Paihia

Contact: 09 402 7678
info@beachsideholiday.co.nz
www.beachsideholiday.co.nz

Tariff: $28–150

GIBBY'S PLACE PRIVATE TOURIST PARK AND ACCOMMODATION
331 Kerikeri Road, Kerikeri

Contact: 09 405 7024
gibbysplace@xtra.co.nz
www.gibbysplace.co.nz

Tariff: $25–$95

KERIKERI TOP 10 HOLIDAY PARK
Aranga Road, Kerikeri

Contact: 09 407 9326
mail@kerikeritop10.co.nz
www.kerikeritop10.co.nz

Tariff: $28–165

NORFOLK MOTEL AND CAMPERVAN PARK
SH 10, Awanui

Contact: 09 406 7515
norfolkmotel@xtra.co.nz
www.norfolkmotel.co.nz

Tariff: $99–150

ORONGO BAY HOLIDAY PARK
5960 Russell Road, Russell

Contact: 09 403 7704
orongobayholidaypark1@xtra.co.nz
www.orongobayholidaypark.co.nz

Tariff: $24–125

PUKENUI HOLIDAY PARK
Lamb Road (off SH 1),
Pukenui, RD 4, Kaitaia

Contact: 09 409 8803
pukenuiholidays@xtra.co.nz,
www.northland-camping.co.nz

Tariff: $26–90

RAWENE MOTOR CAMP
Marmon Street West, Rawene

Contact: 09 405 7720
rawenemotorcamp@hotmail.com
www.rawenemotorcamp.co.nz

Tariff: $24–48

TAUPO BAY HOLIDAY PARK
1070 Taupo Bay Road,
RD 1, Mangonui

Contact: 09 406 0315
info@taupobaypark.co.nz
www.taupobaypark.co.nz

Tariff: $24–120

TAURANGA BAY HOLIDAY PARK
RD 1, Kaeo, Tauranga Bay

Contact: 09 405 0436
holiday@igrin.co.nz
www.taurangabay.co.nz

Tariff: $30–160

TUTUKAKA HOLIDAY PARK
285 Matapouri Road, Tutukaka

Contact: 09 434 3938
www.tutukaka-holidaypark.co.nz

Tariff: $28–140

WAGENER HOLIDAY PARK
220 Houhora Heads Road,
RD 4, Kaitaia

Contact: 09 409 8564
wagenerpark@xtra.co.nz
www.northlandholiday.co.nz

Tariff: $32–50

WAGON TRAIN RV PARK
1265 SH 10, Kerikeri

Contact: 09 407 7889
enquiries@rvparknz.com
www.rvparknz.com

Tariff: $17–85

WAITANGI HOLIDAY PARK
21 Tahuna Road, Waitangi

Contact: 09 402 7866
waitangiholidaypark@xtra.co.nz
www.waitangiholidaypark.co.nz

Tariff: $25–65

WHANGAREI AND SOUTH

ALPHA MOTEL AND HOLIDAY PARK
34 Tarewa Road, Whangarei

Contact: 09 438 6600
info@alphaholidaypark.co.nz
www.alphaholidaypark.co.nz

Tariff: $28–85

BAYLYS BEACH HOLIDAY PARK
24 Seaview Road,
Baylys Beach, Dargaville

Contact: 09 439 6349
motorcamp@baylysbeach.co.nz
www.baylysbeach.co.nz

Tariff: $26–110

BLUE HERON HOLIDAY PARK
85 Scott Road, RD 4,
Whangarei Heads

Contact 09 436 2293
stay@blueheron.co.nz
www.blueheron.co.nz

Tariff: $29–169

CAMP WAIPU COVE
Cove Road, RD 2, Waipu Cove

Contact: 09 432 0410
info@campwaipucove.com
www.campwaipucove.com

Tariff: $18–115

DARGAVILLE HOLIDAY PARK
10 Onslow Street, Dargaville

Contact: 09 439 8296
dargholidaypark@slingshot.co.nz
www.kauriparks.co.nz

Tariff: $28–85

KAMO SPRINGS HOLIDAY PARK
SH 1, 1 km north of Kamo,
Whangarei

Contact: 09 435 1208
kamosprings@xtra.co.nz
www.kamo-springs.co.nz

Tariff: $30–80

MANGAWHAI HEADS MOTOR CAMP
Mangawhai Heads Road,
Mangawhai Heads

Contact: 09 431 4675

Tariff: $24–28

MATAKOHE TOP 10 HOLIDAY PARK
Church Road, Matakohe

Contact: 09 431 6431
www.matakohetop10.co.nz

Tariff: $28–90

WAIPU COVE COTTAGES AND CAMPING
685 Cove Road, 1 km north
of Cove Store, Waipu Cove

Contact: 09 432 0851
covecottages@xtra.co.nz
www.waipucovecottages.co.nz

Tariff: $26–130

WHANANAKI NORTH MOTEL AND HOLIDAY PARK
Main Road, Whananaki North

Contact: 09 433 8896
whananaki@igrin.co.nz
www.whananakiholiday.co.nz

Tariff: $26–90

WHANGAREI FALLS HOLIDAY PARK
12–16 Ngunguru Road,
RD 3, Whangarei

Contact: 09 437 0609
holiday@whangareifalls.co.nz
www.whangareifalls.co.nz

Tariff: $30–54

WHANGAREI TOP 10 HOLIDAY PARK
24 Mair Street, Whangarei,

Contact: 09 437 6856
www.whangareitop10.co.nz

Tariff: $32–95

NORTH AUCKLAND

AQUATIC PARK PARAKAI SPRINGS CAMPING GROUND
150 Parkhurst Road,
off SH 16, Parakai

Contact: 09 420 8998
aquaticpark@xtra.co.nz
www.aquaticpark.co.nz

Tariff: $20–24

LAGOON BAY CAMPSITE
Lagoon Bay, Mahurangi
Regional Park

Contact: 09 366 2000
parks@arc.govt.nz
www.arc.govt.nz

Tariff: $3–5

MARTINS BAY HOLIDAY PARK
287 Martins Bay Road,
RD 2, Warkworth

Contact: 09 425 5655
mbhpark@rodney.govt.nz
www.martinsbayholidaypark.co.nz

Tariff: $20–24

MITA BAY CAMPSITE
Mita Bay, Mahurangi
Regional Park

Contact: 09 366 2000
parks@arc.govt.nz
www.arc.govt.nz

Tariff: $3–5

OCEAN BEACH CAMPGROUND
Takatu Road, Tawharanui
Regional Park

Contact: 09 366 2000
parks@arc.govt.nz
www.arc.govt.nz

Tariff: $5–10

**OREWA BEACH TOP
10 HOLIDAY PARK**
265 Hibiscus Coast Highway, Orewa

Contact: 09 426 5832
obhpark@rodney.govt.nz
www.orewabeachtop10.co.nz

Tariff: $30–95

PINEWOODS MOTOR PARK
23 Marie Avenue, Red Beach,
Whangaparaoa

Contact: 09 426 4526
office@pinewoods.co.nz
www.pinewoods.co.nz

Tariff: $26–110

SANDSPIT HOLIDAY PARK
1334 Sandspit Road,
RD 2, Warkworth

Contact: 09 425 8610
sandspit@xtra.co.nz
www.sandspitholidaypark.co.nz

Tariff: $30–120

SULLIVANS BAY CAMPSITE
Sullivans Bay, Mahurangi
Regional Park

Contact: 09 366 2000
parks@arc.govt.nz
www.arc.govt.nz

Tariff: $5–10

TAKAPUNA BEACH HOLIDAY PARK
22 The Promenade, Takapuna,
North Shore City

Contact: 09 489 7909
info@takapunabeachholidaypark.co.nz
www.takapunabeachholidaypark.co.nz

Tariff: $28–100

TE HARUHI BAY CAMPGROUND
Te Haruhi Bay, Shakespear
Regional Park

Contact: 09 366 2000
parks@arc.govt.nz
www.arc.govt.nz

Tariff: $5–10

TE MURI BEACH CAMPSITE
Te Muri Beach, Mahurangi
Regional Park

Contact: 09 366 2000
parks@arc.govt.nz
www.arc.govt.nz

Tariff: $3–5

WENDERHOLM CAMPGROUND
Schischka Road, Wenderholm
Regional Park

Contact: 09 366 2000
parks@arc.govt.nz
www.arc.govt.nz

Tariff: $5–10

WHANGATEAU HOLIDAY PARK
559 Leigh Road, Whangateau

Contact: 09 422 6305
whpark@rodney.govt.nz
www.whangateauholidaypark.co.nz

Tariff: $20

WEST AUCKLAND

KARAMATURA FARM PADDOCK
Huia Road, Waitakere Ranges
Regional Park

Contact: 09 366 2000
parks@arc.govt.nz
www.arc.govt.nz

Tariff: $3–5

KARAMATURA CAMPGROUND
(accessible only by foot)

Karamatura Valley, Waitakere
Ranges Regional Park

Contact: 09 366 2000
parks@arc.govt.nz
www.arc.govt.nz

Tariff: $3–5

MCCREADIES PADDOCK
(accessible only by foot)

Karekare Road, Waitakere
Ranges Regional Park

Contact: 09 366 2000
parks@arc.govt.nz
www.arc.govt.nz

Tariff: $3–5

ODLINS 2 CAMPSITE
(accessible only by foot)

Lone Kauri Road, Waitakere
Ranges Regional Park

Contact: 09 366 2000
parks@arc.govt.nz
www.arc.govt.nz

Tariff: $3–5

OPANUKU CAMPGROUND
(accessible only by foot)

Mountain Road, Waitakere
Ranges Regional Park

Contact: 09 366 2000
parks@arc.govt.nz
www.arc.govt.nz

Tariff: $3–5

PAE O TE RANGI
(accessible only by foot)

Te Henga Road, Waitakere
Ranges Regional Park

Contact: 09 366 2000
parks@arc.govt.nz
www.arc.govt.nz

PARARAHA CAMPGROUND
(accessible only by foot
at low tide)

Karekare Carpark, Waitakere
Ranges Regional Park

Contact: 09 366 2000
parks@arc.govt.nz
www.arc.govt.nz

Tariff: $3–5

TUNNEL CAMPGROUND
(accessible only by foot
at low tide)

Karekare Carpark, Waitakere
Ranges Regional Park

Contact: 09 366 2000
parks@arc.govt.nz
www.arc.govt.nz

Tariff: $3–5

WHATIPU CAVES CAMPGROUND
(accessible only by foot)

Whatipu Road, Waitakere
Ranges Regional Park

Contact: 09 366 2000
parks@arc.govt.nz
www.arc.govt.nz

Tariff: $3–5

WHATIPU LODGE CAMPGROUND
Whatipu Road, Waitakere
Ranges Regional Park

Contact: 09 811 8860
parks@arc.govt.nz
www.arc.govt.nz

Tariff: $15 per car
(up to 4 people)

AUCKLAND

AVONDALE MOTOR PARK
46 Bollard Avenue, Avondale,
Auckland

Contact: 09 828 7228
avondalemotorpark@xtra.co.nz
www.aucklandmotorpark.co.nz

Tariff: $45–85

SOUTHLAND
EAST AUCKLAND

AMBURY CAMPSITE
Ambury Road, Ambury
Regional Park, Mangere Bridge

Contact: 09 366 2000
parks@arc.govt.nz
www.arc.govt.nz

Tariff: $5–10

BEACH FRONT CAMPSITE
Deerys Road, Tapapakanga
Regional Park

Contact: 09 366 2000
parks@arc.govt.nz
www.arc.govt.nz

Tariff: $5–10

BIG BAY MOTOR CAMP
271 Big Bay Road, RD 4,
Waiuku, Awhitu Peninsula

Contact: 09 235 1132
bigbay@ihug.co.nz
www.bigbaymotorcamp.co.nz

Tariff: $26–120

BLACKBERRY FLATS CAMPSITE
Off East Coast Road, Waharau
Regional Park

Contact: 09 366 2000
parks@arc.govt.nz
www.arc.govt.nz

Tariff: $5–10

BROOK HOMESTEAD CAMPSITE
Brook Road, Awhitu Regional Park

Contact: 09 366 2000
parks@arc.govt.nz
www.arc.govt.nz

Tariff: $5–10

CLARKS BEACH HOLIDAY PARK
226 Torkar Road extension,
Clarks Beach Auckland

Contact: 09 232 1685
cbhp@ihug.co.nz
www.cbhp.co.nz

Tariff: $30–150

CLIFF TOP CAMPSITE
Omana Beach Road,
Omana Regional Park

Contact: 09 366 2000
parks@arc.govt.nz
www.arc.govt.nz

Tariff: $5–10

LOWER MANGATAWHIRI CAMPSITE
(accessible only by foot)
Graeme White Road, Hunua Ranges
Regional Park

Contact: 09 366 2000
parks@arc.govt.nz
www.arc.govt.nz

Tariff: $3–5

**ORERE POINT TOP
10 HOLIDAY PARK**
Orere Road

Contact: 09 292 2774
orerepoint@xtra.co.nz
www.orerepointholidaypark.co.nz

Tarriff: $28–85

PENINSULA CAMPGROUND
Brook Road, Awhitu
Regional Park

Contact: 09 366 2000
parks@arc.govt.nz
www.arc.govt.nz

Tariff: $5–10

PIGGOTT'S CAMPSITE
(accessible only by foot)

Lilburne Road Track, Hunua
Ranges Regional Park

Contact: 09 366 2000
parks@arc.govt.nz
www.arc.govt.nz

Tariff: $3–5

**PORT WAIKATO TOP
10 HOLIDAY PARK**
115 Maunsell Road,
Port Waikato

Contact: 09 232 9857
www.portwaikatoholidaypark.co.nz

Tariff: $24–105

SEA VIEW CAMPSITE
Deerys Road, Tapapakanga
Regional Park

Contact: 09 366 2000
parks@arc.govt.nz
www.arc.govt.nz

Tariff: $5–10

**SOUTH AUCKLAND
CARAVAN PARK**
25 Ararimu Road,
Ramarama, Drury

Contact: 09 294 8903
sacp@ihug.co.nz

Tariff: $26–42

TAWHITOKINO CAMPSITE
(accessible only by foot
at low tide)

Southern end of beach,
Tawhitokino Regional Park

Contact: 09 366 2000
parks@arc.govt.nz
www.arc.govt.nz

Tariff: $3–5

UPPER MANGATAWHIRI CAMPSITE
Moumoukai Road, Hunua
Ranges Regional Park

Contact: 09 366 2000
parks@arc.govt.nz
www.arc.govt.nz

Tariff: $3–5

WAIHEKE ISLAND

POUKARAKA FLATS CAMPSITE
Gordon's Road, Whakanewha
Regional Park, Waiheke Island

Contact: 09 366 2000
parks@arc.govt.nz
www.arc.govt.nz

Tariff: $5–10

AUCKLAND REGIONAL COUNCIL

ABOVE: **Shakespear Regional Park,
Whangaparaoa Peninsula**
RIGHT: **Awhitu Peninsula**
FOLLOWING PAGES: **Tranquil waters
at Whangaroa**

→ LET'S GO CAMPING IN

COROMANDEL

3200 Long Bay Road, 3 km west of Coromandel town

Contact
07 866 8720
lbmccoromandel@xtra.co.nz

Capacity
Long Bay:
26 unpowered / 52 powered

Tucks Bay:
26 unpowered

Open
all year

Bookings
recommended peak season

Price
$15 adult / $8 child unpowered;
$16 adult / $8 child powered

The township of Coromandel makes an excellent base for exploring the northern extremities of the peninsula of the same name, and if you're looking for somewhere to stay out this way, Long Bay will suit you down to the ground. Located just 3 km from the town centre down a quiet no-exit road, Long Bay is both handy and peaceful. This, however, is just part of its charm, because this small, family-run motor camp is also set along two small bays in the Long Bay Scenic Reserve.

Backing the bays, the 23 ha forest reserve is lush and interesting, with the odd remnant kauri — some big, old daddies — as well as a wide variety of other native trees, too, such as puriri, rimu, totara, putaputaweta, nikau and all manner of tree ferns and mosses. The reserve, which can be explored via a couple of tracks, is a significant feature of the Long Bay Motor Camp.

Long Bay itself lies at the entrance to the campsite, the larger and busier of the two areas. All of the powered sites are here, along with several nice tenting nooks (including absolute beachfront) and the facilities block.

There is a definite air of community here, with lots of family holidaymakers making new friends during the summer months. The beach itself is good for swimming and fishing, and there are dinghies and kayaks for hire, a boat ramp and fish-cleaning facilities.

Just over the hill is the happy campers' dream: Tucks Bay — a non-powered area with 26 sites. This picturesque little bay offers lawn-like pitches with a pretty bush backdrop. The somewhat craggy bay is fit for paddling and rock-pooling, and has open sea views. A short, winding road runs over the saddle from Long Bay to Tucks, so you can drive over, walk over or take the pleasant coastal path around the point (it'll take you 10 minutes to walk via coast or hill, so bear this in mind if you're going to and fro to have a shower or do the laundry). Speaking of which: Tucks Bay offers a water supply and long-drop toilets only. All other facilities are at Long Bay.

Those facilities comprise toilets, coin-op showers, kitchen (with a small dining area) and laundry — all fairly basic, a bit old, but perfectly clean and acceptable in all other vital regards. Your affable hosts Gail and Debbie, who run the park on leasehold from the local council, sell basic groceries from their office shop.

TOURISM COROMANDEL / ANDY BELCHER

SCALE CASTLE ROCK FOR GRAND VIEWS OF THE PENINSULA

The start of this two-hour return walk is approximately 5 km from the Coromandel end of the 309 Road. This spiky, pinnacled local landmark (526 m) is thought to be the remains of an eroded volcano that erupted around 12 million years ago. Easy going to begin with, the walk turns into a challenging scramble nearer the top. Those with less energy to burn can instead take a stroll through the Waiau Kauri Grove (3 km further along the 309), where you can get up close and personal with the majestic kauri trees — the largest of which is almost 2 m in diameter. Go on, give it a hug.

TAKE A TRAIN RIDE

The area's most famous conservation project is at Driving Creek Railway (tel 07 866 8703, www.drivingcreekrailway.co.nz; trains daily 10.15am and 2.00pm, more frequently run in summer). It's taken local potter Barry Brickell and his helpers more than quarter of a century to build this astonishing narrow-gauge railway. Your journey starts from the charming and ramshackle potteries, where you can view and buy works by Barry and local artists, before snaking and clacking almost 3 km through regenerating bush. At the end of the line, after climbing about 120 m, you reach the ziggurat viewing platform known as the Eyefull Tower from where there are fabulous views. Your train fare goes towards the restoration project that has seen the planting of thousands of native saplings, including about 1700 kauri. The ride costs $20 per adults, $11 per child and $50 per family.

EXPLORE HISTORIC COROMANDEL TOWN

Once a 10,000-strong community built upon gold mining and kauri logging, today the township is home to fewer than 2000 people, and serves largely as a tourist hub and centre for the peninsula's alternative lifestylers who live in its green and pleasant environs. To get a handle on the town, visit the Goldfield Centre and Stamper Battery (410 Buffalo Road, tel 07 866 7933) or the Mining and Historic Museum (841 Rings Road, tel 07 866 7251). After checking out the local galleries, dine in any one of many decent cateries or head to the famous Coromandel Smoking Company and get yourself a picnic supply of some fine smoked fish. After dark, we'd recommend an outing to one of the town's friendly establishments — the Admiral's Arms is our favourite. For more information, visit www.coromandeltown.co.nz.

**PREVIOUS PAGE: Owharoa Falls, Karangahake Gorge
LEFT: Enjoy a ride on the Driving Creek Railway
FAR LEFT: Northern Coromandel coastline**

TOURISM COROMANDEL / DRIVING CREEK RAILWAY

**Off Waikawau Beach Road,
37 km north of Coromandel
town via Colville**

Contact
DOC Kauaeranga
07 867 9080
www.doc.govt.nz

Capacity
200 unpowered

Open
all year

Bookings
required December and January
07 866 1106

Price
$9 adult / $2 child

PHOTONEWZEALAND / SPID

The northern Coromandel is widely considered to be the most beautiful part of the peninsula, with the bushy Moehau Range at its centre and a fascinating collection of bays along its shore. Any exploration around here will open doors to terrific walks, great beaches and much, much more — accessible by scenic driving routes with stunning views.

The little settlement of Colville, 25 km north of Coromandel town, is your last stop for food and fuel — the general store is fairly well stocked and the café will be open if you're lucky. This is also your last stop for serviced camping; there are several options in the vicinity. From here on in, it's back-to-nature camping, but who could resist with five excellent DOC campsites to choose from?

Waikawau Bay is home to the largest and most popular of the five, the closest to Colville by 20 minutes or so, accessed via a winding gravel road. Once you're down the hill and the dust has settled, you will encounter verdant farmland, fringed by a gorgeous sandy bay that stretches along the coast for 2 km, backed by dunes and the Waikawau River.

The camp is split into two main areas, the larger one on the seaward side of the road, sprawling through interconnected paddocks. A camp office and information board lie at this entrance. On the other side of the road is Pump Paddock, boasting acres of flat, spongy grass and a bit more shade — it's an absolute picnickers' delight.

The facilities here are very basic, with only long-drop toilets, the odd sink and cold showers. However, this beautiful place is a haven for those wishing to get away from it all and you'll find it surprisingly busy during the summer period. That Kiwi families flock here to while away the days is a real testament to their hardiness. No television lounge, not even an ice-cream shop . . .

The beach is fantastic, and will easily eat up the hours. It's great for swimming, diving, fishing, kayaking or just for taking a wander on and spotting birds. Just remember to respect this special and fragile dune environment, home to the endangered New Zealand dotterel (tuturiwhatu) and variable oystercatcher during the breeding season.

Those seeking a more remote experience should keep driving north through Waikawau to Stony Bay, the next DOC campground (52 km from Coromandel; the last 7 km of which is pretty rough and requires good driving skills). It has just 70 sites on a spacious 5 ha, so that should stop the neighbour's soccer ball from knocking your drink over. Stony Bay has long-drop toilets, a water supply, cold showers, barbecues and picnic tables.

MARVEL AT THE SPECTACULAR COASTAL VIEWS ON THE COROMANDEL WALKWAY

Starting at Stony Bay, this walk to Fletcher Bay starts with a well-graded track that leads up the eastern side of the Moehau Range before dropping back down to sea level. There are memorable views all the way, including lookouts over the aptly named Sugar Loaf (221 m) and the Pinnacles offshore (not to be confused with the other Pinnacles, inland). Although this is for the most part an easy walk, you'll need to allow a whole day to get to Fletcher Bay and back (it's six or seven hours return) or you can just walk part of the track and soak up the views. The track can also be biked by those adventurous types who can complete a circuit of the northern peninsula by heading into the hills on the Bridle Track and zipping down towards Sugar Loaf before meeting up with the walkway about three quarters of the way along. Sounds easy? You might want to buy the Kennett brothers' *Classic New Zealand Mountain Bike Rides* book before you take our word for it.

JOIN A FASCINATING NATURE TOUR

The local Moehau Environment Group (tel 07 866 6926, www.meg.org.nz), a local hard-working volunteer group, guides interesting trips around the area, as well as beavering away on environmental projects around north Coromandel. Their summer programme usually runs for about three weeks during January — perfectly timed for you and any children in tow to have some fun and get an education at the same time.

Trips range from half-day jaunts to the rock pools, through to full-on hikes through the hills where you can learn about the kiwi sanctuary. There's even a trip out to Cuvier Island where you can walk amongst saddlebacks, kakariki, skinks and gecko.

Check their website for details, or look out for their printed programme which should be stuck to the outside of the camp shop at Waikawau. Bookings are essential.

**FAR LEFT: Waikawau Bay campsite
LEFT: The Coromandel Coastal Walkway is a favourite with walkers and mountain bikers**

TOURISM COROMANDEL / DREAMLAND DESIGN

**Harsant Avenue, Hahei,
38 km from Whitianga,
28 km from Tairua**

Contact
07 866 3889
www.haheiholidays.co.nz

Capacity
121 unpowered / 203 powered

Open
all year

Bookings
recommended
(essential during peak times)

Price
variable; indicative:
$53 for two people unpowered;
$64 for two people powered

TOURISM COROMANDEL / ANDY BELCHER

Hahei is the quintessential Kiwi summer town, blanketed with pretty holiday homes fronting on to a mighty fine swimming beach with an outlook of shoreline crags and outlying islands. But that's not the only reason people come here: they also come for Cathedral Cove nearby, one of the most photogenic beaches you'll ever see, visited by mammoth hordes that transform Hahei into a car park in the height of the season. Luckily this chaos doesn't last long, because this town can hardly handle it: its amenities largely confined to a petrol station, dairy and café. If you're visiting during the school holidays, be prepared to queue for your popsicle. The rest of the year, normal operations resume — you'll find Hahei a rather quiet and unassuming hamlet.

So here we have an excellent campground in a particularly popular holiday spot. Yet despite this, Hahei Holiday Resort manages to retain a laid-back atmosphere — somewhat of an achievement. While it seems that many of New Zealand's seaside resorts have gone slick and businesslike (which they probably have to, just to survive), Hahei is still hanging a bit loose. Maybe it's because it's family-run and firmly family-oriented, but there's something about this place that encourages fun . . . but that could just be the sunshine going to our heads.

The campground is right next to the beach but sheltered from the coastal breeze by big dunes. (Some powered sites enjoy sea views.) Divided into a number of distinct areas, there are plenty of mature pohutukawa and hedgerows of trees and shrubs. Powered and unpowered sites are largely mixed up, although there are a few tent-only enclaves — the field by the stream is particularly welcoming.

Toilet blocks are dotted around the grounds, with the main facilities block situated by the entrance. They're not the flashest we've seen, but they're certainly functional, clean and well equipped. Some of the many useful extras include a drying room, comfortable television lounge, coin-operated barbecues and a fish-cleaning area. Supplies can be found at the general store, a pleasant five-minute walk away on the main road.

Hahei is named after Hei, said to have arrived on Te Arawa waka with the great explorer Kupe. The Ngati Hei iwi settled this area and one of their old pa sites stands sentry over the bay. Do make the effort to walk up to it — it's just over the stream and up the hill.

AMBLE ROUND THE COAST TO CATHEDRAL COVE

This makes for a very pleasant outing, a walk (one and a half to two hours return) along a well-graded path that undulates from Hahei Beach to the cove (with side tracks to Gemstone Bay and Stingray Bay along the way). The cove gets its name from the mighty arch that extends through the headland. Eroded over thousands of years, you can wander through the arch when the tide's out, laze about on the golden sands or take a dip in the crystal clear waters. At the far end of the cove is another spectacular geological feature, Te Hoho rock — an inshore stack that was most likely created by the collapse of an arch similar to the Cathedral.

DIG YOURSELF INTO A NATURAL HOT POOL AT HOT WATER BEACH

A must-do activity that's all natural and absolutely free, courtesy of the local geology. This landscape was once a frenzy of fiery volcanism, although evidence of that is largely confined to the weathered peaks of dead volcanoes dotted about the peninsula. Just offshore from Hot Water Beach is thought to be a huge reservoir of superheated water — a couple of kilometres under the sea floor — which snakes its way up through the rocks and escapes into the sand on the beach. Armed with a spade, an hour or two either side of low tide you can fashion yourself a therapeutic hot soak and enjoy the seascape while you're at it.

GRAZE AND BROWSE AT COLENSO COUNTRY CAFÉ AND SHOP

This is the sort of place that makes you realise how lucky you are to live in Godzone — great coffee and fine homemade fare in a slightly unlikely location. Whenuakite, about 12 km from Hahei on State Highway 25, is a rural dot on the Coromandel map. At the southern end of the settlement, Colenso sits virtually alone yet attracts many to its door. The café turns out fresh and wholesome meals and snacks which can be enjoyed in the delightful cottage garden, or inside where you will also find a cornucopia of giftware and quality Kiwi-made arts and crafts. Tel 07 866 3725; open daily 10am–5pm, closed August.

TOURISM COROMANDEL / ANDY BELCHER

FAR LEFT: The coastline around Hahei boasts dramatic bluffs, stretches of glorious sand and rocky shores
LEFT: The famous arch of Cathedral Cove

Kauaeranga Visitor Centre, 12 km east of Thames (turn off State Highway 25 along Banks Road, 500 m south of Thames)

Contact
DOC Kauaeranga
07 867 9080
www.doc.govt.nz

Capacity
230 unpowered sites spread over eight campgrounds

Open
some camping areas all year; others summer only

Bookings
not required

Price
$9 adult / $2 child

Home to the greatest expanse of walking and tramping tracks in the Coromandel, the Kauaeranga Valley forms part of the Coromandel Forest Park, which spreads itself in patches from one end of the peninsula to the other. Although the valley was brutally logged of its kauri over a 60-year period from around 1870, it remains a satisfying place to visit, where original forest giants can still be seen — northern rata, rimu and tawa and even the occasional kauri — alongside a healthy collection of regenerating species. Not far from Thames, the gateway to the Coromandel, Kauaeranga Recreation Reserve offers a vastly different experience to that of the sandy beaches of the coast. This is a quiet, green place of dappled light and an aroma of wood sap.

The shiny new DOC visitor centre lies 12 km from the Thames turn-off, with the last 2 km unsealed. From here the road runs a further 9 km (all gravel), with the valley's myriad attractions accessible along its length. To find out more, get a copy of DOC's *Coromandel Recreation Information* leaflet ($1) available at the visitor centre or downloadable from DOC's website.

Steep-sided to begin with, the valley opens out into a bush-clad wonderland. It boasts short walks to suit everyone from go-getter to granddad: nature trails, lookout tramps and minor detours to picnic spots and swimming holes. There are longer, more challenging tracks that take you deep into the ranges, and up to some of the area's most lofty peaks such as The Pinnacles (773 m). Relics of the logging era, including old camps, dams and water races, are also spread throughout the valley.

There are eight DOC campsites alongside the valley road. They're much of a muchness: welcoming flat pitches close to the river with plenty of room, some nestled into bushy, private nooks. Cooking platforms and barbecue grates are provided, as are toilets, with some sites providing shelter for cooking out of the rain.

This is back-to-basics camping, so you'll need to be self-sufficient. Remember to take cash for your registration envelope (or pay at the visitor centre when it's open) and take your rubbish out with you.

PHOTONEWZEALAND / LYNETTE MILL

THINGS TO SEE AND DO IN KAUAERANGA VALLEY

FOLLOW IN THE FOOTSTEPS OF KAURI BUSHMEN ON THE KAUAERANGA KAURI TRAIL

Pack tracks built between the 1870s and 1920s provide access to some of Kauaeranga's most stunning scenery. The main entry point for the tracks is at the road end, 9 km beyond the visitor centre. From here a mere 20-minute constitutional will get you to a viewing point for the Billygoat Falls, but to truly get amongst it you'll need to head off on a longer mission. Getting to Hydrocamp (a now derelict campsite used by workers to put in power lines to the east coast in the 1940s) will take around one and a half hours via the Webb Creek route and about two and a half hours via Billygoat Basin. Another couple of hours will see you atop the spiky monoliths, The Pinnacles. These are well worth visiting, but to get from the road end to The Pinnacles and back in one day is a long day's walking. We think the best way to do it all *and* enjoy it is to spend a night at the rather luxurious — by DOC standards — Pinnacles Hut ($15 adult / 7.50 child). Or, if you don't mind lugging the tent in, camping is possible at Billygoat Basin and beside the Pinnacles Hut ($7.50 adult / 3.50 child). More information can be obtained from DOC's *Kauaeranga Kauri Trail* leaflet ($1).

TAKE A DIP IN HOFFMAN'S POOL

After all that walking you're going to need to soak your feet and rinse the sweat off, right? About a kilometre from the visitor centre, this lovely swimming hole on the Kauaeranga River is an ideal spot for a picnic and a swim. Other great places for a splash about can be found close to the Hotoritori and Shag Stream campgrounds.

BRING A BIKE!

Those with reserves of energy — and two wheels — can ride one of the two mountain bike tracks that start from Hotoritori campground. There's a 750 m loop for beginners and a 4 km one for the eager. Not enough? There's always riding up and down the main drag — all 16 km of it . . . there's nothing like a bit of gravel road to improve your skills.

ABOVE: The craggy Pinnacles as seen from the air on the eastern side of the Coromandel
LEFT: From the valley floor at Hikuai, the Pinnacles stand out starkly on the skyline

BEACHAVEN MOTEL AND HOLIDAY PARK
21 Leo Street, Waihi Beach
Contact: 07 863 5505
beachavenwaihi@xtra.co.nz
www.beachaven.co.nz
Tariff: $32–180

BLEDISLOE HOLIDAY PARK
Little Waihi Beach, (near Te Puke)
Contact: 07 533 2157
info@bledisloeholiday.co.nz
www.bledisloeholiday.co.nz
Tariff: $22–55

BOWENTOWN BEACH HOLIDAY PARK
Seaforth Road, Waihi Beach
Contact: 07 863 5381
info@bowentown.co.nz
www.bowentown.co.nz
Tariff: $35–180

COROMANDEL MOTEL AND HOLIDAY PARK
636 Rings Road, Coromandel
Contact: 07 866 8830
enquiries@coromandelholidaypark.co.nz
www.coromandelholidaypark.co.nz
Tariff: $24–170

DICKSON HOLIDAY PARK
Victoria Street, Tararu, Thames
Contact: 07 868 7308
enq@dicksonpark.co.nz
www.dicksonpark.co.nz
Tariff: enquire for tariff

HARBOURSIDE HOLIDAY PARK
135 Albert Street, Whitianga
Contact: 07 866 5746
info@harboursidewhitianga.co.nz
www.harboursidewhitianga.co.nz
Tariff: $30–135

HOT WATER BEACH HOLIDAY PARK
790 Hot Water Beach Road, Hot Water Beach
Contact: 0800 2 HOTBEACH
info@hotwaterbeachholidaypark.co.nz
www.hotwaterbeachholidaypark.com
Tariff: $30–110

KARANGAHAKE RIVER LODGE AND CAMPERVAN PARK
45 River Road, RD 4, Karangahake
Contact: 07 862 8481
info@river-road.co.nz
www.river-road.co.nz
Tariff: $30–100

MERCURY BAY HOLIDAY PARK
121 Albert Street, Whitianga
Contact: 07 866 5579
mercurybayholidaypark@xtra.co.nz
www.mercurybayholidaypark.co.nz
Tariff: $36–180

MIRANDA HOLIDAY PARK
595 Front Miranda Road, Miranda
Contact: 07 867 3205
mirandaholidaypark@xtra.co.nz
www.mirandaholidaypark.co.nz
Tariff: $40–195

OTAUTU BAY FARM CAMP
257 Port Jackson Road, Colville
Contact: 07 866 6801
otautubaycamp@xtra.co.nz
Tariff: $25–29

PAPA AROHA HOLIDAY PARK
Colville Road, RD 4, Papa Aroha
Contact: 07 866 8818
www.papaaroha.co.nz
Tariff: $26–58

SEABREEZE TOURIST PARK
1043 Tairua–Whitianga Road (SH 25), RD 1, Whenuakite
Contact: 07 866 3050
info@seabreezetouristpark.co.nz
www.seabreezetouristpark.co.nz
Tariff: $20–130

SETTLERS MOTOR CAMP
101 Leander Road, Whangamata
Contact: 07 865 8181
settlersmotorcamp@xtra.co.nz
Tariff: $26–60

**SHELLY BEACH TOP
10 HOLIDAY PARK**
243 Colville Road, Coromandel

Contact: 07 866 8988
shelly@world-net.co.nz
www.shellybeachcoromandel.co.nz

Tariff: $32–145

TAPU MOTOR CAMP
SH 25, Tapu

Contact: 07 868 4837
tapumotorcamp@xtra.co.nz
www.tapumotorcamp.co.nz

Tariff: $20–40

TE PURU HOLIDAY PARK
473 Thames Coast Road
Te Puru, Thames

Contact: 07 868 2879
tepuruholidaypark@xtra.co.nz
www.tepuruholidaypark.co.nz

Tariff: $32–95

**WAIHI BEACH TOP
10 HOLIDAY PARK**
15 Beach Road, Waihi Beach

Contact: 07 863 5504
info@waihibeach.com
www.waihibeach.com

Tariff: $36–227

WHANGAMATA MOTOR CAMP
Barbara Ave, Whangamata

Contact: 07 865 9128
adbrien@xtra.co.nz

Tariff: $24–65

TOURISM COROMANDEL

Granite Wharf, near Port Jackson

BAY OF PLENTY, EASTLAND AND TE UREWERA

11 MCLAREN FALLS PARK

McLaren Falls Road, 18 km southwest of Tauranga (off State Highway 29)

Contact
Tauranga District Council
07 577 7000
www.tauranga.govt.nz

Capacity
sufficient (all unpowered)

Open
all year

Bookings
not required

Price
$5 adult (under 16 free)

If you're looking to explore the Bay and its myriad attractions from a base offering more personal space and tranquillity, McLaren Falls is for you.

The Bay of Plenty is unquestionably bountiful in many regards, including sand, surf and sunshine. And while Captain Cook let the cat well and truly out of the bag when he named it, being the home of the world's finest fuzzy fruit has made it all the more famous (well, at least within New Zealand anyway). Not even an influx of migrant Aucklanders can detract from its appeal as a holiday destination ripe for your exploration.

The beaches *are* beautiful, which is why the best of them are liberally fringed with urban development. If you're looking to explore the Bay and its myriad attractions from a base offering more personal space and tranquillity, McLaren Falls is for you. Just a 20-minute drive inland from downtown Tauranga, this waterside park offers trees, trees and more trees — as well as the undeniably picturesque Lake McLaren, created in 1925 when the Wairoa River was dammed for a hydroelectric power plant.

The 750 ha park is popular year-round, especially on summer weekends when the locals favour it as a picnic spot. As for its obvious charms as a camping destination, those same locals have been hiding this light under a bushel, for sure. That situation, however, may well change once folk hear about the new information centre and ablution block which will make McLaren Falls even more inviting for the unpowered camper. That said, this is primarily a park not a campground, so only the bare necessities are on offer.

You can freedom camp around the park, except where signs say otherwise. There are two established, flat fields, which have toilets and spigots on hand. Closest to the entrance (and information centre) is a waterside field with a sheltered aspect, encircled by trees. The lake can be seen between their trunks while on the opposing shore hills rise up, grazed by sheep. We hope you like sheep, because there are a few hundred of them roaming the park itself. (Do they nibble your chocolate biscuits if you leave them unattended?) The second field is further on, a little way up a hill with more exposure to the sunshine. There's just one long-drop toilet here.

Both camping areas have picnic tables. Neither are great drainers, so in the wet, pitch on high ground. There's no public shelter either, although the ranger may be able to sort you out a bed in one of the on-site hostels if things turn to mush. You'll meet the rangers — they reside on site and drive around the camp to collect your fees.

And here's an important note: the park gates are open 8am–7.30pm in summer, 8am–5.30pm in winter. Either side of these times, you're either in or you're out!

PARK UP IN THE PARK

Tree-huggers will be pleased to know that McLaren Falls Park contains one of the North Island's best collections of trees. It is also home to a diverse range of birdlife, which you may meet on explorations via a network of pleasant paths. The lake offers year-round trout fishing (licence required), but for those who prefer terrestrial animals, Marshall's Animal Park, (tel 07 543 3734, www.marshallsanimalpark.co.nz), located within the park's grounds, offers opportunities to meet Tibetan yaks, shire horses and chinchillas, among many other unusual creatures. It's open daily in the summer school holidays and Wednesdays and Thursdays 10am–2pm the rest of the year.

GET WITH THE GLOW WORMS

These can be viewed along one of the park's short walkways or, for the more adventurous, by kayak . . . in the dark. Blair and his team at Waimarino Adventure Park (tel 07 576 4233, www.waimarino.com) will take you on a truly unique and exciting kayaking trip after dark to visit the secret glow-worm canyon. Trips depart from the edge of Lake McLaren, with all equipment provided.

EXPLORE THE PLENTIFUL BAY

Highlights include gorgeous beaches (Waihi Beach, the Mount, Papamoa . . .), adventure sports, excellent walks, a brilliant new municipal gallery and heaps of fabulous eating and drinking (especially on Tauranga's waterfront Strand). Visit www.bayofplentynz.com for detailed information.

TAURANGA DISTRICT COUNCIL

PREVIOUS PAGE: The road to East Cape
ABOVE: McLaren Falls Park in glorious autumnal colours

**Ohiwa Harbour Road
(off State Highway 2), 14 km
west of Opotiki, 35 km east
of Whakatane**

Contact

07 315 4741

www.ohiwaholidays.co.nz

Capacity

60 unpowered / 120 powered

Open

all year

Bookings

recommended peak season

Price

$18 adult / 10 child

GEOFF MARSHALL / PHOTONEWZEALAND

The Bay of Plenty coastline lavishes its visitors with beach after beach of dazzling beauty, punctuated by gnarled pohutukawa trees and golden sand dunes. Conveniently for campers there are numerous campgrounds very near the ocean, and a very nice bunch they are, too. If you're heading east, however, our pick is Ohiwa Harbour. Why's that? Well, because this splendid campground is not only situated on a sandspit with a gorgeous beach out front, but it's also bent around a bird-filled tidal harbour and backed by a bushy nature reserve. Now that's lavish.

The owners of Ohiwa Family Holiday Park are certainly doing their bit to enhance this unique natural environment. Since they bought the campground almost 20 years ago they've been helping to restore the dunes in front of it. The pitches closest to the beach used to be but a stone's throw away from the high-tide mark; today they are several hundred metres away. The endangered New Zealand dotterel (tuturiwhatu) and oystercatchers nest here in summer, so be sure to use the pathways to the beach rather than walking through the dunes willy-nilly.

That's not the only hard work the owners have undertaken, because this is also one of the smartest holiday parks in New Zealand. The grounds are highly manicured, with prickle-free lawn pitches landscaped into excellent terracing — almost everyone gets a view. A picturesque combination of young pohutukawa and palms offer shade and a bit of privacy — and in high summer, you'll need it. Although not quite as sardine-like as some, this place is absolutely packed over the holidays, wall-to-wall with families in their homes-away-from-home. If you're after a little P and Q, we recommend you visit in the off season or try to score a site along the beachfront or down the far end (that's the campsite numbers starting with Ds or Es).

This super-slick operation has an extensive array of facilities, all immaculate and in excellent condition. The two kitchen blocks have good washing-up space along with the necessary electricals, including an oven. There's sheltered outdoor dining plus a barbecue area and fish-cleaning sinks. Children will be well distracted with kayak hire (see page 63), a couple of rope swings, a toddlers' playground and the incredible jumping pillow, a big inflatable jump-o-rama. Watch your child bounce around wildly with other children like hankies in a tumble dryer. Makes you wish you were young enough to give it a go . . .

Internet is available, both Wi-Fi and at terminals in the games room, which also has television, air hockey and table tennis. The office shop has bread, milk, ice cream, newspapers, bait and other basic supplies. And just when you thought it couldn't get any better: an espresso bus visits during peak season.

THINGS TO SEE AND DO
NEAR OHIWA HARBOUR

HEAD FOR THE HILLS AND GET A VIEW FROM THE PA

Starting just along the road from the campground, this 40-minute walk climbs through regenerating native bush before breaking out into farmland near the top of the hill. The views from the pa site are fantastic — over the harbour and across to Ohope Beach, and out to smouldering Whakaari (White Island) 50 km to the north. On the way back down, take the right fork: this track leads you down a steep path that brings you out at the back of the campground.

HIT THE BEACH

Wander through the dunes, keeping an eye and ear out for the ginger-tinged dotterels pripping and pweeping as you go. There's room for everyone on this expansive beach, whether you're up for a spot of bat down, kite-flying, sandcastle building, throwing a longline out for tonight's tea or just relaxing with a book. It's also a good spot for boogie-boarding, body surfing and safe swimming when conditions are right.

KAYAK TRANQUIL OHIWA HARBOUR

A few hours can easily be whiled away exploring these estuarine waterways, which cover around 26 sq km in all. It's rich in plant and birdlife, so bring your camera and binoculars in a dry bag if you can — if you're lucky you may spot a banded rail (moho-peruru), fernbird (matata) or even the well-camouflaged bittern standing frozen amongst the reeds with its beak pointed skywards. At low tide, over three quarters of the harbour bed is exposed — so check tide times to avoid getting left high and dry. You can hire kayaks from the camp office.

WHAKATANE TOURISM

LEFT: **Ohiwa Family Holiday Park**
ABOVE: **While away the hours on Ohiwa Harbour**

13 MARAEHAKO BAY

State Highway 35, 90 km northeast of Opotiki, 245 km from Gisborne

Contact
07 325 2685

Capacity
ample unpowered

Open
all year

Bookings
not required

Price
$12 adult / $8 child

If you were setting out on a journey to find the best camping spot in New Zealand, your imagination might conjure up a golden cove, its waters a pool of sparkling blue, flanked by craggy points and backed by bird-filled native bush.

If you were setting out on a journey to find the best camping spot in New Zealand, your imagination might conjure up a golden cove, its waters a pool of sparkling blue, flanked by craggy points and backed by bird-filled native bush. Big, old pohutukawa would stand along the foreshore, their gnarled trunks and twisting branches entwining into a canopy of scarlet explosions. At Maraehako Bay you have reached this destination.

The Hei whanau owns and works the farm here, located along arguably the most beautiful stretch of the East Cape road. They have set aside this beachside field for their visitors. There's not much to it, at least in the way of facilities: just a bunker-like building housing a kitchen, showers and toilets, and some rubbish bins. But this little camping spot is simply magic, complete with a backdrop of verdant, fern-covered hills from where a stream runs down to meet the sea. The stony beach is steeply pitched but largely safe for swimming, the family says, in favourable conditions.

There's a real 'freedom camping' feel here that the presence of the facilities and tiny office-cum-shop thankfully do little to dispel. There are no powered sites, no permanents and nothing to book. Just come on in and pick your spot. Bold souls will probably want to peg out under the pohutukawa, in some of the most scenic and unspoilt waterfront sites in the country. It can get a bit blowy up the front, however, so bring long tent pegs or be prepared to rock your bits and pieces down. It's also a bit stony, so bring a thick sleeping mat too. For greater comfort and shelter from the breeze, camp in the open on the grassy field, or tuck yourself away in the shade at the foot of the hill.

Bea Hei looks after the camp and runs the shop which sells bread, milk and ice cream (open peak season only). You can bring your dogs if they're good. The showers have hot water, but note that water must be treated before drinking.

If the weather treats you mean, there's accommodation at the Maraehako Bay Retreat at the western edge of the bay, run by Bea's brother, Hamai. Between them they can hook you up all sorts of fun activities, including kayaking and fishing (see page 65).

SEE THE SEA. HANG OUT. DO NOUGHT.

Noodle around in the freshwater stream. Have a swim. Catch a fish (or at least give it a go). Suck an ice block — every day. Throw a banger on the barbecue. Read a book. Play catch or have a kick-around. Throw a stick for the dog. Sit in the shade and chew the fat. Let time drift slowly by. Be glad that despite all that you hear about Kiwi coastal camping dying out, we still have plenty of special places to go.

RING THE RETREAT AND SEE WHAT FUN'S ON OFFER

Also run by the Hei family, the Maraehako Bay Retreat (tel 07 325 2648, www.maraehako.co.nz) arranges all sorts of activities as well as running a lodge for those non-camping types. Why not hire a kayak? It's the perfect way to explore the bay and its interesting landforms, and hopefully spot some wildlife. Dolphin-watch, diving and all sorts of fishing trips are also on offer, hosted by a local expert and departing from the lodge. They can also arrange other adventures for you, such as horse trekking, guided walks, and a visit to the local marae. These are relaxed, unscheduled adventures, tailored especially for you. So if you really want to get to know the East Cape and its people, here's a great opportunity.

Absolute beachfront camping at Maraehako Bay

SARAH BENNETT AND LEE SLATER

167 Wharf Road (off State Highway 35), Tolaga Bay, 56 km northeast of Gisborne, 272 km from Opotiki

Contact
06 862 6716
tolagabayholidaypark@msn.com

Capacity
80 unpowered / 50 powered

Open
all year

Bookings
recommended peak season

Price
$12 per person unpowered /
$14 per person powered

SARAH BENNETT AND LEE SLATER

To anyone who has either been to or merely heard of Tolaga Bay, its historic wharf is probably what springs to mind. Sitting at the southern end of Tolaga's long, sandy crescent, its striking form stretches way, way out over the water, silhouetted against a backdrop of limestone bluffs. Perhaps it's just our inclination towards the salt-crusted remnants of New Zealand's maritime heritage, but we think it's worth camping here for the wharf alone. The wharf is, however, deteriorating at an alarming rate. Fortunately it has recently been classified as a place of outstanding historical significance, so with luck that will help local campaigners raise enough funds for the restoration work needed to safeguard its future.

To our great satisfaction, the Tolaga Bay Holiday Park sits right next to the wharf, separated from the beach by only a driftwood-covered dune. The grounds are somewhat unremarkable: a flat, rectangular field, covered in sandy grass, with a row of Norfolk pines plotted along the length of the dune. An old-school playground and unflash facilities block sit in the middle, around which is laid out a grid of fairly exposed sites. Around the edges, however, are a sizeable number of more sheltered, private sites — the best being down the far end of the park where a belt of macrocarpa offers shade from the heat and sneak-through peeks of the estuary.

In high summer the campground is full of lively family groups, the sort that make fun out of fresh air and sunshine. Sand-dusted children scrabble about with their boogie-boards or bike around the park yapping their heads off. The fisherfolk launch their dinghies throughout the day, in pursuit of some kaimoana for tea. Maybe it's this shared love of the seaside — or simply its relatively small size and down-home atmosphere — that gives this places its particularly laid-back and sociable atmosphere.

The facilities block is basic but entirely functional, and offers the bonus of piped music throughout. (There's nothing like a bit of 70s soft rock to help you through a bucket of dishes!)

The kitchen has the necessary electricals, including an oven. There's a fish-cleaning sink and a couple of worn barbecues. The no-frills playground will provide a few minutes' diversion for the youngsters, although the beach is where the real fun is had. A tractor is available for boat launching, and kayaks can also be hired.

The campsite shop has only the most basic supplies such as milk, bread and ice blocks; it's open during the summer holidays. Otherwise, your closest service town is Tolaga Bay, 3.5 km away — a sleepy hamlet, with a takeaway shop, pub, a couple of cafés and a few shops.

VISIT COOK'S COVE

Not far east of Tolaga Bay, this cove proved such a happy anchorage for the *Endeavour* in October 1769 that it was named after the captain himself. See for yourself what all the fuss was about by taking the walkway (two and a half hours return), which starts just 300 m from the campground. A well-formed track leads through manuka forest before reaching a lookout (125 m above sea level) with a wonderful vantage of the cove below. Having descended to the flats and come upon the stile, you can head left for the hole in the rock known to Maori as Te Kotere-o-te-Whenua. It's well worth the five-minute walk to see the natural archway used as a shortcut between the two coves; Tolaga Bay can be seen through the gap. From the stile you can also head right to the Cook monument (15 minutes; a good spot for a picnic) or continue on to the cove and its northern headland.

LEFT: Tolaga Bay wharf
ABOVE: Cook's Cove — just one of many places that bear the great explorer's name

WALK THE WHARF

At 660 m long, Tolaga Bay Wharf is reputed to be the longest in the southern hemisphere. Once the lynchpin of local trade and the shipping point for massive quantities of wool and livestock, the wharf — built between 1926 and 1929 — is now a more tranquil place to visit. Arguably one of New Zealand's most romantic waterside landmarks, the wharf is favoured for fishing (gurnard and kahawai are common catches) or just an amble to the end and back. It is possible to leap off it, as you will almost certainly see someone doing. It's particularly magical at dawn and dusk, when the light plays in its shadows, and on the water and the layered cliffs behind. Mesmerising.

Perhaps it's just our inclination towards the salt-crusted remnants of New Zealand's maritime heritage, but we think it's worth camping here for the wharf alone.

Te Urewera National Park, State Highway 38, 62 km northwest of Wairoa, 160 km southeast of Rotorua

Contact
06 837 3826
www.lake.co.nz

Capacity
15 unpowered / 44 powered

Open
all year

Bookings
required all year

Price
$12 adult / $5 child

Oh, the joys of the New Zealand road trip, where you get to use the words 'gravel' and 'highway' in the same sentence. So described, State Highway 38, 95 km of which is unsealed, joins the east coast town of Wairoa to State Highway 5 just south of Rotorua. This road winds through Te Urewera National Park, passing Lake Waikaremoana along the way. The motor camp sits proudly on its shore at Opourau, also known as Home Bay.

This is the largest of the North Island's national parks, 212,673 ha of rugged wilderness, centred around the Ikawhenua, Huiarau and Kahikatea Ranges. The southern end of the park is punctuated by uplifted and eroded escarpments, such as the famous Panekiri Bluff. Should you be fit enough to make it to the top, you will see for yourself that this is a landscape of incredible density — a seemingly endless web of thickly forested ridges and valleys stretching into the distance. Much of the park is inaccessible except to the hardcore back-country tramper and those undertaking the five-day Great Walk around the lake.

There is, however, much to be enjoyed without straying too far from the campground, including plenty of nature trails and day walks. It's a famously good fishery, too, with both rainbow and brown trout in good quantity and size — the average weight is allegedly 1.75 kg, with some reported catches in excess of 3 kg. This explains why the camp brims with boats, trailers and lifejacketed children. Covering a relatively small area, the grounds are dotted with chalets and cabins. There are two camping areas: one skirting around the central facilities block — busy but close to the kitchen — and the other a little further away, on the lake edge. This is our preferred spot — sites numbered from the early 30s upward. Swimming is possible here, although be prepared for waterfowl poop.

The central amenities block is sturdily built of timber with hard-wearing facilities. There is a spacious kitchen, which has an oven as well as the standard appliances including plenty of hotplates. There's also a water boiler, which is particularly helpful as the tap water was unpotable on our last visit. There are dining tables indoors, but the best place to eat is on the veranda, where you can enjoy views of the toetoe-fringed lake and moored pleasure boats. It's a very pretty sight, particularly when the light begins to fade.

The bathrooms are decked out in charming retro Formica, but could do with a scrub. Other facilities include a fish-cleaning sink, gas barbecues and a telephone booth. The camp office is located in the general store, which is well stocked with all manner of goods, including hot pies, bad novels, petrol — and a swarm of fishing flies.

DOC

LEFT: **Lake Waikaremoana Motor Camp**
ABOVE: **Te Urewera National Park**
— a place of deep, dense forest and
fascinating landforms

WALK IN THE WOODS

Much of Lake Waikaremoana is surrounded by dense, virgin forest, making for many a fascinating outing — so long as you know where you're going. To get your bearings, visit the Aniwaniwa DOC Visitor Centre (tel 06 837 3803, open daily), reached from the campground via the Black Beech Walk (30 minutes each way). Sadly inadequate for such a jewel of a national park, the visitor centre is currently confined to the basement due to rotten timber in the floors above. With any luck there'll be a new centre soon (check DOC's website for updates). However, helpful staff can still sort you out with maps and information on this remarkable environment and its rich Maori history. The centre is also the starting point for a number of short and all-day walks (as detailed in the DOC pamphlet *Lake Waikaremoana Walks*). A terrific half-day option is heading to Lake Waikareiti via the lake track (an easy hour each way), although it can also be completed as a loop on the Ruapani Circuit (six hours clockwise). This is a lovely walk to a wonderful lake, but even more adventure awaits if you get the boatshed key from DOC (see below). If you're not keen on boating but want to see a little bit more of the environs, keep walking clockwise along the lake edge for about 10 minutes until you come to the sheltered crescent-shaped bay. Isn't this the most divine lake-swimming spot you've ever seen? Go on, get your duds off. No one's watching.

POKE YOUR OAR INTO ONE OF NEW ZEALAND'S MOST PRISTINE LAKES

Before you set off to Lake Waikareiti, pick up the boatshed key and lifejackets from the DOC visitor centre, for which a modest fee is payable. Aluminium dinghies await you at the lake edge. Once upon the crystal waters, you will see that what the lake lacks in size it certainly makes up for in charm, being dotted with six little islands and surrounded by a pleasing mix of hummocky forest and wetlands. It's a quiet, serene place with an other-worldly feel.

GO CRUISING ON THE BIG LAKE

Created over 2000 years ago when a huge landslide dammed the Waikaretaheke River, Lake Waikaremoana ('sea of rippling waters') is a haven for boaties of all persuasions. If you don't have your own craft, kayak hire or tours are available with Waikaremoana Guided Tours (tel 06 837 3729), or you can get out the easy way on the local water taxi. Home Bay Shuttles (tel 06 837 3800, www.waikaremoana.com) offers various drop-offs and pick-ups allowing you to walk part of the main track or stop off somewhere for a spot of fishing. They also run short cruises, one of which scoots across to the far side of the lake to view a petrified forest, while another will get you close to a waterfall. You can arrange your water taxi service and get your fishing licence at the camp office.

BAY OF PLENTY

ACCOMMODATION TE PUNA
Cnr Minden and Auckland–
Waihi Roads (SH 2), Te Puna,
RD 6, Tauranga

Contact: 07 552 5621
tepuna.motel@xtra.co.nz
www.accommodationtepuna.co.nz

Tariff: $34–160

ATHENREE HOT SPRINGS AND HOLIDAY PARK
1 Athenree Road,
Athenree, Bay of Plenty

Contact: 07 863 5600
hotsprings@xtra.co.nz
www.athenreehotsprings.co.nz

Tariff: $32–160

AWAKERI HOT SPRINGS HOLIDAY PARK
SH 30, RD 2, Whakatane

Contact: 07 304 9117
awakeri.springs@xtra.co.nz
www.awakerisprings.co.nz

Tariff: $20–90

BAY VIEWS MOTEL AND HOLIDAY PARK
195 Arawa Avenue, Maketu
(near Te Puke)

Contact: 07 533 2222
bayviews@xtra.co.nz
www.bayviews.co.nz

Tariff: $20–100

BEACH HOLIDAY PARK
Town Point Road, Maketu
(near Te Puke)

Contact: 07 533 2165
bhp@xtra.co.nz
www.maketubeach.co.nz

Tariff: $20–115

COSY CORNER HOLIDAY PARK
40 Ocean Beach Road,
Mount Maunganui

Contact: 07 575 5899
stay@cosycorner.co.nz
www.cosycorner.co.nz

Tariff: $30–135

GOLDEN GROVE HOLIDAY PARK
73 Girven Road, Mount Maunganui

Contact: 07 575 5821
www.golden-grove.co.nz

Tariff: $24–90

MOUNT MAUNGANUI BEACHSIDE HOLIDAY PARK
1 Adams Avenue (at the base of
the Mount), Mount Maunganui

Contact: 07 575 4471
info@mountbeachside.co.nz
www.mountbeachside.co.nz

Tariff: $26

MURPHY'S HOLIDAY CAMP
SH 2, Matata (between
Te Puke and Whakatane)

Contact: 07 322 2136

Tariff: enquire for tariff

OHOPE BEACH TOP 10 HOLIDAY PARK
367 Harbour Road,
Ohope Beach

Contact: 07 312 4460
enquiries@ohopebeach.co.nz
www.ohopebeach.co.nz

Tariff: $36–285

OMOKOROA THERMAL HOLIDAY PARK
165 Omokoroa Beach Road,
RD 2, Tauranga

Contact: 07 548 0857
stay@omokoroa.co.nz
www.omokoroa.com

Tariff: $36–150

OPOTIKI HOLIDAY PARK
39 Potts Avenue, Opotiki

Contact: 07 315 6050
opotiki.holidays@xtra.co.nz
www.opotikiholidaypark.co.nz

Tariff: $50–110

PACIFIC PARK CHRISTIAN HOLIDAY CAMP
1110 Papamoa Beach Road,
Papamoa

Contact: 07 542 0018
office@ppchc.co.nz,
www.ppchc.co.nz

Tariff: $26–99

SAPPHIRE SPRINGS THERMAL POOLS AND HOLIDAY PARK
274 Hot Springs Road,
RD 2, Katikati

Contact: 07 549 0768
sapphire.springs@xtra.co.nz
www.sapphiresprings.net.nz

Tariff: $32–250

SILVER BIRCH HOLIDAY PARK AND MOTEL
101 Turret Road, Tauranga

Contact: 07 578 4603
silverbirch@xtra.co.nz
www.silverbirch.co.nz

Tariff: $30–105

TAURANGA TOURIST PARK
9 Mayfair Street (off
15th Ave), Tauranga

Contact: 07 578 3323
www.taurangatouristpark.co.nz

Tariff: $22–70

THORNTON BEACH HOLIDAY PARK
163 Beach Road, Thornton,
RD 4, Whakatane

Contact: 07 304 8296
www.thorntonbeach.co.nz

Tariff: $30–110

TIROHANGA BEACH MOTOR CAMP
SH 35, Tirohanga Beach, Opotiki

Contact: 07 315 7942
tmcamp@xtra.co.nz,
www.tirohangabeachmotorcamp.co.nz

Tariff: $28–85

WHAKATANE HOLIDAY PARK
McGarvey Road, Whakatane

Contact: 07 308 8694
whak@xtra.co.nz,
www.whakataneholidaypark.co.nz

Tariff: $60–85

EASTLAND

SHOWGROUNDS PARK MOTOR CAMP
20 Main Road, Makaraka,
Gisborne

Contact: 06 867 5299
camp@gisborneshow.co.nz
www.gisborneshow.co.nz

Tariff: $22–40

TE ARAROA HOLIDAY PARK
SH 35, Main Road,
Te Araroa, East Cape

Contact: 06 864 4873
bill.martin@xtra.co.nz

Tariff: $36–80

TE KAHA HOLIDAY PARK, MOTEL AND CAFE
SH 35, Te Kaha

Contact: 07 325 2894
tekahahp@xtra.co.nz
www.tekahaholidaypark.co.nz

Tariff: $16–130

WAIKANAE BEACH HOLIDAY PARK
Grey Street, Gisborne

Contact: 06 867 5634
motorcamp@gdc.govt.nz
www.gisborneholidaypark.co.nz

Tariff: $24–87

→ LET'S GO CAMPING IN

ROTORUA, TAUPO AND THE CENTRAL PLATEAU

Tarawera Falls Road, 27 km southwest of Kawerau

Contact
DOC Rotorua
06 348 3610
www.doc.govt.nz

Capacity
30 unpowered

Open
all year

Bookings
recommended peak season

Price
$7 adult / $2 child

PREVOUS PAGE: **DOC's Whakapapa Visitor Centre**
ABOVE: **Lake Tarawera with Mount Tarawera in the background**
RIGHT: **Tarawera Falls**

Once upon a time the Pink and White Terraces at Lake Rotomahana were considered to be one of the wonders of the world. In June 1886, however, Mount Tarawera roared to life in a now legendary display of raging fire and billowing clouds of ash. The volcano's cataclysmic awakening changed the surrounding landscape forever, burying everything surrounding it and obliterating the famous terraces. Around 150 people were killed, including 15 in the village of Te Wairoa, the ruins of which can be visited from the Rotorua side of the lake (see page 77).

Both despite and because of this catastrophe, the Lake Tarawera area is fresh and tranquil — so much so you'd hardly believe this relatively recent history save for the bald, flat-topped mountain which looks quite lately spent. A powerful and other-worldly presence in the landscape, even the most sceptical may find themselves somehow spellbound in its shadow.

Tarawera is the deepest and second largest of the Rotorua lakes, and great swathes of its shore are accessible only by boat. A few small settlements dot the western side; the rest is punctuated only by pristine and sheltered bays, trailheads and the odd boat ramp. There are also two DOC campgrounds, but only one is accessible by road — via Kawerau — and what a peculiar road it is.

Between Kawerau and Lake Tarawera are vast blocks of privately owned pine forest, and to reach Te Tapahoro Bay you must first obtain a forest access permit from the visitor centre in Kawerau ($4; open daily; tel 07 323 7550). This grants you access to the road, largely in good nick with only a few potholes of note. The plantation goes on and on — a sea of the same old trees with few landmarks with which to gauge your position or progress. The forest stops abruptly as you reach the scenic reserve, however; the view suddenly opens up and you can see across the lake to the distant shore. A steep hillside lies on one side, the mighty mountain itself towers on the other. It's incredibly picturesque — and just wait till you survey it from the jetty . . .

Camping ranges over several undulating clearings, none with lake views but no matter. The forested slopes curtain a lovely encampment, with plenty of bush for privacy and shade. There are two picnic shelters with benches and tables, and long-drop toilets dotted all over. Two stalls are set up for solar-shower use.

It is important to note that the gates to the forest close at 8.30pm during daylight saving, and at 7.30pm the rest of the year. A camp manager is in residence during peak times.

WALK TO THE FALLS

If you're inclined to a walk, a must-do while you're here is the walk along the river to the majestic Tarawera Falls (two hours one way). While many of New Zealand's most famous falls are pretty much a straight-down dump, these take a more wayward path, one which sees them bounce and cascade over 65 m in a much more enchanting fashion. The source of the falls is a river that runs underground further upstream, seeping through fractured and eroded rock. At the falls it finds its exit point, gushing forth from an impressive cliff, thought to be the end of a lava flow that poured from Mount Tarawera around 11,000 years ago. The river runs fairly fast, so should you fancy a swim look out for the swimming spot about one and a half hours from the outlet. (The falls can also be accessed from a car park about half an hour's drive from the campground.)

HIKE TO HUMPHRIES

Another good trip on foot is the walk to Humphries Bay (two and a half hours one way). The track follows the edge of Lake Tarawera and climbs inland through dense forest before descending into the bay, on the northern arm of the lake. This scenic picnic and camping spot is accessible only by boat or on foot, making it a good option for those seeking a little solitude.

WHAKATANE TOURISM

A powerful and other-worldly presence in the landscape, even the most sceptical may find themselves somehow spellbound in the shadow of Mount Tarawera.

GO FOR A WANDER AND PONDER THE WONDER OF NATURE

The jetty makes a good port of call. A pretty little thing it is, too, jutting out over very inviting, clear water. (A swim may be had, although it may pay to bring your beach shoes — the bottom is quite stony.) If you have access to a kayak or other small watercraft, this is the place to launch it. The views across the lake, up to the maunga and back towards the campground are stunning. Pause and reflect: the 1886 eruption caused widespread damage here, destroying or burying much of the vegetation. For over a century, the forest has been slowly recovering, with regeneration taking hold more quickly on the lower, more fertile slopes. Before the eruption, these slopes were forested with a mixture of rata, rimu and totara. The resulting devastation and subsequent vegetation succession has seen it replaced by a mixture of kamahi, kanuka, rewarewa and colourful northern rata and pohutukawa.

723 Tarawera Road, Tikitapu (Blue Lake), 9 km southeast of Rotorua

Contact
07 362 8120
www.bluelaketop10.co.nz

Capacity
100 unpowered / 75 powered

Open
all year

Bookings
recommended peak season

Price
$17 adult / $9.50 child (1–14 years) unpowered; $20 adult / $10 child powered

Prosaically named for the colour of its waters, the Blue Lake is known to Maori as Tikitapu, the place where a sacred (tapu) tiki pendant was lost by a chief's daughter.

Only a wafer-thin crust of earth separates the bustling town of Rotorua from piping hot magma below, and you'd think this would put people off visiting. Yet the legions who pass through each year seem utterly unconcerned at the explosions of steaming water and the boiling hot mud . . . not even the pervasive eggy smell can put them off, so strong is the magnetism of this town's incredible thermal attractions. If you wish to discover (or rediscover) this dynamic area but sleep in a quiet corner without the odour, it's well worth making the 10-minute drive from downtown to the Blue Lake Holiday Park.

Blue Lake is one of four small lakes which sit between the larger lakes, Rotorua and Tarawera. (The others are Lake Rotokakahi or the Green Lake, Okareka and Okataina.) Prosaically named for the colour of its waters, the Blue Lake is known to Maori as Tikitapu, the place where a sacred (tapu) tiki pendant was lost by a chief's daughter. Along with the other lakes it lies within a volcanic caldera. The colour of its waters comes from rhyolite and pumice on the lake bed, just 20 m down at its deepest point. These calm, sapphire waters are a lovely sight, made all the more so by being encircled by forest. Alongside the lake is a large grassy reserve — popular with daytrippers, of which there are many.

This is a welcoming holiday park, set over 5.7 ha, right across the road from the lake edge. But that's not the only reason this is the most pleasant in the Rotorua area. Although it's a big campground — and busy all summer long — its gentle terraces and mature landscaping make it surprisingly restful. At the front, close to the lake, some boat and road noise can be heard, but as you reach the upper fields you will find lots of room and plenty of peace.

The bulk of the sites are excellent, with good shade, shelterbelts and picnic benches. Two facilities blocks have all the necessaries, and are in absolutely A1 condition. The larger of the two has a dining room and a pleasant, covered barbecue patio, with a spa pool room alongside. In another corner of the park there's a flash new games room with more barbecuing facilities outside.

Blue Lake is very popular for watersports events, including kayaking and rowing regattas, triathlons and water-skiing competitions. Events are held over many summer weekends, and some will prevent you from enjoying your own activities on the lake at certain times of the day. To check the sports schedule in advance, visit www.envbop.govt.nz and search for 'lake closures'.

To make your own watersport fun, kayaks, canoes and fishing boats can be hired from the office, where fishing licences are also available. Staff can help you with bookings for all sorts of local activities, and direct you to the glow-worm grotto if you ask nicely. The shop next to the office is well stocked, and offers instant gratification in the way of hot pies and ice cream.

BIKE THROUGH THE REDWOODS WHAKAREWAREWA FOREST

This is one of New Zealand's best mountain biking parks (www.redwoods.co.nz), suitable for bikers of all ages and abilities. With over 90 km of trails you could ride here for days without covering the same ground. To get your bearings, pop into the visitor centre on Long Mile Road where you can buy a trail map ($5, which goes towards track upkeep and development). Bikes can be hired from several shops in town, as well as from Planet Bike (tel 07 346 1717, www.planetbike.co.nz) which also offers guided trips, bike drops and shuttle runs. For those without wheels, there are plenty of walker-only tracks, six of which begin at the visitor centre.

CIRCUIT THE LAKE ON FOOT

The Blue Lake Walk is a 5.5 km, two hour circuit passing through both native and exotic forest. If you fancy a dip, a welcoming option is the small beach at the southern end of the lake — it's well away from the hubbub of the campground and reserve. Just up from the beach towards the road is the lookout over lakes Tikitapu and Rotokakahi, or the Blue and Green Lakes as European settlers named them. The track begins at the northwestern corner of the Blue Lake reserve, at the far end of the main beach.

VISIT THE BURIED VILLAGE OF TE WAIROA

Tarawera's violent eruption of 1886 rent a 7 km scar in the mountainside, in the process burying the surrounding countryside in a blanket of hot ash and mud, including Te Wairoa and two other smaller villages (read more about this on page 76). After the eruption no greenery could be seen within a 15 km radius of the mountain. Just five minutes' drive from the campground at Te Wairoa is a small museum along with excavated Maori whare and settlers' homes. It's a fascinating place to visit, offering not only the stories of that tragic event but also an educational insight into a bygone era. Tel 07 362 8287, www.buriedvillage.co.nz.

GIOVANNI VILLASECA

Tikitapu or Blue Lake

Huka Falls Road,
4 km north of Taupo

Contact
Taupo District Council
07 376 0617
www.taupodc.govt.nz

Capacity
(sufficient unpowered)

Open
Labour Weekend to Easter
maximum stay: seven days

Bookings
not required

Price
free

Its natural beauty
is obvious, sitting
on the banks of the
Waikato River, which
slips gracefully by
in a shade of deep,
emerald green.

The biggest blue jewel studding the New Zealand landscape, Lake Taupo well deserves the praise heaped on it for its many splendours, including its expansive waters and the view of snowy-peaked volcanoes from its shores. The town is very pleasant, too. And with a raft of exciting activities on its doorstep, plenty of places to eat and drink, and satisfying shopping to boot, it's no wonder Taupo is a tourist drawcard. It's well set up to handle it.

Campers, however, may well be frustrated by their options. While there are four very acceptable holiday parks around town, and another one south along the lake at Motutere, they're all fairly municipal or close to the road. If you're looking for camping au naturel, your choices are seriously limited. Not even DOC comes to the rescue here. There is, however, a glimmer of hope: Reid's Farm — just five minutes' drive from town and even closer to Huka Falls.

Run by the local council (who controversially closed their town campground in 2006), Reid's Farm is a reserve with untapped potential; even as it stands in slightly 'rustic' condition it remains unparalleled in the area. Its natural beauty is obvious, sitting on the banks of the Waikato River, which slips gracefully by in a shade of deep, emerald green.

Reid's Farm is on the way to the Huka Falls, on the 'tourist loop' road along which are dotted various other attractions such as the The Honey Hive, Huka Prawn Park and the Huka Jet base. The reserve ranges along the river bank, with terraces landscaped in sympathy with its natural undulations and interesting rock formations. A disparate collection of plants such as old fruit trees, pines and young plantings of natives beg questions of an untold heritage. (Who was Reid? What's his story?) Very popular in summer (it is free, after all), you'll have to be in quick for the pick of the pitches during the holidays.

Competing for a park up are day-users — Sunday drivers, picnickers and kayakers who put their boats in at the riverbank. It's come one come all, and unfortunately this has included vandals. These largely local hoony types have been known to make a racket, break the odd beer bottle and light fires, threatening the reserve with closure. The council has tried to clamp down: a security patrol now passes through daily, and a caretaker may also be in residence. Things appear much improved, but even so the future of Reid's Farm hangs in the balance. We really hope it stays open (and we'd be prepared to cough up some camp fees to help that happen).

The facilities are totally back-to-basics: long-drop toilets but no spigot — bring your own water. You can, however, bring your dog if it's friendly and you're handy with the plastic bag. No fires please.

WATCH THE HUKA FALLS FALL

Not far from where the Waikato River — New Zealand's longest — is born from the waters of Lake Taupo, it's forced through a narrow granite canyon before being dumped 11 m into a maelstrom of spray. You can see why Maori named these falls Hukanui (big foam). Crossing the river, a footbridge offers good vantage points and access to other viewing areas and short walks. The Huka Falls can be reached on foot from Reid's Farm via Huka Falls Road — it'll take about half an hour.

DOC / HELEN MITCHELL

The Huka Falls are a must-see for anyone visiting the Taupo region

SEEK ADVENTURE IN TAUPO

As the adrenaline capital of New Zealand, Taupo has an unnerving assortment of pants-wetting options available . . . how brave are you feeling today? Skydiving perhaps, from 4500 m, freefalling through thin air, the ground rushing up to meet you? Or maybe bungy jumping — a 47 m boing over the Waikato River on a big rubber band? A jet boat ride, blowing your hair back and spinning your eyeballs around? Or maybe a quiet day on the river, fly-fishing for trout? (You might still get your pants wet.) The efficient i-SITE staff can help connect you to your destiny (tel 07 376 0400, www.laketauponz.com).

HAVE A (FREE) HOT SPA

The falls lie at one end of the Huka Falls Walkway, an hour-long riverside amble to Spa Thermal Park, on the edge of Taupo township. En route, a rocky creek gushes its hot contents into the river, warming the waters where they meet. You'll have no trouble finding this spot: look for the bridge and the eroded footholds where people have slipped themselves into the drink.

Whakapapa Village (Tongariro National Park), Bruce Road (off State Highway 48), 49 km southwest of Turangi

Contact
07 892 3897
www.whakapapa.net.nz

Capacity
8 unpowered / 45 powered

Open
all year

Bookings
recommended

Price
$17 adult / $10 child

So that's snow and a live volcano. Sounds like a great place for camping, doesn't it?

Mount Ruapehu is primarily synonymous with skiing, and with sporadic eruptions that hurl hot rocks and mud down its slopes. So that's snow and a live volcano. Sounds like a great place for camping, doesn't it?

Rest assured, Whakapapa Holiday Park at the Whakapapa Village at the foot of Mount Ruapehu is a totally safe proposition and most likely to be snowless in summer (although you never know). It is also a very rare beast — a campsite within the boundary of a national park that has powered sites and a range of facilities.

Designated a World Heritage site in 1991, Tongariro National Park is centred upon the three mountains that stand proudly on the volcanic plateau — Ruapehu is the big daddy, home to the Whakapapa and Turoa skifields; the others are Tongariro — famous for the Alpine Crossing, one of New Zealand's most spectacular day walks; and Ngauruhoe, known in certain circles as Mount Doom. With plenty to do in and around the village itself and with options for dining out, this campground makes an excellent base for exploring the environs.

Leased by DOC to private operators, this holiday park offers the best of both worlds: a woodsy park in a spectacular natural setting with facilities that you won't find in your average DOC campground. Although fairly close to the bushline, it's a very leafy spot, with sites nestled in seclusion under a canopy of mature mountain beech. Mount Ruapehu can be glimpsed here and there between the trees. The Whakapapanui Stream crashes down beside the campground, accessible via several tracks — some places are perfect for a picnic or for dipping a toe in the water, should you wish to see one of your own bodily parts go numb and turn blue in front of you.

There's one central amenities building: a well-maintained, no-nonsense affair. Hobs aplenty and stainless steel benchtops for miles, the kitchen is particularly functional, clean as a whistle and big — there'll be no fighting for cooking space here.

Other facilities include a laundry, drying room, Wi-Fi internet, coin-operated barbecue and recycling stations. There are numerous cabin options should the weather turn to custard (or perhaps ice cream). The on-site shop sells daily newspapers and basic supplies and can help you with bookings for local activities. The holiday park is within the national park boundary so no fires or dogs are permitted.

Don't forget your woolly jumper and the four-seasons sleeping bag. This is, after all, the highest-altitude serviced campground in the land.

GET THE LOW-DOWN ON THE NATIONAL PARK AT THE DOC WHAKAPAPA VISITOR CENTRE

Learn about the area — its geology, ecology, history and culture — through excellent interpretive displays and a couple of short films. The maunga are obviously the main attraction here, so you'll find the DOC centre particularly interesting if you're a budding volcanologist or rock-hound. Perfect for a rainy afternoon, the toasty centre has a shop with good books, gifts, and an array of snuggle-worthy merino wear — very convenient if you need tramping socks or a woolly hat. DOC staff will help you explore the park in a safe and happy fashion, with advice on tracks and conditions. The centre is a three-minute walk from the holiday park and is open daily, all year round (tel 07 892 3729).

TRAMP THE TONGARIRO ALPINE CROSSING

New Zealand's most famous one-day walk is readily accessible from the village, and campsite staff can set you up with transport to the trailhead, just 15 minutes' drive away. This is a long and challenging tramp that should only be attempted by fit and well-equipped walkers. Those people, however, will be amply rewarded with spectacular volcanic landscapes, steaming vents, beautiful coloured lakes and the conical perfection of Ngauruhoe up close. If you have a little less time or energy to burn there are numerous interesting short walks from the village and nearby — DOC has a leaflet that details these.

EAT AT THE CHATEAU'S PIHANGA CAFÉ

Its location within the grand hotel must surely account for its quality and consistency — we've certainly never had a bad meal here yet. Serving up a range of surprisingly inexpensive meals to suit all — from soup and salads to gourmet pies and hot, tasty stews — this is the prefect place for one-pot-wonder-weary campers to treat themselves without breaking the bank. And there's more good news on the culinary front: the other places in town are pretty good, too. You might want to try coffee and cake on a picnic bench outside the tearoom. (Tel 07 892 3809, www.chateau.co.nz.)

The maunga are obviously the main attraction here, so you'll find the DOC centre particularly interesting if you're a budding volcanologist or rock-hound.

The Tongariro Alpine Crossing is your chance to tread Mount Doom

ROTORUA

AFFORDABLE WILLOWHAVEN HOLIDAY PARK
31 Beaumont Road,
Ngongotaha, Rotorua

Contact: 07 357 4092
bookings@willowhaven.co.nz
www.willowhaven.co.nz

Tariff: $20–85

COSY COTTAGE INTERNATIONAL HOLIDAY PARK
67 Whittaker Road, Rotorua

Contact: 07 348 3793
stay@cosycottage.co.nz
www.rotoruaholidaypark.co.nz

Tariff: $30–89

REDWOOD HOLIDAY PARK
5 Tarawera Road, Rotorua

Contact: 07 345 9380
reservations@redwoodpark.co.nz
www.redwoodparkrotorua.co.nz

Tariff: $90–130

ROTORUA FAMILY HOLIDAY PARK
22 Beaumont Road,
Ngongotaha, Rotorua

Contact: 07 357 4289
stay@rotoruafamilypark.co.nz
www.rotoruafamilypark.co.nz

Tariff: $55–92

ROTORUA THERMAL HOLIDAY PARK
Old Taupo Road
(south end), Rotorua

Contact: 07 346 3140
holidayparkrotorua@xtra.co.nz

Tariff: $24–80

WAITETI TROUT STREAM HOLIDAY PARK
14 Okona Cres,
Ngongotaha, Rotorua

Contact: 07 357 5255
stay@waiteti.com
www.waiteti.com

Tariff: $18–105

TAUPO AND THE CENTRAL PLATEAU

ALL SEASONS HOLIDAY PARK TAUPO
16 Rangatira Street, Taupo

Contact: 07 378 4272
reservations@allseasons.nzl.com
www.taupoallseasons.co.nz

Tariff: $28–115

GOLDEN SPRINGS MOTEL, HOLIDAY PARK AND RESTAURANT
SH 5 (between Rotorua and
Taupo), Golden Springs

Contact: 07 333 8280
golden-springs@farmside.co.nz
www.goldenspringsholidaypark.co.nz

Tariff: $25–90

GREAT LAKE HOLIDAY PARK
406 Acacia Bay Road, Taupo

Contact: 07 378 5159
gtlake@xtra.co.nz
www.greatlake.co.nz

Tariff: $32–115

LAKE TAUPO TOP 10 HOLIDAY RESORT
28 Centennial Drive, Taupo

Contact: 07 378 6860
office@taupotop10.co.nz
www.taupotop10.co.nz

Tariff: $18–245

OASIS MOTEL AND HOLIDAY PARK
426 SH 41, Tokaanu
(5 minutes from Turangi)

Contact: 07 386 8569
oasismotelstokaanu@xtra.co.nz
www.oasismotel.co.nz

Tariff: $40–80

RAETIHI HOLIDAY PARK AND CABINS
10 Parapara Road, Raetihi

Contact: 06 385 4176

raetihiholidaypark@ihug.co.nz
www.raetihiholidaypark.com

Tariff: $30–50

TAUMARUNUI
HOLIDAY PARK
SH 4 (4 km south of
Taumarunui), Taumarunui

Contact: 07 895 9345
taumarunui-holiday-park@xtra.co.nz
www.taumarunuiholidaypark.co.nz

Tariff: $26–65

TAUPO DEBRETTS SPA RESORT
Napier–Taupo Highway, Taupo

Contact: 07 378 8559
www.taupodebretts.com

Tariff: $40–180

TONGARIRO HOLIDAY PARK
SH 47, Tongariro

Contact: 07 386 8062
info@thp.co.nz
www.thp.co.nz

Tariff: $26–80

TURANGI CABINS
AND HOLIDAY PARK
13 Te Reiti Tamara
Grove, Turangi

Contact: 07 386 8754
cabinsgalore@xtra.co.nz
www.turangicabins.co.nz

Tariff: $22–40

WAIRAKEI NATURAL
THERMAL VALLEY
SH 1 (south of SH 1 and
5 intersection), Wairakei
Park, Taupo

Contact: 07 374 8004
johnrichards@wave.co.nz

Tariff: $26–85

→ LET'S GO CAMPING IN

WAIKATO, TARANAKI AND MANAWATU

**61 Marine Parade, Raglan,
48 km west of Hamilton**

Contact
07 825 8283
www.raglanholidaypark.co.nz

Capacity
100 unpowered / 100 powered

Open
all year

Bookings
recommended peak season

Price
$15 adult / $7.50 child

> The long-established surfing culture has shaped the town of Raglan, as has its out-of-the-way location. It is sweet, salty and unspoiled, regarded by many as one of our prettiest towns.

The township of Raglan is inextricably linked with surfing, being home to several of New Zealand's best surfing beaches. One in particular — Manu Bay — is said to boast the world's longest left-hand break. Now surfing's not for everyone and most of us can barely face a half-metre roller in the shallows without getting dumped in a heap. However, the long-established surfing culture has shaped the town of Raglan, as has its out-of-the-way location. It is sweet, salty and unspoiled, regarded by many as one of our prettiest towns.

Enjoying Raglan's charms couldn't be easier for campers. The holiday park is in an enviable spot, just a five-minute walk from the main street, reached by a picturesque footbridge. Located on Te Kopua Recreation Reserve, the campground was established in 1938, a fairly perfunctory set-up until £10 was donated in 1950 for the purpose of planting some trees.

Surrounded by an estuary on three sides, the campground has a relatively tranquil feel — or at least it does when it's not high summer and full of lively families, or when small aircraft take off from the airstrip next door. This is a big camp, and really busy over the Christmas holidays. The sites are drawn up in a pretty tight grid, with sparse trees for privacy or shade — that £10 doesn't seem to have gone very far.

Unpowered campers get the best sites, along the edges of the park and down the far end. These also offer the bonus of some shade and easy beach access, just beyond the dunes. Speaking of which: although the grounds are grassy, be prepared for lashings of sticky black sand. Not that we're complaining: it's nice to see that camp management have resisted the temptation to pave a network of roads and pathways through the place. Seventy years on, it still has a paddock look about it.

Over the dunes from the camp is the main beach, which enjoys a super outlook over the entrance to Raglan Harbour — you can see and hear the breakers crashing into the bar from the Tasman Sea. There's decent swimming here, and magnificent sunsets.

The holiday park has two big amenity blocks. The main block has the lion's share of amenities including plenty of gas hobs, a games room (with air hockey) and television lounge, plus a pleasant outdoor dining and barbecue area. There's also a grassy area for mucking about on set in front of a small amphitheatre — the scene of many shows such as sandcastle competitions, concerts and film evenings. The second block, at the rear of the camp, has been tailored for big groups, with a catering-size gas oven and large dining area under an awning.

The camp has the feel of a workhorse, with the facilities in reasonable order but not unduly fussed-over with the air freshener and gardening gloves. However, it's a comfortable camp in an interesting corner of Aotearoa, and that's good enough for us.

THINGS TO SEE AND DO NEAR RAGLAN

LEARN TO SURF AT NGARUNUI BEACH

Raglan is the country's number-one surfing destination and Ngarunui is the perfect place to learn the basics. Raglan Surfing School (tel 07 825 7873, www.raglansurfingschool. co.nz) will get you going. You're almost certain to get up on the board on your first lesson, apparently. If you can't cope with that raging success — or embarrassment — it's still a great beach, the best in the area for swimming (with lifeguards in summer). It's a spunky place to hang out, with beautiful ocean views and bronzed bodies straight out of *Baywatch* (or perhaps *Piha Rescue*).

HANG OUT IN RAGLAN

Take a wander round one truly pretty town. By day there's browsing to be had in the surf shops and galleries, followed by a flat white and a bite to eat in one of several decent cafés along the main street. When the sun goes down, the town livens up. Late night bars and the heritage Harbour View Hotel regularly host live music, particularly in summer when Raglan attracts some top bands. And with just a 10-minute walk from camp to town, there'll be no squabbles over who has to be the designated driver.

SCALE MOUNT KARIOI IN THE PIRONGIA FOREST PARK

This strenuous walk is not for the faint-hearted, but rewards with jaw-dropping views along the coastline and of Raglan, Aotea and Kawhia harbours. On a clear day you can also see Mount Taranaki, Pureora, Maungamangero and Te Aroha in the distance. It takes about two and a half hours to get to the lookout and another hour to get to the summit (756 m). Don't worry if you can't make it all the way to the top though, as there are great vantage points along the way. To get to the trailhead from Raglan, drive south along Whaanga Road until you get to the Te Toto Scenic Reserve car park.

PREVIOUS PAGE: A big break on Surf Highway 45
LEFT: Raglan Harbour

PHOTONEWZEALAND / GERHARD EGGER

State Highway 3, 26 km north of New Plymouth, 61 km south of Mokau

Contact
06 752 3643
www.onaerobayholidaypark.co.nz

Capacity
51 unpowered / 71 powered

Open
all year

Bookings
recommended peak season

Price
$12.50 adult / $6 child

SARAH BENNETT AND LEE SLATER

Located just off the coastal road between New Plymouth and Mokau (onthe way to Te Kuiti), Onaero Bay has been a public domain since 1904. Today it is visited by daytrippers and by lucky overnighters who get to enjoy great camping with decent facilities in a park now run by the New Zealand Motor Caravan Association. It may not look particularly enticing from the road, but don't be fooled — beyond that fence is Taranaki's loveliest camping ground.

Here, within a small cove, the muddy-bottomed Onaero River breaks free from its narrows and wends beside a driftwoody dune before streaming out over a stony patch of sand. At this end of the beach, low tide leaves little, shallow pools, perfect for short-legged people to paddle about in, or a ready-made moat for a sandcastle. At the other end of the beach, the black sandy bottom is clear of stones and good for swimming. Fishing is a popular pastime, too, with kahawai to be had off the beach, and snapper further offshore.

Flanking the bay are high cliffs, eroded by wind and water to reveal their earthy layers — starkly contrasting like two-tone coconut ice. Fluffy-topped toetoe clings to them like an unroped climber, while just offshore doomed stacks stand orphaned, topped with gardens of remnant bush. To the north the coast stretches for miles into the hazy distance; out on the horizon the Pohokura gas platform can be seen poking unexpectedly out of the sea.

The campground is divided over two areas. On the near side of the river the bulk of the powered sites can be found, along with the office / shop, one of the two facilities blocks and a few cabins. In desperate times, television can be watched in the kitchen here — according to managers Reese and Judi, it will pick up *Coronation Street*, so that's a relief. The best spots on this side are right down the front, with T1 and T4 absolute corkers — directly overlooking the river mouth out to the bay.

Over the creaky bridge is a welcoming camping field (and public domain), as proudly maintained as any urban park. A row of unpowered sites sit along the foot of a hill, with an attractive backdrop of native plantings and Norfolk pines. The playground sits in the middle, surrounded by a spacious grassed area, irresistible for running around on. Along the river bank are yet more delightful sites, a mixture of powered and unpowered (T18 is tenters' heaven).

The facilities block serving the field is fairly new and in excellent shape, with the kitchen glinting in stainless steel. It has a tiny bit of room for indoor dining. Outside are picnic benches for alfresco meals, and barbecues can be hired from the office. The laundry is here, too.) The showers require a token (50 cents), available from the office along with milk, bread, ice and other essentials. Your cheerful hosts offer smiles for free. The closest place for further supplies is the Four Square at Urenui, 2.5 km up the road.

THINGS TO SEE AND DO NEAR ONAERO BAY

MAKE A MUD PIE

Running through the middle of the campground, the Onaero River offers hours of entertainment for the younger folk, whether splashing about in its slow waters, paddling up and down in a kayak (for hire from the office) or fossicking around in piles of sun-bleached driftwood. The river's muddy banks make for dirty, squidgy, slippery fun, the perfect antidote to squeaky clean modern life. (An on-the-spot outdoor shower makes for easy cleaning, thank goodness.)

HELP THE CAMPAIGN FOR REAL ALE

Whitecliffs Organic Brewery (tel 06 752 3676, www.organicbeer.co.nz) is 7 km north of Onaero Bay on State Highway 3. Here you'll find great, wholesome beer in a pleasant location. It has two award-winning brews on offer: Mike's Mild and Mike's Lager. They're certified organic and claimed by co-owner Jill to be hangover free — but you might want to test that theory for yourself. The tasting room / shop has cider and other treats, too. Keep an eye on their website — when the on-licence comes through, you'll be able to sup a few ales on the spongy lawn out back. Make sure you've got your designated driver sorted before you set out, or buy some bottles to take away.

WALK ABOVE AND BELOW THE WHITE CLIFFS

The coast between the Pukearuhe Stream and Tongaporutu River is home to a vertiginous line of sedimentary cliffs, arches and stacks sculpted by the endless pounding of the Tasman Sea. You can see them up close via the White Cliffs Walkway. About 10 km north of Onaero Bay, turn left into Pukearuhe Road and follow the road to the end; the walk starts at the boat ramp. The track heads inland through farmland to Mount Davidson then along the ridgeline, where you're met with dramatic views of the North Taranaki coastline. From here, descend to the Waipangau Stream via hundreds of wooden steps and follow the stream valley until it reaches the sea and the real stars of the show — the White Cliffs (Parininihi). From here you can follow the beach back to Pukearuhe, but only two hours either side of low tide — check the newspaper or ask at the camp office for tide times.

VENTURE TARANAKI / ROB TUCKER

FAR LEFT: **Looking north from Onaero Bay**
LEFT: **White Cliffs — just like Dover except totally different**

OAKURA BEACH HOLIDAY PARK

2 Jans Terrace, Oakura, 15 km southwest of New Plymouth

Contact
06 752 7861
www.oakurabeach.com

Capacity
60 unpowered / 110 powered

Open
all year

Bookings
essential peak season

Price
$15 adult / $8 child unpowered;
$16 adult / $8 child powered

REBECCA COWLEY

Just 15 minutes' drive south of New Plymouth, the beach at Oakura is one of the most family-friendly along the Taranaki coast, known for its safe swimming (patrolled by lifeguards), surf to suit all levels, and facilities such as showers, toilets, a playground and a café. Walkers can enjoy nearby nature reserves, while indulgent types will love the buzzy little high street with its galleries and gift shops, a couple of eateries and a decent pub. Thank goodness that there's a campground befitting this sweet and summery seaside town.

Oakura Holiday Park enjoys an enviable position at the far end of the beach, well beyond the hubbub in front of the surf lifesaving and boardriders' clubrooms. Beyond the campground is the entrance to the reserve. From here it's an enjoyable 2 km walk along the coast to Ahu Ahu Beach and a short hop across the rocky spit to Weld Road Beach Reserve picnic area.

The holiday park has several different camping areas, and the best sites are in hot demand throughout the busy months. That said, a large proportion enjoy million-dollar views. Putting the squeeze on things are the 'erosion events' (as the camp owners call them) that are whittling away the waterfront row; many of these primo unpowered tent sites have shrunk to half their original size. Does that sound close enough to the ocean for you?

The failsafe way to keep the sand out of your hair and the kids off your pitch is to camp in either Kaitake or Land's End — sheltered valleys away from the main beach block. However, if you're looking for roomy, quiet(er), beachside, unpowered sites, ask for one of the sites numbered 16 to 26, towards the reserve end of the camp. As for the electrified people, they'll be only too pleased with the terraced rows and grandstand views of the Tasman Sea.

The beachside sites are reasonably exposed, so remember your sun hat or awning. There are two tidy amenities blocks with similar facilities although the larger of the two — in the middle of the beach block — offers the bonus of ocean views. Outdoor cold-water showers will rinse off all that black sand. There's Wi-Fi internet, too.

The camp office shares its building with The Terrace Takeways (open daily in summer, tel 06 752 1190), famed for its gourmet pies, pizza and 'meal of the day': a home-cooked dinner that you can collect of an evening (phone ahead to reserve your share). They also stock very basic groceries, coffee and ice cream, which you can linger over in their pleasant courtyard.

VENTURE TARANAKI / ROB TUCKER

BEHOLD MIGHTY MOUNT TARANAKI, THE PINNACLE OF EGMONT NATIONAL PARK

Just a five-minute drive south of Oakura, Lucy's Gully gives access to the national park and the Kaitake Range. For the fit and surefooted, the loop walk (three hours) to Patuha Trig (682 m) affords a head-swivelling 360-degree view of the coastline, fertile farmland and the conical peak of Taranaki. If you want to actually set foot on it, visit the North Egmont Visitor Centre, clearly signposted from Egmont Village on the New Plymouth to Stratford Road (State Highway 3), about 35 minutes from Oakura. Sitting nearly 1000 m above sea level, the visitor centre has great views down to the coast — unless of course you're clouded in. Worry not a jot if you are: there's plenty to divert you including information displays, a video presentation and a café. Numerous short walks start from here, and it is also the trailhead for the summit track. This is a popular and achievable day-tramp for the fit, but you'll need to do your homework, be extremely well prepared and be sure of good weather. Visit www.doc.govt.nz for essential pre-tramp information, and be sure to check in at the DOC centre to leave your intentions. Taranaki is not only the most climbed mountain in New Zealand, it has also claimed the most lives.

SOAK UP SOME CULTURE IN NEW PLYMOUTH

This ascendant city is home to Puke Ariki (www.pukeariki.com) — a most excellent and stylish museum; and also the Govett-Brewster Art Gallery (www.govettbrewster.com), arguably the best provincial art gallery in New Zealand. As well as presenting a wide range of contemporary exhibitions, the gallery is home to the Len Lye collection. Never heard of him? See his Wind Wand waving around on the New Plymouth foreshore . . . and there are plenty more kinetic wibbly-wobblers where that came from.

When the children have reached their boredom threshold, whisk them off to Pukekura Park for ice cream and a row on the lake. This stunning park is the Mayfair of the New Zealand Monopoly board — as voted by the public, nationwide.

If you're anywhere near New Plymouth in the summer, don't miss Pukekura Park's legendary Festival of Lights.

FAR LEFT: Oakura Beach Holiday Park
LEFT: The conical peak of Mount Taranaki, 2518 m

Heads Road (via Lower Glenn Road, off State Highway 45), 8 km west of Manaia

Contact
06 274 8577

Capacity
12 unpowered / 23 powered

Open
all year

Bookings
recommended peak season

Price
$20 per site (2 adults, 2 children) unpowered / powered

Taranaki boasts some of the country's best surf beaches and the majority of them are only a short drive from Kaupokonui.

The highway following the semi-circular coast of Taranaki from New Plymouth through to Hawera is known as Surf Highway 45, named for the legendary surf breaks accessed off it. Perhaps the highway is slightly misnamed, however, for while the surf itself remains completely out of view for most of the 105 km journey, the classic cone of Mount Taranaki is omnipresent. Maybe it should be called Mountain Highway 45 instead?

One of the roads leading off that surf / mountain highway transports you to the tiny coastal settlement of Kaupokonui. And having travelled through your typical Taranaki landscape — swathes of thickly grassed fields being chomped by a gazillion cows — the sudden drop down to the bay springs a big surprise. For here, where the Kaupokonui River meets the sea, the land is cut into two distinct pieces: green fields on one side, mammoth black sand dunes on the other. It's a startling contrast, one that gives this campground the 'wow' factor.

Owned by the local council, managed by a supportive society and taken care of by Tony, Kaupokonui campground sits on the near side of the river, tucked around the corner from the ocean, nestled against a low hill covered in a combination of gnarled old macrocarpa and native plantings. Here, a terraced bank at the river mouth has been groomed into an inviting camping area, the bulk of the sites laid out along its edges. There are a couple of cabins and a 10-bed backpackers, as well as a clutch of cute, privately owned baches.

In the middle is a block of power sites laid out tidily in a grid. As is so often the case, unpowered campers enjoy some of the best sites, with several along the terrace edge overlooking the river and out to the sea just a few hundred metres away. Looking inland, Mount Taranaki peers over the top of the hills. Virtually all the sites are shadeless, so don't forget your hat.

The amenities block is old, but clean and tidy nonetheless. The kitchen and laundry are equipped with the essentials, including two freestanding stoves. A shop (open Labour Weekend to Easter) sells sweets, hot pies, ice creams and the like, along with other critical essentials such as tomato sauce, bread and milk. Your next closest option is the Four Square at Manaia.

Next to the modern playground are two wonky slides chuting down to a picturesque reserve which runs along the grassy river edge below the campground terrace. The reserve has picnic tables shaded by a row of Norfolk pines, and public toilets (seriously run-down but still tidy and considerably stocked with loo paper). From here, a footbridge crosses the river to the aforementioned dunes and the rugged beach.

Little to do, little to see. It's just a little bit of weird and wonderfulness by the sea.

HANG TEN ALONG SURF HIGHWAY 45

Taranaki boasts some of the country's best surf beaches and the majority of them are only a short drive from Kaupokonui. There are breaks aplenty from here through to New Plymouth (visit taranakisurf.tripod.com for more details). Consistent Tasman swells and beaches facing north, south and west mean there are always waves to catch somewhere. Most beaches are accessible by road, but some require that you cross private land: get the local low-down and be sure to get permission first.

GET BLACK SAND BETWEEN YOUR TOES

Across the footbridge there's an outlandish landscape to explore. One option is to follow the river to its mouth, where you'll reach a beach of Smitheresque boulders and hardy gulls. Swimming can be enjoyed in favourable conditions, and the fishing is good, so they say. (There are whitebait in the river, too.) Otherwise, head up into the volcanic duneland. The views along the coast are impressive, as are those inland — although largely confined to peeks of that ever-present mountain, endlessly spying on you. The dunes are great for larking about on, particularly if you've got yourself a boogie-board. A word of warning: keep clear of the crumbling cliff edge, and beware of the wild cows that range freely in the dunes. We don't know what they're up to, but they have a mighty strange look in their eyes.

Kaupokonui River

HAVE A SNACKY IN OPUNAKE

Besides decent food, there are several good reasons to stop in this vibrant little town. It has a sheltered crescent beach — patrolled by lifeguards in summer — alongside which is a domain and ice cream shop, making it even sweeter still. (There are glow worms, too, if you know where to look.) The main street has surfie shopping and one of Taranaki's best cafés, Sugar Juice (42 Tasman Street, tel 06 761 7062). If you've overindulged on ice cream or pies, you can always walk it off on the Opunake Walkway (7 km, two and a half hours return). Opunake is 27 km from the Kaupokonui campground.

> The views along the coast are impressive, as are those inland — although largely confined to peeks of that ever-present mountain, endlessly spying on you. The dunes are great for larking about on, particularly if you've got yourself a boogie-board.

HAMILTON AND WAIKATO

CAMBRIDGE MOTOR PARK
32 Scott Street, Cambridge

Contact: 07 827 5649
cambridgemotorpark@paradise.net.nz,
www.cambridgemotorpark.co.nz

Tariff: $28–95

HAMILTON CITY HOLIDAY PARK
14 Ruakura Road, Hamilton

Contact: 07 855 8255
hchp@xtra.co.nz
www.hamiltoncityholidaypark.co.nz

Tariff: $30–100

KAWHIA CAMPING GROUND
73 Moke Street, Kawhia

Contact: 07 871 0863
kawhiacampingground@xtra.co.nz
www.kawhiacampingground.co.nz

Tariff: $32–65

LAKE HAKANOA MOTOR CARAVAN PARK
5 Taihua Street, Huntly

Contact: 07 828 3363

Tariff: $20–50

MATAMATA AERODROME CAMPING GROUND
SH 27, Waharoa, Matamata

Contact: 07 888 8386

Tariff: $12–17

OPAL HOT SPRINGS AND HOLIDAY PARK
Okauia Springs Road,
RD 1, Matamata

Contact: 07 888 8198
info@opalhotsprings.co.nz
www.opalhotsprings.co.nz

Tariff: $22–100

OTOROHANGA HOLIDAY PARK
20 Huiputea Drive, Otorohanga

Contact: 07 873 7253
billie@kiwiholidaypark.co.nz
www.kiwiholidaypark.co.nz

Tariff: $30–105

OTOROHANGA KIWI TOWN HOLIDAY PARK
7 Domain Drive, Otorohanga

Contact: 07 873 8279
waikiwi@ihug.co.nz

Tariff: $25

TE AROHA HOLIDAY PARK AND HOT POOLS
217 Stanley Road, Te Aroha

Contact: 07 884 9567
marta@xtra.co.nz
www.tearoha-info.co.nz/HolidayPark

Tariff: $20–90

TE KUITI CAMPING GROUND
1 Hineranga Street, Te Kuiti

Contact: 07 878 8966
tewaka@hotmail.com

Tariff: $18–55

TOKOROA MOTOR CAMP
22 Sloss Road, Tokoroa

Contact: 07 886 6642
tokoroa.camp@orcon.net.nz
www.tokoroamotorcamp.co.nz

Tariff: $15–80

WAINGARO HOT SPRINGS
2263 Waingaro Road, Ngaruawahia

Contact: 07 825 4761
waingaro.hot.springs@clear.net.nz
www.waingarohotsprings.co.nz

Tariff: $28–90

WAITOMO TOP 10 HOLIDAY PARK
12 Te Anga Road, Waitomo
Caves Village, Waitomo

Contact: 07 878 7639
www.waitomonz.co.nz

Tariff: $38–122

TARANAKI AND WANGANUI

AVRO MOTEL AND CARAVAN PARK
36 Alma Road, Wanganui

Contact: 06 345 5279
bookings@wanganuiaccommodation.co.nz
www.wanganuiaccommodation.co.nz

Tariff: $30–120

BELT ROAD SEASIDE HOLIDAY PARK
2 Belt Road, New Plymouth

Contact: 06 758 0228
info@beltroad.co.nz
www.beltroad.co.nz

Tariff: $30–110

**BIGNELL STREET MOTEL
AND CAMPERVAN PARK**
86 Bignell Street, Wanganui
Contact: 06 344 2012
info@bignellstreetmotel.co.nz
www.bignellstreetmotel.co.nz
Tariff: $12–75

**CASTLECLIFF SEASIDE
HOLIDAY PARK**
1A Rangiora Street, Wanganui
Contact: 06 344 2227
holidayparks@xtra.co.nz
www.castlecliffholidaypark.co.nz
Tariff: $26–85

FITZROY BEACH HOLIDAY PARK
Beach Street, Fitzroy,
New Plymouth
Contact: 06 758 2870
fitzroybeach@xtra.co.nz
Tariff: $24–95

KING EDWARD PARK MOTORCAMP
70 Waihi Road, Hawera
Contact: 06 278 8544
Tariff: $28

**NEW PLYMOUTH
TOP 10 HOLIDAY PARK**
29 Princes Street, Fitzroy,
New Plymouth
Contact: 06 758 2566
info@nptop10.co.nz
www.nptop10.co.nz
Tariff: $34–180

OPUNAKE BEACH HOLIDAY PARK
Beach Road, Opunake
Contact: 06 761 7525
opunakebeach@xtra.co.nz
www.opunakebeachnz.co.nz
Tariff: $27–75

**STRATFORD TOP
TOWN HOLIDAY PARK**
10 Page Street,
Stratford, Taranaki
Contact: 06 765 6440
stratfordholpark@hotmail.com
www.stratfordtoptownholidaypark.co.nz
Tariff: $25–95

THE TARANAKI EXPERIENCE
PO Box 302 Hawera, Taranaki
Contact: 06 278 6523
stay@taranaki-bakpak.co.nz
www.mttaranaki.co.nz/retreat/camphouse
Tariff: $50–225

WHANGANUI RIVER TOP 10 HOLIDAY PARK
460 Somme Parade, Wanganui
Contact: 06 343 8402
wrivertop10@xtra.co.nz
www.wrivertop10.co.nz
Tariff: $34–165

RANGITIKEI, MANAWATU AND TARARUA

**ASHHURST DOMAIN
CAMPING GROUND**
Napier Road, Ashhurst
Contact: 06 326 8203
www.pncc.govt.nz
Tariff: enquire for tariff

BRIDGE MOTOR HOME PARK
2 Bridge Street, Bulls
Contact: 06 322 0894
bullsmotel@infogen.net.nz
Tariff: $28–50

DANNEVIRKE HOLIDAY PARK
Christian Street, Dannevirke
Contact: 06 374 7625
dannevirkeholidaypark@xnet.co.nz
Tariff: $30–96

FEILDING HOLIDAY PARK
5 Arnott Street, Feilding
Contact: 06 323 5623
info@feildingholidaypark.co.nz
www.feildingholidaypark.co.nz
Tariff: $25–80

PAHIATUA CARNIVAL PARK
Glasgow Street, Pahiatua
Contact: 06 376 6340
karolynjana@slingshot.co.nz
Tariff: $12–20

**PALMERSTON NORTH
HOLIDAY PARK**
133 Dittmer Drive,
Palmerston North
Contact: 06 358 0349
palmerstonnorthholidaypark@xtra.co.nz
Tariff: $28–75

**TAIHAPE RIVERVIEW
HOLIDAY PARK**
Old Abbatoir Road, Taihape
Contact: 06 388 0718
taihape.riverview.holidaypark@xtra.co.nz
Tariff: $25–70

PREVIOUS PAGE: **Whanganui River**
LEFT: **Waitomo Caves**

→ LET'S GO CAMPING IN

HAWKE'S BAY AND WAIRARAPA

State Highway 2, 40 km north of Napier, 79 km southwest of Wairoa

Contact
DOC Napier
06 834 3111
www.doc.govt.nz

Capacity
30 unpowered

Open
closed for lambing,
August–September

Bookings
not required

Price
$5 per person

Some spots on earth . . .
inspire in their owners
a very special affection
. . . an occult sympathy
betwixt the elementals
of the soil and those who
touch its surface with
their feet.

— *Herbert Guthrie-Smith*

If you're reading this book it's probably safe to assume you're an earthy type, the sort who appreciates many different aspects of the New Zealand landscape. Maybe, like us, you've embarked on a journey that has led you to question your surroundings. What is that strange plant? How did that rock form like that? There is also, of course, the question of who. From Maori middens to early colonists, we all leave our impression on the landscape in one way or another.

In northern Hawke's Bay, Tutira is a place with stories to tell. Today it's a country park, but it was once the home — and now the legacy — of one of New Zealand's most famous pioneering farmers, Herbert Guthrie-Smith. Not content simply to work the land, here was a man who both questioned and found answers, in the process evolving into a naturalist and writer.

Guthrie-Smith took on the lease of Tutira in 1882, when it was a hard-bitten sheep station of some 8100 ha. The land became his passion, and nearly 40 years later his book, *Tutira: the Story of a New Zealand Sheep Station* (1921), was published. An incredibly detailed personal and ecological account, it tells of his labours and the changes that occurred as he sought to capture the history of the landscape and preserve it for future generations. His deep connection with Tutira would last the rest of his life and into the next — he died and was buried here in 1940.

Having relinquished various leases and subdivided parcels for soldiers returning from the First World War, only 810 ha of the original Tutira station remained after Guthrie-Smith's death — which was left in trust to the New Zealand public as a recreation reserve and wildlife refuge. And this is the Tutira Country Park you can enjoy today, managed by DOC.

Having travelled through typical Hawke's Bay pastures — largely bare and dry — Lake Tutira appears as an inviting oasis. Encircled by trees and surrounded by hilly padocks, it's a very pretty scene. There are two lakeside camping areas: one near the entrance and quite close to State Highway 2 (but just far enough away); the other a kilometre or so further along the lake-edge road. This is our pick. This gently sloping camping field has lots of graceful shady trees and spongy grass — a postcard would have picnickers lying about underneath them, for sure. Good sites can be found all over the field, and there's quite a few spaces on the lake edge, alongside the shelter, which are particularly suitable for bigger vans. From here there's a tranquil view across the water towards the opposite shore.

There are few facilities: just long-drop toilets and water spigots. If you need supplies, Tutira General Store (open daily) is just 4 km north on the highway.

THINGS TO SEE AND DO NEAR TUTIRA

GET OUT ON SWAN LAKE

Lakes Tutira and neighbouring Waikopiro together cover nearly 500 ha of serene waters bordered by rushes, sedges and weeds. In the past two decades, significant efforts have been made to reoxygenate the lake and replant large areas surrounding it. Results have generally been good — the water is now relatively clear, with large numbers of swan, mallard duck and scaup calling the place home. To get out amongst them you'll need to bring your own kayak or dinghy (no motorised craft are allowed). There's swimming, too (if you don't mind the odd skim of bird poop), although check all signs by the lake: toxic algae sometimes bloom here.

TAKE A SEAT AT TABLE MOUNTAIN

From the campsite you can embark on a grand circuit (four hours return) on the Tutira Walkway Long Loop. About half way around you'll reach Table Mountain Trig (487 m), where you can rest up and enjoy panoramic views of the Kaweka and Maungaharuru ranges and, on a clear day, the Hawke's Bay coast from Mahia Peninsula to Cape Kidnappers. A shorter option is to combine the Kahikanui and Galbraith's tracks. This involves about an hour's gentle stroll through pine forest and farmland with views over the lake. Track starts are signposted from the farthest camping area and shown on the interpretive displays.

About half way around the Tutira Walkway Long Loop you'll reach Table Mountain Trig (487 m), where you can rest up and enjoy panoramic views of the Kaweka and Maungaharuru ranges and, on a clear day, the Hawke's Bay coast from Mahia Peninsula to Cape Kidnappers.

PHOTONEWZEALAND / LEE WILSON

PREVIOUS PAGE: Te Mata Peak
LEFT: Table Mountain

Waipatiki Beach, 33 km north of Napier, 99 km south of Wairoa

Contact

06 836 6075

waipatiki@xtra.co.nz

Capacity

24 unpowered, 16 powered

Open

all year

Bookings

recommended peak season (minimum stay of five nights during peak)

Price

$20 adult / $8 child

Cooling off shouldn't be too much of a problem though, for right out front is the stream, banked by reeds and flowing to the fun-filled lagoon.

The Hawke's Bay landscape is farms, farms, farms . . . from mountain to coast, as far as the eye can see. This is a situation not entirely conducive to camping — the best spots being either up in the mountains (such as Kuripapango, see page 104), or theoretically, at the beach. The trouble is, a large part of the Hawke's Bay shoreline is exposed, shingly or steeply pitched — particularly the inhospitable beach between Napier and Te Awanga. Either side of this stretch, however, the beaches are better, such as the popular expanses of Ocean Beach and Waimarama south of Napier. To the north, our pick is Waipatiki Beach, where there's a farm that doubles as a campground.

Waipatiki Beach is half an hour's drive north of Napier. From the State Highway 2 turn-off the road takes a 10 km rollercoaster ride along the hilltops before beginning its descent to the bay. At the top of the hill you encounter Waipatiki Scenic Reserve, an important coastal forest remnant and just one of many reasons to visit this picturesque spot.

Waipatiki township is a down-home, beach-holiday delight — a clutch of predominantly board-and-batten baches tucked into the bush. Or at least it *was*. A fancy new subdivision announces that the cat is out of the bag. The farm park, however, lies like an island in time, separated from the settlement by a stream and paddocks.

Follow the farm rules and shut the gate as you enter. Greeted by rusty tractors and the odd farmyard animal, you may wonder what you're in for. Well, we can tell you: ducks, chooks, horses, turkeys and sheep, amongst others. You're also in for a bit of a surprise, because if you keep on truckin' past the sheds and beyond the second gate, a little ripper of a campground will come into view.

Set against a hill and just 300-odd metres from the beach, this small, particularly tent-friendly camp offers rows of pitches on several terraces — almost all commanding sea views. There are few trees for shade, so bring your beach umbrella or awning. Cooling off shouldn't be too much of a problem though, for right out front is the stream, banked by reeds and flowing to the fun-filled lagoon.

The amenities block is dependable and clean. A small kitchen has the usual appliances including an oven, while outside is a shady barbecue pagoda, the hub of much socialising of an evening. The lounge will do the trick on a rainy day — as will a handful of cute little cabins, although these are very popular so book early.

Owners Bill and Ann run a shop from their office which stocks little more than ice, frozen bread and milk — but that's better than nothing as there's no other shop for miles.

ENJOY WAIPATIKI'S WALKS

Close to the camp is a 40-minute walk through Waipatiki Domain. This rare remnant of coastal bush features some very old kahikatea (one possibly 650 years old) and other shapely natives such as nikau palms and various ferns. You'll probably see a few birds along the way. Further up the valley, the DOC-managed 64 ha Waipatiki Scenic Reserve offers similar arboreal delights, sadly rare in these parts. Fortunately, in 1952, livestock was fenced out of the reserve area, allowing the understorey to regenerate beneath the canopy. Take the loop walk (just over an hour) and see how the bush has bounced back. Other Waipatiki walks include the coastal tracks, which on a clear day afford views north to Mahia Peninsula and south to Cape Kidnappers. All these walks are detailed in a pamphlet available from the camp office.

PHOTONEWZEALAND / LEE WILSON

Waipatiki Beach

FLOAT DOWN TO THE LAGOON ON YOUR LILO

Before being uplifted by the notorious Napier earthquake of 1931, the waterway here was an estuary, from which early Maori used to enjoy an abundant supply of flounder, hence the name Waipatiki — *wai* is water, *patiki* flounder. Today, the lagoon makes a wonderful, watery playground, particularly suitable for little ones and for those wishing to float a little boat or play with a beachball. Safe swimming is always possible in the lagoon, but the beach can be pretty good, too, and is popular for swimming and boarding. Be careful how you go, though — the sea conditions will dictate safety and there are *Piha Rescue* traps here such as rips, holes and backwash.

> Today, the lagoon makes a wonderful, watery playground, particularly suitable for little ones and for those wishing to float a little boat or play with a beachball.

Napier–Taihape Road, 75 km northeast of Taihape, 76 km west of Napier

Contact

DOC Hawke's Bay

06 834 3111

www.doc.govt.nz

Capacity

50 unpowered

Open

all year

Bookings

not required

Price

$5 per person

Quiet and tranquil, Kuripapango is a place where you'll feel blissfully alone. There are few distractions — perhaps just a little reading, walking, and surveying the lie of the land — so this really is back-to-basics camping, just like the sign says.

For the purpose of getting from A to B, it couldn't be more logical for a road to run direct from Taihape to Napier, despite the fact that the Kaweka and Ruahine ranges lie in the way. Indeed, in the spirit of pioneering road-building — the spirit in which New Zealand's most improbable roads were built, such as Haast and Arthur's passes, or Skippers Canyon in the extreme — these low mountains proved little impediment. The middle portion of this handy route is known as 'Gentle Annie', a name bestowed upon it ironically by diggers who negotiated what was then a precipitous, narrow, rocky track in their rush to find gold. That, however, was the 1860s, and Annie has since matured into a much easier route.

Well over a century ago the land along this route was converted from forest to grazing, and was frequently passed through by travellers who stopped at the farming settlement of Kuripapango in its midst. It's hard to believe it today, but Kuripapango once boasted two hotels, a general store, saddler's shop, blacksmith, and stables. Now there are a just a handful of dwellings, a drove of horses and presumably the odd human (although none were sighted on our visit).

The hotels long gone, Kuripapango still makes a logical overnight stop on a journey from Napier to Taupo, and DOC can oblige you with two campgrounds. A sign reads 'basic camping in a natural setting', and that 'natural setting' is Kaweka Forest Park, a curious tract of 27,720 ha of mountain country. A little under a sixth of that area is planted in pine; the rest being regenerating bush, recovering from a legacy of fire and browsing both by farm animals and the usual raiders: deer, goats, pigs, rabbits and possums. With its eroded peaks and runaway pine it's by no means the most beautiful forest you'll see, but it certainly has its charms.

Cameron is the original campground, just a short walk from Kuripapango, a more recently established, larger campsite a little further removed from the road. This is the better of the two, sitting on a terrace above the Ngaruroro River, which twists and turns through these parts. Steep, bush-clad valley walls shelter the camp, while a particularly dramatic escarpment towers over it at the end.

With acres to spare there's room for everyone, including ample flat terrain for campervans and caravans and nooks and crannies for tenters. Shade and privacy can be found among the manuka scrub and grassland. Your water supply comes from the river, which requires a two-minute walk down a slightly tricky gravel path — and a three-minute walk up again. (And don't rush in if lugging it made you thirsty: that water must be boiled before drinking.) On our last visit, water flows allowed a chilly dip in the swimming hole, accessible from a stony beach.

CLIMB A (LOW) MOUNTAIN

Standing at the gape of the Ngaruroro Valley, Mount Kuripapango (1250 m) offers a far-reaching vista of both the Kaweka and Ruahine ranges. And if you're lucky — as we were on a fine but blustery late summer's day — you can see all the way out to Hawke's Bay and Cape Kidnappers. This moderately strenuous walk is three and a half hours return from the Cameron campground or two and a half hours return from the Lakes car park (drive 3 km from the campground towards Napier, then turn left onto a gravel road and drive for another 6 km). If you're going up via this track, look out for the short detour after about 30 minutes. A lookout captures impressive views inland across to the eroded Rogue Ridge and down to the Kuripapango Lakes.

DO YOUR BIT FOR CONSERVATION: PULL UP A PINE

The Kaweka Forest Park is home to a diverse range of flora, primarily regenerating kanuka and manuka lower down (with some remnant beech and podocarp in the valley floors) and, higher up, hardy subalpine species such as brown tussock, mountain daisies, hebe and the weird-looking Dracophyllum (one botanist quite rightly says this tree looks like it's been drawn by Dr Seuss). There is, however, an interloper: the North American Pinus contorta or lodgepole pine, which competes aggressively with the native vegetation. You can do your bit to repel this invader by pulling out a few wilding pines as you happen upon them.

ENJOY ONE OF NEW ZEALAND'S MOST UNDERRATED SCENIC DRIVES

Travelling through farmland to forestry and wilderness, the Napier–Taihape Road has been known as tortuous, twisting and thick with gravel. It's much less formidable since tarsealing began in earnest, although the presence of logging trucks means you still have to keep your wits about you. This is an unusual drive, the road rolling along the hilltops for much of the way, affording open views. That's because Kaweka Forest Park is surrounded by high-country runs — vast backblocks of homogeneous pasture, closely hewn and dotted with livestock. Close to camp, where the farmland runs out and forest begins, the landscape changes dramatically. Combined with the Kaimanawas, this is one of the largest tracts of wilderness country in the North Island, although scarred hillsides and acres of pine forest speak of its exploitation.

Kaweka Forest Park

DOC

Jetty Road, Castlepoint,
64 km west of Masterton

Contact

06 372 6705

www.castlepoint.co.nz

Capacity

20 unpowered / 42 powered

Open

all year

Bookings

recommended peak season

Price

$21 adult / $10.50 child

ABOVE: **The view from**
Castlepoint Holiday Park
RIGHT: **Castlepoint lighthouse**

The North Island's east coast between Cape Kidnappers and Cape Palliser is home to little more than a dozen tiny settlements, determined little dots on the map toughing it out in a rugged reality. The coast's stony beaches and wind-bitten cliffs are the terminal face of rolling uplands, bookending the extensive farming plains of Hawke's Bay and the Wairarapa. Blanketed in nibbled, yellowed grass, this area is a farming heartland, where the stream is a watering hole for hot livestock and trees serve as welcome shade or to hold the odd gully together. Hardly a holiday destination; only hardy campers need apply here.

There are about a half-dozen campsites along this shoreline, and our pick of the bunch is at Castlepoint. For a starter it's the most picturesque of the many beaten paths to the coast. Bordered by cow parsley verges, the road sweeps through a mellow rural scene. Many a pleasing vista opens up along the way — green fields of fluffy sheep, willowed creeks, cabbage tree swamp, patches of bush and pockets of pine forest.

Castlepoint itself is a bach settlement most famous for its lighthouse. Oh, what a lucky breed those lighthouses are, always occupying — the whole world over — the most dramatic extremities of the land. Castlepoint lighthouse is no exception, lying appropriately within the bounds of a scenic reserve which boasts a number of spectacular geographical features, including a limestone reef and lagoon. All these fascinations are readily accessible at the far end of the town.

The holiday park rolls out the welcome mat at the entrance to the settlement. Accessed through a promising colonnade of phoenix palms, it occupies the seafront on a windswept beach. There are several camping areas to choose from: a beachfront block, a few hill terraces and sheltered spots up the back popular with tenters looking to escape the prevailing nor'wester. It's a hardy campground: there are few trees towards the front of the camp, so shade is hard to come by, and the terrain is tough and dusty with sparse patches of grass. Happily though, homely potted plants and flowerbeds soften a few edges. Someone here's making an effort to pretty things up.

That would be owners Pauline and Ian, who took out a Qualmark 'most improved campground' award in 2008. Their hard work is evident all around the grounds, particularly in the main facilities block — a solid Kiwi classic, the 'Colin Meads' of the ilk. It's in excellent nick. The kitchen has the necessary appliances including an oven, while the annexe offers both dining and lounge.

The sandy beach out front offers safe swimming in favourable conditions, and surfboards can be hired from the office. Basic groceries and fuel can be bought at the general store and tearoom, which bakes a most acceptable afghan.

CASTLEPOINT HOLIDAY PARK

GET YOUR COBWEBS BLOWN AWAY

The Castlepoint lighthouse first beamed out in 1913, and has since remained a welcoming beacon for Kiwi and international sailors alike — it's the first sign of landfall for American ships bound for Wellington. It's a handsome sight, both from down low and on high, and to get to it one needs only to take the Lighthouse Walk (30 minutes return). From this vantage point there are fantastic views over the settlement and beach, and south towards the lagoon and rock. Chances are it'll be blowing a hooley: wind speeds in excess of 200 km per hour have been recorded here. So hang on to your hat and try not to let the treacherous seas below distract you from your footing. Spellbinding drama.

PHOTONEWZEALAND / MIKE HEYDON

FROLIC IN NEW ZEALAND'S LUNAR LAGOONA

As well as the lighthouse, Castlepoint Scenic Reserve contains a collection of fascinating landforms: a limestone reef, lagoon, sand dunes and Castle Rock. Between them they support a unique ecosystem, the focus of restoration efforts by DOC. Especially precious is the rare Castlepoint daisy, although many other interesting plants and creatures can be seen, such as katipo spiders (well, maybe you don't want to actually *see* one), white-fronted terns and reef herons to name but a few. The ocean beyond is visited by dolphins, seals and occasionally small whales. Humans frequent the reserve, too, most of whom will be mucking around in the sheltered lagoon with its gentle shallows, with the odd breaker rolling through the inlet. It's a strange and wonderful place, great for paddling, sandcastling, swimming, surfing and fishing. You might want to keep a look out for aliens: this crazy landscape feels like another planet.

SCALE THE ROCK

Named by Captain Cook in 1770, Castle Rock dominates the skyline here with its 162 m fortress-like form. Those with a head for heights and a good set of lungs can reach the top via the Deliverance Cove track (one and a half hours return), signposted from the reserve car park. Crouch low on the steep section near the top — it can get blustery. Keep an eye out for lounging fur seals and penguins around the rocks.

10 Dublin Street West, Martinborough

Contact
06 306 8946
www.martinboroughcamping.com

Capacity
18 unpowered / 16 powered

Open
all year

Bookings
recommended peak season and essential on event weekends (e.g. Toast Martinborough and Alana Estate concert)

Price
$17 adult / $10 child

With its wide, sleepy streets lined with cute-as-a-button century-old cottages, Martinborough is an ideal town for walkers and cyclists.

Surrounded by a patchwork of pasture and pinstripes of vines, Martinborough (population around 1300) remains one of New Zealand's most charming towns, one thankfully not twee'd-up and overrun with tourists, as is the fashion of late. And despite being a distinctly wine-sodden area it is not, as you might expect, pretentious or particularly affluent, but rather a grafter, populated largely by farmers, grape growers, and the necessary service-folk who ensure that the wheels stay well oiled. That's not to say it isn't popular with visitors — it most certainly is. This explains the presence of numerous respectable cafés and restaurants in the town, a drawcard in their own right.

With its wide, sleepy streets lined with cute-as-a-button century-old cottages, Martinborough is an ideal town for walkers and cyclists. It takes little over 20 minutes to walk from one side to the other. Around a leafy square in the middle of town are the restaurants and shops, along with other attractions such as the Wine Centre and cinema. If this sounds like the sort of place you'd like to noodle around for a day or two, we recommend Martinborough Village Camping, on the edge of town just 600 m from the square.

Surprisingly unfettered by the township save for the presence of the municipal swimming pool next door, this small leasehold campground on a council-owned recreation reserve enjoys a largely rural setting, bordered by paddocks and vineyards. It's come a long way since we started camping here a decade ago, with a programme of improvements well underway. While a few mature trees stand assuringly at its centre, younger plantings have yet to reach a really useful age but nevertheless add to an already pleasant environment for both tents and vans. Between the trees and beyond the fences, the Tararuas and Martinborough hills can be seen in the distance.

The two timber amenities buildings are newly erected and smart, joined together by a deck on which a barbecue area is set up. The bathrooms are particularly pleasing, mirrors and liquid soap dispensers speaking volumes of the consideration managers Lisa and Frank have given their visitors. The kitchen and lounge area is relaxed and comfortable, and features useful extras such as internet access (kiosk and Wi-Fi internet) and tourist brochures. Kitchen appliances include hotplates and a microwave, but no oven. The laundry is as tidy as your mother's might be.

Not only fabulously convenient, the village campground is just a nice place to hang out. Enjoy your cheese and pinot noir at the picnic tables, or go next door to the pool (open Labour Weekend to Easter). When you're ready to see the sights, just pop on those comfy shoes or hire a bicycle from the office. It couldn't be easier.

THINGS TO SEE AND DO
NEAR MARTINBOROUGH

BEHOLD THE PRIMEVAL POWER OF CHICKEN WIRE, PLASTER OF PARIS AND KIWI INGENUITY

A 20-minute drive northeast of Martinborough, Stonehenge Aotearoa is a full-scale adaptation of the Salisbury Stonehenge, carefully orientated on a grassy knoll overlooking the Wairarapa Plain and the Tararuas. It's a fascinating place to visit, with an excellent pre-tour talk and audio-visual presentation followed by an encounter with the henge itself — a pretty surreal sight, day or night. Hear how these huge obelisks aided exploration of the universe and unlocked the great mysteries of navigation and survival. Learn about constellations, aliens and ancient beliefs, and find out why you're not really an Aries. They've got big telescopes, too. Tours are a bargain at $10; bookings essential. Open daily, Ahiaruhe Road, Carterton. Tel 027 246 6766, www.stonehenge-aotearoa.com.

ENJOY A GLASS OR TWO OF THE TOWN'S MAIN EXPORT

Although the region's first grapes were planted way back in 1883, the prohibition movement of the 1890s soon put the cork back in the bottle. Winemaking was revived here only in the early 1980s after a government report announced that Martinborough had similar terroir to Burgundy in France. Since that time the number of vineyards has ballooned to around forty. The area enjoys an impressive international reputation for its wines, with many a gold medal being won by local pinot noir, riesling and sauvignon blanc. The Martinborough Wine Centre (Kitchener Street, tel 06 306 9040, www.martinboroughwinecentre.co.nz) is an easy place to taste and buy, although a more fun way is to get out amongst the grapes on two wheels (see Bike the Vines).

BIKE THE VINES

Beautiful scenery and a high concentration of vineyards make Martinborough ideal for a wine trail. You can reach plenty of them on foot, but for those with sound balance and a modicum of self-control, we recommend a bicycle. They can be hired from the campground or in town (Martinborough Bicycle Hire, 28 Puruatanga Road, tel 06 306 8920; bus tours are available if you prefer, see www.wairarapanz.com). Prior to setting off on your grape ride, pick up a copy of the *Wairarapa and Martinborough Wine Trail* booklet, available all over town. It will help you keep your bearings (maybe).

> The area enjoys an impressive international reputation for its wines, with many a gold medal being won by local pinot noir, riesling and sauvignon blanc.

PHOTONEWZEALAND / MIKE HEYDON

Vines at Escarpment Vineyard, with the Martinborough Hills behind

**Mount Holdsworth Road,
17 km northwest of Masterton
(signposted off State Highway 2,
2 km south of Masterton)**

Contact
DOC Masterton
06 377 0700
www.doc.govt.nz

Capacity
150 unpowered

Open
all year

Bookings
not required

Price
$6 adult / $2 child

This river valley has long been a favoured access point to the forest, with numerous early naturalists venturing this way to fondle and pluck its many wonders.

An enticing wilderness within a stone's throw of the capital, the Tararua Forest Park was the first to be established in New Zealand, founded in 1954. At the core of the park, a range of towering peaks extend all the way from the Manawatu Gorge in the north to the Rimutaka Saddle in the south, a distance of more than 50 km. Two of its highest mountains are Mount Mitre (1571 m) and Mount Hector (1529 m), both presenting a decent uphill challenge. Indeed, the Tararuas seem irresistible to trampers; today the park is as popular as ever for its tracks and other recreational opportunities, despite some dubious weather. Its proximity to Cook Strait makes for high winds, mist and frequent rain, but fortunately that's largely towards the tops. The Tararuas' sheltered flats will surely see you right . . .

The forest park is accessible from both Kapiti in the west (see page 116), and from several points on the Wairarapa side, the most popular of which is Holdsworth. This river valley has long been a favoured access point to the forest, with numerous early naturalists venturing this way to fondle and pluck its many wonders. Guided parties began climbing to the summit of Mount Holdsworth (1470 m) way back in the 1890s, and the early twentieth century saw enterprising tour operators putting considerable effort into track-building and hosting visitors in their lodges. This is evident in the facilities you see today: well-formed walks and interpretive displays; picnic, camping and parking areas; legendary swimming holes; and a ranger in residence.

Coming from Masterton, the drive from State Highway 2 is typically rural, but as you reach the park boundary pasture gives way to thick forest. Lying at the foot of fairly steep hills and alongside the Atiwhakatu Stream, a large grassy flat is split into two areas — one apiece for campers and day-users.

There is plenty of room to camp and no reason to have neighbours unless you wish to. Plenty of shady nooks can be found around the perimeter of the main field, but with a steady flow of day visitors through here in the summer holidays, we prefer to pitch further up on the elevated alcoves. These offer lovely camping, shelter and privacy, with bush all around. They are perfect for families or groups.

The DOC shelter is a bit rough and ready, and other facilities are minimal. Long-drop loos are dotted around, as are water spigots. The good news is that delightful (soapless) bathing can be had in one of numerous fantastic swimming holes along the stream. It's not even that cold!

HEAD FOR THE HILLS

Three walking tracks start from the campground, two of them involving some inevitable uphill slog. This effort will be amply rewarded, however, with views of the mountains, valleys and the mosaic pattern of the Wairarapa plain. We suggest the 360-degree panorama enjoyed from Rocky Lookout on the Gentle Annie track (two hours return). For the fit and intrepid the track continues onward and upward towards the boardwalks of boggy Pig Flat and Powell Hut further on. The six-hour return walk to the hut is a demanding one, but boasts some of the most expansive views in the park. The 30-bunk serviced hut is rather impressive and popular with trampers on the two- to three-day Holdsworth–Jumbo circuit. A good overnight option is to stay at the hut and then make the hour-long climb up to the summit of Mount Holdsworth in the morning before heading back down to the campground the same way or via the East Holdsworth Track. The Tararuas have a notorious reputation for severe weather at any time of year, so trampers should be experienced, well prepared and vigilant.

PHOTONEWZEALAND / MIKE HEYDON

The Tararua Ranges and Waiohine River — the gorge in the foothills is a splendid place for a daytrip

HEAD FOR SOME MORE HILLS

An alternative entrance to the forest park is further south at Waiohine Gorge (signposted off State Highway 2, 4.5 km south of Carterton). A smaller recreational reserve with more secluded, excellent camping and picnicking facilities, the gorge is dramatic and handsome, well worth a day visit or overnight stay. The main drawcard here (especially for families or non-trampers) is the river: the swimming hole below the campground is heavenly, with the stony river beach next to it very pleasant for soaking up some sun while marvelling at the gorge's bluffs and forest. There's also a good day tramp from here: the Lower Waiohine Track (three hours return), a somewhat boggy excursion that skirts along the top of the gorge for most of the way. The track involves crossing a 94 m long suspension bridge, which is a bit of a thrill.

NAPIER AND HAWKE'S BAY

AFFORDABLE WESTSHORE HOLIDAY PARK
88 Meeanee Quay, Westshore, Napier

Contact: 06 835 9456
westshoreholiday@xtra.co.nz
www.westshoreholidaypark.co.nz

Tariff: $24–110

BAY VIEW MOTEL AND HOLIDAY PARK
43 Petane Road, Bay View, Napier

Contact: 06 836 6933
bayviewhotelnap.pc@xtra.co.nz

Tariff: $22–100

BAY VIEW VAN PARK
Cnr Main and Onehunga Roads,
Bay View, Napier

Contact: 06 836 6064
bayviewvanpark@paradise.net.nz
www.bayviewvanpark.co.nz

Tariff: $30

ESKDALE CARAVAN PARK
Yule Road, Eskdale, Napier

Contact: 06 836 6864

Tariff: $24–40

KENNEDY PARK TOP 10 RESORT
11 Storkey Street, Napier

Contact: 06 843 9126
info@kennedypark.co.nz
www.kennedypark.co.nz

Tariff: $36–195

MOUNTAIN VALLEY ADVENTURE LODGE
408 McIvor Road, RD2, Napier

Contact: 06 834 9756
clive@mountainvalley.co.nz
www.mountainvalley.co.nz

Tariff: $20–80

RIVER'S EDGE HOLIDAY PARK
Harker Street, Waipawa

Contact: 06 857 8976
paddy.mccloskey@paradise.net.nz

Tariff: $20–90

RIVERSIDE MOTOR CAMP
19 Marine Parade, Wairoa

Contact: 06 838 6301
riversidemotorcamp@clear.net.nz
www.riversidemotorcamp.co.nz

Tariff: $30

WAIPUKURAU HOLIDAY PARK
SH 2, Waipukurau

Contact: 06 858 8184
ypuk.holidaypark@xtra.co.nz

Tariff: $25–100

WAIRARAPA

CARTERTON HOLIDAY PARK
Belvedere Road, Carterton

Contact: 06 379 8267
cartertonholidaypark@contact.net.nz

Tariff: $20–85

GATEWAY MOTEL AND HOLIDAY PARK
Lake Ferry Road (3 km from Lake
Ferry Beach), Lake Ferry

Contact: 06 307 7780
gatewaypark@xtra.co.nz

Tariff: $20–85

→ LET'S GO CAMPING IN

KAPITI AND WELLINGTON

Otaki Gorge Road, 19 km southeast of Otaki (signposted off State Hightway 1 just south of Otaki)

Contact
DOC Wellington
04 384 7770
www.doc.govt.nz

Capacity
150 unpowered

Open
all year

Bookings
not required

Price
$6 adult / $2 child

....

Running right alongside is the Waiotauru River, babbling swiftly by and offering a refreshing splash on a summer's day; there are several good swimming pools nearby should you desire total immersion.

....

The Tararuas have long been a favoured getaway, particularly for wired Wellingtonians looking to unwind the spring coiled by the working week. Otaki Forks, on the western side of the range, is the most popular entrance to the forest park, being the trailhead for a well-established track network with plentiful huts. The mountains are a tramper's paradise, but some car-accessible foothill clearings — and close proximity to State Highway 1 — mean it's perennially popular with daytrippers and campers, too.

Here in this pretty valley the Otaki River is met by both the Waiotauru River and Waitatapia Stream — hence the name 'Forks'. Terraced river flats surrounded by regenerating bush-clad hills yield plenty of natural fun, whether it's picnicking, bird-spotting, swimming, kayaking, mountain biking or just exploring the valley — old stone walls and rusty boilers bear testament to the interesting human history of the area. Whether you just want to hang out or venture further into the park, Schoolhouse Flat campground will suit you down to the ground.

The last 5 km of the access road is unsealed, and sidles along the river while negotiating undulating narrows and some tight bends. Keep driving on from Boielle Flat (the day-use area) and past the warden's house until you reach Schoolhouse Flat. This campsite, spread over a large area, has an open aspect, plenty of flat, spongy ground, and ample shade and decent private nooks to be had if you strike it lucky during the busy season. Running right alongside is the Waiotauru River, babbling swiftly by and offering a refreshing splash on a summer's day; there are several good swimming pools nearby should you desire total immersion.

The campsite has recently had some attention lavished on it, hence the handsome new toilet block (flushers no less, and a washing-up sink). Besides this, facilities are confined to the occasional cooking platform and rubbish bins. A total fire ban is in place — the year-round resident warden will enforce that rule, collect your fees and check that you're a happy camper.

Tararua Forest Park can also be accessed from the eastern (Wairarapa) side: see page 110.

TAKE A HIKE

You can embark on many different walks starting at the campground — from a three-minute loop to an all-day up-the-hill-and-back-again. Our favourite is the Waitewaewae Track (three hours return) that passes through a variety of regenerating native bush to an old log hauler, a remnant of the area's sawmilling history. There's a good picnicking spot at Papa Creek, about 10 minutes before the log hauler. There are several other half-day options, detailed in DOC's *Otaki Forks* leaflet (available online or from visitor centres). Keen trampers will probably already know that Otaki Forks is also the starting point for the epic four to five-day (46 km) circuit that takes in the magnificent Tararua Peaks, with side trips to Mount Crawford (1462 m) and Mount Hector (1529 m), returning to Otaki Forks via the Fields or Penn Creek tracks. There is also, of course, the Southern Crossing, a two- to three-day slog across the invariably claggy tops (highest point: Mount Hector) from Otaki to Kaitoke.

SWEETEN YOURSELF UP WITH BROWN SUGAR

Right on State Highway 1, a few hundred metres north of the Otaki Gorge Road turn-off, the terrific Brown Sugar Café (tel 06 364 6359) is housed in a heritage building built as stables in the late 1920s. It has become a favoured stop for food-lovers travelling up and down the country, famed for its scrumptious food and delightful environment. Deli-style sandwiches, pastries and cakes compete for attention with a blackboard menu of breakfast and all-day light meals, including fresh salads and lovely ham off the bone. If it's fine, eat in the cottage garden. The children will love it and so will you.

PHOTONEWZEALAND / GEOFF MARSHALL

PREVIOUS PAGE: Kapiti Island
ABOVE: Fishing for flounder at Otaki River estuary with Tararua Ranges behind

**180 Wellington Road, Paekakariki,
30 km north of Wellington**

Contact
(04) 292 8292
www.paekakarikiholidaypark.co.nz

Capacity
30 unpowered / 150 powered

Open
all year

Bookings
required Christmas period only

Price
from $13 adult / $7 child

Despite its capacity this holiday park remains relatively restful, with ample privacy, the well-planned plantings of mature pohutukawa and Norfolk pines lending shade and shelter for warbling birds. Adding cheery colour are the odd geranium, lily and fuchsia.

It absolutely positively proclaims that it's a fabulous tourist town, so why is it that there's no camping in Wellington city? Perhaps it's the wind, wont to rip a tent clean off the ground even if it's rocked out with breeze blocks? Or maybe it's the fault lines, which might open up in a magnitude eight, swallowing the unsuspecting van?

We jest of course, but it remains true that there are very limited options in the capital for campers and vanners, whether passing through from the ferry crossing or wishing to hang out for a few days. The Top 10 Holiday Park in Petone offers all the necessities, located just a 15-minute drive from the city. However, for those heading in or out on State Highway 1 — or indeed looking to explore the Kapiti Coast — the Paekakariki Holiday Park, 35 minutes' drive away, offers a quieter, more natural and more interesting experience.

Paekakariki is the sweetest of the Kapiti Coast's towns. Sitting proudly upon hillocks above a long stretch of beach, many of its residents enjoy striking views out to Kapiti Island, along the coast, and far away to the South Island. Queen Elizabeth Park — the last swathe of natural duneland along the Kapiti coastline — is accessible from the northern end of town. The holiday park is right next to the entrance to the park, down the end of Wellington Road, a five-minute minute drive north from the highway turn-off.

This is a very quiet corner of Paekakariki; once inside the gates you'd never know you were so close to the highway. The holiday park is like Dr Who's TARDIS— it's much bigger than it looks from the outside. As you venture inward it expands in all directions, with hedgerowed alcoves, streamside nooks and a particularly pleasant, largely unpowered field down the very end (this is our pick — sites numbered in the 120s, although perhaps not when the group lodge is occupied).

There are two ablution blocks — dated but still clean, tidy and in good nick. One block has a small but homely television lounge, while the other has gas barbecues. The kitchens have the usual small appliances and hotplates, but no ovens. As well as a playground set-up, there's a sandpit and trampoline. Dog Bay, a fenced alcove, offers sanctuary for your four-legged friend.

A camp store is open over the summer holidays, selling ice and treats for the children. Further afield, the Beach Store (ten minutes' walk along the foreshore) has coffee and ice cream, although this is really just a ruse to get you to look at their fancy designer wares. There's a lovely park next door to the store, too, with goalposts for a kick around. The main shops (dairy, deli and cafés) are back where you entered town over the railway lines.

This is an excellent family camp in many regards, and will serve you well whether you're looking to stay for a while or just passing through.

HANG OUT AT THE BEACH

It's a three-minute walk from the camp gate to the beach, crossing Queen Elizabeth Park with its excellent adventure playground, run-around area and picnic tables. The beach is patrolled by lifeguards in summer and enjoys a spectacular vista out to Kapiti Island. A good beach on a great day, it's much less so when the wind blows — this isn't far from Wellington, after all. When the tide's in the waves roll right up, leaving only a sliver of sand — the time to swim or stroll is definitely around low tide.

EXPLORE QUEEN ELIZABETH PARK

This is one of the last remaining areas of relatively unchanged dune and wetland that once stretched northward all the way to Foxton. Luckily for you there are 650 ha of it right here on your camping doorstep. As well as the usual seaside fun, there are plenty of opportunities for walking, biking, horse riding and picnicking and lots of room to run around. For the anoraks, the Wellington Tramway Museum is located at the McKays Crossing entrance to the park. All aboard for the 2 km tram ride to Whareroa Beach — running at weekends, public holidays and daily in January, weather permitting (tel 04 292 8361, www.wellingtontrams.org.nz).

PHOTONEWZEALAND / PAUL KENNEDY

VISIT KAPITI ISLAND

One of the New Zealand's most important nature reserves, Kapiti is home to endangered bird species including the little spotted kiwi, takahe, saddleback, and hihi (stitchbird). Tui, bellbird, weka, kaka, kereru and the North Island robin are also commonly seen in the island's shrubland and forest, while on the lagoon and along the coast you're likely to spot scaup, grey teal, royal spoonbill, shag, a variety of gull species and the ubiquitous oystercatcher. It's a veritable twitchers' paradise! A 90-minute walk to the island's 521 m summit, Tuteremoana, rewards with magnificent 360-degree views. There are two options for visiting the island, which is 5 km offshore — either self-guided excursions or guided tours. For further information, advice and bookings, contact the Wellington DOC visitor centre (tel 04 384 7770 or email wellingtonvc@doc.govt.nz).

LEFT: **Paekakariki, with Raumati in the distance beyond Queen Elizabeth Park**
FOLLOWING PAGE: **Zealandia — the Karori Sanctuary in Wellington**

OTHER CAMPGROUNDS IN KAPITI AND WELLINGTON

HOROWHENUA / KAPITI COAST

BYRON'S RESORT
20 Tasman Road, Otaki
Beach, Kapiti Coast

Contact: 06 364 8119
byrons.resort@xtra.co.nz
www.byronsresort.co.nz

Tariff: $30–150

EL RANCHO (WAIKANAE CHRISTIAN HOLIDAY PARK)
Kauri Road, Waikanae

Contact: 04 902 6287
www.elrancho.co.nz

Tariff: $22–90

FOXTON BEACH MOTOR CAMP
1 Holben Parade, Foxton Beach

Contact: 06 363 8211

Tariff: $24–42

HIMATANGI BEACH HOLIDAY PARK
30 Koputara Road,
Himatangi Beach

Contact: 06 329 9575
www.himatangibeachholidaypark.co.nz

Tariff: $27–85

HYDRABAD HOLIDAY PARK
Forest Road, Waitarere Beach

Contact: 06 368 4941
hydrabad@paradise.net.nz
www.waitarerebeachcamps.co.nz

Tariff: $30–65

LEVIN MOTOR CAMP AT PLAYFORD PARK
38 Parker Ave, Levin

Contact: 06 368 3549
levin.motor.camp@xtra.co.nz

Tariff: $30–85

LINDALE MOTOR PARK
Ventnor Drive (off SH 1),
Paraparaumu

Contact: 04 298 8046
lindalemotorpark@xtra.co.nz

Tariff: $29–90

WAITARERE BEACH MOTOR CAMP
133 Park Ave, Waitarere Beach

Contact: 06 368 8732
wbmc@paradise.net.nz
www.waitarerebeachcamps.co.nz

Tariff: $30–48

WELLINGTON

AOTEA CAMPING GROUNDS
3 Whitford Brown Ave, Porirua

Contact: 04 235 9599

Tariff: $26–70

CAMP ELSDON
18 Raiha Street, Porirua

Contact: 04 237 8987
www.campelsdon.co.nz

Tariff: $20–32

HARCOURT HOLIDAY PARK
45 Akatarawa Road, Upper Hutt

Contact: 04 526 7400
harcourtholidaypark@xtra.co.nz
www.harcourtholidaypark.co.nz

Tariff: $30–100

WELLINGTON TOP 10 HOLIDAY PARK
95 Hutt Park Road,
Lower Hutt

Contact: 04 568 5913
www.huttpark.co.nz

Tariff: $40–160

→ LET'S GO CAMPING IN

MARLBOROUGH AND NELSON

Port Underwood Road, 24 km north of Blenheim, 33 km south of Picton (turn off State Highway 1 at Tuamarina, 9 km north of Blenheim); 36 km to Picton via Port Underwood

Contact

DOC South Marlborough
03 572 9100
www.doc.govt.nz

Capacity

20 unpowered sites

Open

all year

Bookings

not required

Price

$6 adult / $1.50 child

This combination of terrific views, sandy beach, good swimming, shady walks and birdsong afford welcome relief from the sauna of flat and arid midsummer Blenheim — it's well worth the 25-minute drive.

Cloudy Bay is the ocean terminus of the Wairau Plain, the huge, vine-striped flat through which Marlborough's largest river, the Wairau, flows — all the way from the mountains of Nelson Lakes National Park, 160 km up the valley. The bay is interesting for many reasons, not least of all that Captain Cook named it cloudy, when it hardly ever is: Blenheim claims the crown of New Zealand's sunniest town more often than not.

But the bay holds far greater intrigue. Amateur archaeologists have long been excavating artefacts around the Wairau Bar and the lagoons to the south. However, recent digs have unearthed bones of both Haast's eagle and moa, along with a stone adze, middens and a hangi pit, prompting at least one anthropologist to purport that Cloudy Bay is where the first Polynesians came ashore in New Zealand.

There are geological curiosities, too. Running through the plain, the Wairau Fault dissects the landscape: to the north, the schisty peaks of the Richmond Range; to the south, the Wither Hills, greywacke coated in siltstone and sandstone — low, eroded, and parched for most of the year. Whites Bay is a small cove at the foot of the northern ranges, lying in the bushy foothills of Mount Robertson (1036 m). It has a spectacular vantage of Cloudy Bay: the brutal shoreline and a panorama of the Wither Hills and the White Bluffs, beyond which Cape Campbell can be seen in the distance. All of this — and more — can be surveyed on the drive over the hill to Whites Bay (and also on the Rarangi–Whites Bay Walkway, see opposite).

The campground is set on the only sandy, safe swimming beach within the arc of Cloudy Bay (there's a lifeguard patrol in summer). The campground's landscaped grounds are in great shape, their plantings having reached a useful and attractive maturity. Close to the main car park, historic cable-station house (the original Cook Strait telegraph cable used to come ashore here) and picnic area are a few secluded camping nooks and appealing roadside spots. These offer the advantage of easy beach access, as well as several toilets, changing rooms and a cold-water shower, all housed in the surf lifesaving club rooms. This area, however, will be teeming with daytrippers during the summer holidays so at this time your best bet is the top field — about a two-minute walk up the hill. It's quieter, with alcove sites and a small toilet block. Both top and bottom areas have picnic benches, tiny cooking shelters and spigots.

This combination of terrific views, sandy beach, good swimming, shady walks and birdsong afford welcome relief from the sauna of flat and arid midsummer Blenheim — it's well worth the 25-minute drive.

SAMPLE A SAUV OR TWO

Mention New Zealand wine and Marlborough sauvignon blanc is most likely to spring to mind. And it's no wonder, with Marlborough's 500-odd grape growers growing 56 per cent of the country's grapes — that's approximately 16,000 ha of vines, around 75 per cent of which is sauv blanc. This vast winemaking region has almost tripled in size since 2002, and at last count there were 109 wineries, many of which welcome visitors. That's a lot of wine tasting! Get started by picking up the Marlborough Wine Trail map from the Blenheim i-SITE. Numerous tour operators will guide you round the grapes, or you can hire bikes and pedal yourself.

WALK IN BOTH DIRECTIONS

Two good walks start at opposite ends of Whites Bay. The Black Jack Track (one and a half hours return) begins with a rather humdrum climb through the bush before reaching a ridge above precipitous bluffs from where there are dizzying views north to the many coves of Port Underwood and across Cook Strait to the North Island. On the way back down you'll get intermittent but expansive views across Cloudy Bay to the White Bluffs, and beyond Clifford Bay to Cape Campbell. The Inland Kaikoura Range rises above the tops of the Wither Hills. The walk from the other end of the beach, the Rarangi–Whites Bay Track (two hours return), offers views with a similar aspect, while at Rarangi itself you can enjoy a 20-minute return walk to Monkey Bay or have a wander along Rarangi Beach and the coastal reserve.

WANDER INTO THE WITHERS

Just a five-minute drive (or 30-minute walk) from Blenheim town centre, the Wither Hills Farm Park's recently upgraded car parks and toilet facilities reflect its increasing popularity. Ranging over the gentle hills on the south side of town, the park boasts 23 well-graded tracks (many with mountain biking permitted) covering over 50 km in all. Various lookout points offer fine views of the valley below, and — if you get high enough — northeast out to Cloudy Bay and the North Island, and southeast to the Inland Kaikoura Range and its tallest mountain, Mount Tapuae-o-Uenuku (2885 m). A good option is the Mount Vernon Lookout (422 m), one hour's walk from the Redwood Street entrance. Pick up a map from the Blenheim i-SITE or download a copy from www.marlborough.govt.nz. No dogs are allowed in the park, as it is still a working farm with real live sheep.

SARAH BENNETT AND LEE SLATER

**PREVIOUS PAGE: The bountiful pleasures of a Marlborough vineyard
ABOVE: A view down to Whites Bay and across to Cloudy Bay and the Wither Hills**

Onahau Bay, Queen Charlotte Sound, 40 km northwest of Picton, 32 km east of Havelock (also accessible by boat from Picton)

Contact
03 573 4048
www.mistletoebay.co.nz

Capacity
100 unpowered

Open
all year

Bookings
Recommended during summer holidays and Easter

Price
$15 adult / $5 child
(under fives free)

Mistletoe Bay is a restful place to while away a few days. As pretty as a picture, its glassy waters lie surrounded by regenerating bush; a small jetty juts into the bay from where visitors are conveyed in and out over the waves.

The Marlborough Sounds — Pelorus, Kenepuru and Queen Charlotte — are a labyrinth of waterways with a thousand bays, bound by bushy ridgelines and studded with islands. Between them they offer seemingly endless opportunities for adventure. It is, however, hardly groundbreaking news that many of the sounds' most beautiful places are down winding gravel roads or accessible only by boat, for those along the beaten track are typically bach clad and boat ramped, awash with visitors all summer long. Those seeking solitude will be pleased to discover that DOC services a multitude of campsites dotted throughout the extremities of the sounds, but if you're looking for something a bit easier to access, a little bit of Marlborough Sounds magic can be found in Mistletoe Bay, where you'll have only a handful of cabin-dwellers and campers for company.

Mistletoe Bay is in fact a small cove at the head of Onahau Bay in the Grove Arm of Queen Charlotte Sound, not far — as the crow flies — from Picton, and just a stone's throw from Portage, over the hill in Kenepuru Sound. The Queen Charlotte Track passes across the hills above and accounts somewhat for the popularity of Mistletoe: it makes a logical stop for walkers and bikers. It's also less than an hour's drive from Picton, on a winding but almost entirely sealed road (there's just a short stretch of gravel from the main road down to the bay).

Mistletoe Bay is a restful place to while away a few days. As pretty as a picture, its glassy waters lie surrounded by regenerating bush; a small jetty juts into the bay from where visitors are conveyed in and out over the waves. A stream trickles down through the small valley, emptying into a shallow, muddy beach, perfect for paddling and poking about on for crabs and shells. The grassy foreshore invites camp chairs and blankets, picnics and sunbathing. You could chill out here all day long.

The camping area slopes gently up the hill behind the bay. Carpeted in lush grass, sites have a fairly open aspect. Those around the edges enjoy some shelter from the bush, but some are well short of shade at high noon. This campsite isn't suitable for caravans or big campervans, although there are cabins, a backpackers and a bach available for rent.

Facilities include a recently completed ablution block (with hot showers and an environmentally friendly grey-waste recycling system) and a basic kitchen with stovetop, oven, microwave and fridge — an upgrade is planned for the near future. There are sheltered dining tables and a barbecue so you can sizzle a sausage.

The campsite is self-registration, although up the hill is the caretaker's house where you can buy ice blocks and other basics in summer. And you can feel good about buying that Trumpet: the camp trust puts any profits back into 'maintaining and improving our resource for future generations'. Nice one.

CRUISE THE SOUNDS ON THE HISTORIC *WINSOME II*

Based at Mistletoe Bay, this handsome 11 m motor launch was built in 1924 and employed in World War Two by the New Zealand Air Force as an operational support vessel. She now plies the sounds, taking visitors on customised cruises and fishing trips. A variety of options are available, from a two-hour jaunt to a full-day adventure (www.classiccruises.co.nz, tel 021 375 444). Water taxi operators can also ship you around. There are numerous operators including Cougar Line (www.cougarline.co.nz, tel 03 573 7925) who offer 'Cruise 'n' Walk' options designed to suit all.

GO FOR A PADDLE

A great way to explore Onahau Bay and the Grove Arm is by kayak, which can be hired by the half- or full day at the campground. Fishing rods and bait are also available should you wish to try your hand at reeling in some kaimoana for dinner. The famous sounds blue cod is off the menu, sadly, as overfishing has forced the closure of the fishery until at least 2012 (so return those little fellas back to the water). Of course you'll probably only catch a spotty, anyway . . .

TRAMP OR BIKE THE QUEEN CHARLOTTE TRACK

With stunning views and varied terrain, this popular 71 km track runs between historic Ship Cove (a regular port of call for Captain Cook on the *Endeavour*) and Anakiwa (home of Outward Bound). The track can be walked in either direction and picked up at various points, including by taking a short walk up the hill from Mistletoe Bay. From this point, two day-walks can be embarked on: either head west towards Torea Saddle (two and a half hours, 7.5 km one way); or southeast towards Anakiwa (three and a half hours, 12.5 km one way). Mountain bikers can make a terrific loop by cycling to Torea Saddle via the track, popping down to Portage for a spot of lunch, then returning to Mistletoe via the rollercoaster Kenepuru Road. Hard work, but well worth the effort. (www.qctrack.co.nz)

The Queen Charlotte Track often follows the ridgeline, affording bird's-eye views such as this one over The Portage

DESTINATION MARLBOROUGH

**Pelorus Bridge, State Highway 6,
18 km west of Havelock,
40 km east of Nelson**

Contact

Camp office
03 571 6019
p.b.cafe@xtra.co.nz
www.doc.govt.nz

Capacity

23 unpowered / 14 powered

Open

all year

Bookings

recommended peak season

Price

$10 adult / $5 child unpowered;
$11 adult / $5 child powered

*Set amid the grandeur
of towering kahikatea,
our tallest native tree,
the ground is carpeted
with closely mown
grass. Bordered by
bush, alcoves provide
attractive pitching with
a degree of shade and
privacy.*

Sitting roughly halfway between Blenheim and Nelson, Pelorus Bridge has long been a favoured halt for travellers. And this pitstop has never been nicer, with the tearooms in stellar form — it's worth a special trip for these alone — clean toilets, short walks for stretching the legs and an easily accessible river with the most inviting, clear pools to swim in.

The bridge, rest area, tearooms and camping ground lie within a DOC-managed scenic reserve, one of the last remnants of river flat forest in Marlborough, bless it. (The only reason it remains intact is because it was set aside for a town that was never built; the reserve was created in 1912.) Hidden away in its forest is Kahikatea Flat, a delightful unpowered campsite. Compact and shapely, it's about as refined as a DOC campground gets.

Don't let its proximity to busy State Highway 2 put you off; in fact this will be in your favour if you don't have your own transport: both Kiwilink and the K Bus stop by every day. Besides, the campsite is well away from the kerfuffle, a good 300 m or so down a driveway through the forest. At its entrance, next to the tearoom, is the rainy-day lounge — a small but comfortable affair with little in the way of amusements.

Set amid the grandeur of towering kahikatea — our tallest native tree — the ground is carpeted with closely mown grass. Bordered by bush, alcoves provide attractive pitching with a degree of shade and privacy, while in the centre is a lawn big enough for swingball, hacky sack or a restrained game of bat down. You'll be entertained whether out on the field or sitting on the sidelines. Behind the amenities block is an odd but inviting pup tent area, set in a grove of skirt-wearing wheki-ponga. Riverside pitching can be had by a lucky few, although pretty much every spot's a lucky one in this magical place. It even has glow worms.

The amenities block, simple and dependable with joyously retro styling, has hot showers and a laundry but no kitchen. Gas burners are provided in the sheltered cooking areas annexed to the building.

Next door is the aforementioned tearoom (run by the campground managers) which stocks basic supplies such as bread, milk, postcards and ice cream. This is also the camp office, and there's a card phone, too. Powered sites and cabins are available next to the outdoor education centre (which has a hall and bunkrooms for hire) on the other side of the bridge.

THINGS TO SEE AND DO
AROUND PELORUS BRIDGE

POP YOURSELF INTO
THE PELORUS RIVER

Along the riverbank you'll find numerous places to slip yourself into the drink — just follow the wet footprints or ask the people with dripping hair and towels over their shoulders. There are rock ledges for leaping off and clear waters will help you safely assess your jump (do be careful, though: people have hurt themselves here). The river conditions change according to water levels, but in the right spot at the right time, this is sublime river swimming.

ENJOY HEAVENLY HOME
BAKING AT THE TEAROOMS

We find this little café simply impossible to pass by. But don't go looking for a sandwich: they make very few. Their forte is pastry, and not even the fact that they nuke them can spoil the appeal of their pies: venison, wild boar, bacon and egg. Oh, and the cakes . . . fantastic tan square, citrus slice, carrot cake . . . all as fresh and sweet as a Marlborough cherry, but not nearly as good for you. Enjoy your deliciously buttery lunch alfresco on the deck or on a picnic bench. Open daily from 8am until around 6pm.

STROLL ALONG THE RIVER
OR HEAD INTO THE HILLS

Three short walks (each half to three quarters of an hour) explore the fertile lowland forest and riverbanks of the Pelorus. On the east side of State Highway 6 is the Totara Path, looping through forest containing giant totara — favoured by Maori for carving and building waka. A short detour off this track takes you down to the river and a good swimming spot. The opposite side of the river can be explored by crossing the bridge to the Circle Track, an easy stroll with the bonuses of a suspension bridge and views of the river junction where the Rai meets with Pelorus. On the tearoom side of the road, the Tawa Walk leads from the carpark to a series of river terraces via a path punctuated by mighty rimu and kahikatea. Those who indulged in both pie *and* cake at the tearooms might wish to burn off a few more calories on the Elvy Waterfalls Track (two hours return) and Trig K Track (four hours return). The latter provides views of the surrounding countryside. Both of those tracks are signposted off the Tawa Walk, close to the campground.

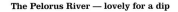
The Pelorus River — lovely for a dip

DESTINATION MARLBOROUGH

Totaranui Road,
Abel Tasman National Park,
32 km east of Takaka

Contact
DOC Totaranui camp office
03 528 8083
www.doc.govt.nz

Capacity
425 unpowered

Open
all year

Bookings
required 1 Dec–10 Feb
(bookings open 1 July)

Price
$12 adult / $6 child (peak);
$8 adult / $4 child (off-peak)

This still feels like back-to-nature camping, with a host of small camping fields divided by mature shelterbelts, and numerous nooks for the lucky ones. No site is further than a minute from the beach.

Totaranui Bay is towards the northern end of the famously fabulous Abel Tasman National Park. Surrounded by some of the best remnant native bush in the area, its 1 km long beach is swathed in golden sand, while behind it are large open grassy flats — previously part of the farm here. The homestead, Ngarata (built in 1914), still stands. A significant historical building, it's a rare example of a Californian-style bungalow constructed of board and batten. The farm was sold to the Crown in 1948 and nowadays the Totaranui estate is managed by DOC.

What once were paddocks are now camping fields and large reserves allocated for day use. Spread far and wide, the campground accommodates up to 850 people, making it the largest DOC campground in New Zealand. But it still fills up, with early booking required to secure a site during peak season. Despite the throng, however, this still feels like back-to-nature camping, with a host of small camping fields divided by mature shelterbelts, and numerous nooks for the lucky ones. No site is further than a minute from the beach.

All sites are unpowered, and among them are big fire pits with wood supplied — the hub of much socialising of an evening. There are six ablution blocks: the toilets are flushers, but the showers have only cold water, so you may want to bring your solar shower. Simple laundry facilities comprise tubs and wringers.

The DOC visitor centre is open daily from Labour Weekend until Easter. Interpretive displays are set up in the foyer, while staff will answer queries and issue maps and passes. They don't, however, handle bookings for water taxis and the like, although all necessary information is available, as are phonecards for the box outside. Absolute necessities are also for sale, such as insect repellent, gas canisters, ice and chocolate bars. There's no bread or milk, so stock up well before you tackle the hill — you don't want to drive that last 12 km of winding gravel road unnecessarily.

TAKE THE WEIGHT OFF YOUR FEET

There's a surfeit of activities to be enjoyed at Totaranui. For a starter, there's heaps of room for lounging around, and although the beach may be swelteringly hot and shadeless at high noon, near the shore there are plenty of suitable trees under which you can lay out your blanket, eat your cheese and pickle sandwich, and have a wee nana nap. Bliss! The golden, sandy beach offers excellent swimming, while at the north end an estuary has safe paddling and hypnotic rippling waters where the stream babbles out to the sea. At this end there are also two boat ramps and a trailer park; water-skiing is allowed in the designated area. Bicycles can be ridden around the reserve's roads, too.

SEE THE PARK FROM THE WATER

A boat is a thrilling way to explore the national park, and unsurprisingly there are many water taxis zipping to and fro just in front of the DOC visitor centre. Drop-offs and pick-ups can be easily arranged according to both established schedules and your particular needs — look for the timetables and contact details at the visitor centre. Kayaking is also popular, allowing you to reach secluded bays and beaches that are inaccessible on foot. Golden Bay Kayaks (www.goldenbaykayaks.co.nz, tel 03 525 9095), based at Tata Beach, offers guided tours and freedom rentals for the northern part of the park between Golden Bay and Totaranui.

DISCOVER WHAT MAKES A WALK 'GREAT'

From Totaranui you can head north or south along the subtropical Abel Tasman Coast Track, where golden sand and lush forest meet clear blue waters. North towards Separation Point, an easy 45-minute track reaches Anapai Bay, one of the park's finest beaches. Will you be able to resist a swim? Other notable walks from the campground include the Pukatea Walk (30 minutes return), which rambles through the only part of Totaranui that wasn't burnt or felled to create farmland. For a more elevated view, take the Lookout Rock Track towards Pigeon Saddle. This one-hour return walk passes through higher altitude forest containing mature rata, red beech, rimu, matai and miro — trees much less prevalent on the flats, where they were logged out.

Mutton Cove, Abel Tasman National Park

DOC / GARRY HOLZ

**Tukurua Beach Road,
off State Highway 60,
18 km north of Takaka**

Contact
03 525 9742
www.goldenbayholidaypark.co.nz

Capacity
150 unpowered / 74 powered

Open
all year

Bookings
recommended peak season

Price
$16 adult / $8 child unpowered;
$17 per adult powered

This campground is a national treasure and exactly the sort of place that people have in mind when they talk about the glory of Kiwi coastal campsites.

Forgive the grand statement, but this campground is a national treasure and exactly the sort of place that people have in mind when they talk about the glory of Kiwi coastal campsites and how we should celebrate and save them. Run by Paul and Jude — particularly hardworking and cheerful hosts — this holiday park offers quintessential family-oriented beachside camping.

So what is it that makes it so special? Location for a start. More or less smack-bang in the middle of Golden Bay, it's 1 km from the main road to the camp gates, down a road which allows beach access for campers only. From here you can access all the area has to offer — whether it's bird-spotting on Farewell Spit, walking in the two nearby national parks (Abel Tasman and Kahurangi) or taking the kids to Bencarri Nature Park to feed the eels. And it's only a 15-minute drive to arty Takaka and its new supermarket.

What else? Well, the beach is a water-baby's delight. It's relatively sheltered, with a bush backdrop; some shade can be found along the shoreline should you need it. The beach's sandy bottom and gentle incline make it ideal for tentative swimmers and those on little legs, while the stream outlet offers more wet fun.

The campground itself is 40 years old with plenty of mature trees to show for it. A shelterbelt keeps the coastal breeze at bay, while hedgerows and graceful silver birches provide privacy and shade. Towards the back of the camp there's ample open grass for running around on.

Tukurua does get busy over the Christmas holidays, but those who stay here during this time will likely find this life-affirming: gaggles of children larking about till sundown while their parents recharge their batteries with endless cups of tea and cold beers. It's a great place to make friends, with a high proportion of tents rather than vans.

The amenities are excellent. The main kitchen, albeit small, has the necessary appliances as well as hotplates (but no oven). Note that fridge space can get tight in peak season, although a spacious freezer will help you keep things iced up. The dining area has a table, a small television and one internet terminal. The second kitchen is smaller with similar cooking facilities but little room for loitering. Showers cost 50 cents and last just five minutes: not only does this save water and power, it stops the teenagers from hogging them. The coin-op laundry has washers and dryers and washing lines outside.

Extra facilities include a shop in the office (stocking basic groceries), a handful of cabins and a boat ramp.

FOLLOW IN THE FOOTSTEPS OF THE BAY'S GOLD PROSPECTORS

The well-graded Kaituna Track (an old pack-horse track) follows the Kaituna River through dense native forest, passing the remains of old gold workings from the mid-1800s. An hour's stroll will get you to an idyllic spot by the river — the Forks — where you can rest on a rock and dip a toe in the water. Beyond the Forks the track is suitable only for experienced and fit trampers, so you may wish to turn around here and head back to the car park and the irresistible Naked Possum Café (tel 03 524 8433, www.nakedpossum.com). Enjoy all sorts of snacks and tasty meals (including terrific venison pies), hopefully in great weather in the garden bar. There's also a possum tannery on site. The Kaituna Track trailhead is 15 km from Collingwood: take the Collingwood–Bainham road, turn right onto Carter Road and then drive 4 km to the car park.

VISIT NEW ZEALAND'S LONGEST SAND SPIT

Farewell Spit is more than 30 km long and still growing. This wind-blown and dynamic landscape is home to an internationally renowned nature reserve and bird sanctuary — a huge variety of birds can be spotted here (more than 90 species have been recorded). The spit is best known for its migratory wading birds, including the tenacious bar-tailed godwits that arrive here during summer after travelling more than 12,000 km from Siberia and Alaska. Walkers can explore the first 4 km of the spit via a network of tracks starting near the visitor centre. However, guided tours will show you so much more: your options are Farewell Spit Eco Tours (tel 03 524 8257, www.farewellspit.com) and Farewell Spit Nature Experience (tel 03 524 8992, www.farewell-spit.co.nz).

SHELL OUT FOR A TREAT AT THE MUSSEL INN

Built in 1992, this unashamedly rustic pub is a Golden Bay institution. The main drawcard is its fine ales — including the legendary Captain Cooker — brewed on site using traditional methods. But wait, there's more! Their food is also delicious; a small menu offers wholesome fare with lashings of salad. Sit outside on the veranda or under the trees and enjoy a pint or two and a bowl of mussels while listening to one of the regular live music acts — sound like a good night out? The Mussel Inn is only a five-minute drive from the holiday park, but you can walk it in an hour: along the beach, up Washbourn Road, then left onto State Highway 60. Do check the tide times first — you could get wet feet. (Tel 03 525 9241, www.musselinn.co.nz.)

PHOTONEWZEALAND / IAN TRAFFORD

Farewell Spit

Kerr Bay, Nelson Lakes National Park, 87 km south of Nelson (via State Highway 6 and Tophouse), 102 km southwest of Blenheim (via State Highway 63)

Contact
DOC St Arnaud
03 521 1806
www.doc.govt.nz

Capacity
30 unpowered / 9 powered

Open
all year

Bookings
essential during peak season

Price
$10 adult / $5 child unpowered;
$12 adult / $6 child powered

The Kerr Bay campsite has proximity to the lake and good walks to recommend it, too. The surrounding bush is handsome indeed, emanating the unmistakable aroma of sweet, sticky beech.

Sitting more or less at the crossroads of the Wairau Valley, the Motueka Valley Highway and the Buller Gorge through to the West Coast, Nelson Lakes is a small but diverse national park that serves its visitors well, whether they are just breaking a journey or seeking adventure among the mountains and lakes. Established in 1956, the 102,000 ha park is situated at the northern end of the Southern Alps, a geography clearly evident in its mountainous landscape. At an altitude of around 660 m, two significant lakes lie in the glacial river valleys: Lake Rotoiti ('little lake') and Lake Rotoroa ('long lake'). Surrounding them are ranges of craggy peaks, marked by a starkly drawn bushline above which the dense beech forest halts abruptly, giving way to rocky tops smattered in clumps of alpine plants.

There are several serviced camping areas in the park, but the one with the most on offer is at Kerr Bay, on the shores of Lake Rotoiti. Only 100 m or so from the lake edge, the camping area is particularly tent friendly, with ample room for pitching over grassy and gently sloping terrain. A few private nooks can be claimed by the early birds.

Powered sites are set in their own area, a little bit closer to the flash new amenities block — the focus of some public criticism due to its hefty price tag. We reckon it's worth every penny: this is a high-use recreational area, and we droves of outdoorsy folks do sincerely appreciate a generous quantity of spider-free flushers, so thanks for that, DOC. There are coin-op hot showers and a laundry in the same building. Across the way, the old-school Blechynden day shelter has cooking benches with sinks, hotplates, dining tables, and coin-op barbeques. The water is drinkable, and there's recycling facilities to boot.

The Kerr Bay campsite has proximity to the lake and good walks to recommend it, too. The surrounding bush is handsome indeed, emanating the unmistakable aroma of sweet, sticky beech. Restoration efforts have meant that, compared to many native forest enclaves in New Zealand, the birdsong here is impressive. Many different birds may be seen if you stand still for long enough, so let's hope the sandflies will allow it.

About a five-minute walk up the road is the DOC visitor centre, which is well worth a visit, particularly if you're keen to embark on a tramp or just wish to learn more about the fascinating natural history and heritage of the area.

DAWDLE TO ST ARNAUD VILLAGE

Just a ten-minute stroll via the pleasant Black Valley walk (near the bridge by the campsite), St Arnaud is the place to get your various tanks filled up. Alpine Lodge (tel 03 521 1869, www.alpinelodge.co.nz) has an inviting public bar with high stud and wood beams, savvy service, satisfying meals and pleasant streamside garden bar. Highly recommended. The village also sports a general store offering fuel, basic groceries and various instant gratifications.

GO JUMP IN THE LAKE

Very seldom does nature present such a perfect opportunity. With its neat, shingly shore dropping swiftly to clear depths, and the small jetty emphatic in its invitation to run and jump, this is your chance to enjoy one of nature's great cleansings. The view across the lake will surely lure you in, as will the jeers of your companions who reckon you'll never do it, even as you stand there in your togs, psyching yourself up. The water *is* jolly frigid, and you *will* be more or less hypothermic in the 30 seconds it takes for you to doggy-paddle back to shore, but c'mon . . . what are ya? Man or mouse? If the answer is mouse, you can always plant yourself on one of the lakeside benches, contemplate the majesty and watch the swans glide by.

TAKE A WALK IN THE PARK

There are numerous walks starting from the campground, including the easy Bellbird and Honeydew paths. These take you through a snippet of the 5000 ha of lakeside beech forest currently being restored as part of the Rotoiti Nature Recovery Project. Keep your eyes and ears peeled as there are many birds to be encountered along the way, including bellbird (how did you guess?) and tui. For the fit, the steep climb up to Parachute Rocks (five hours return) and the ridge beyond (1680 m altitude) makes a tip-top day-tramp, affording spectacular views. Our favourite, however, is the Mount Robert summit loop (three to four hours), accessed from the car park 3 km beyond the West Bay campground. A climb of an hour or so up the aptly named Pinchgut Track ascends to the exposed top of Mount Robert, from where the breathtaking 360-degree vista will likely knock your socks off. Do try and keep them on, however — it's very cold up here. The track back down to the trailhead is all non-stop lake views. Both Parachute Rocks and Mount Robert are fair-weather tramps, virtually pointless in poor visibility and more than a little treacherous in a wet, alpine fog. The DOC visitor centre has interpretive maps, intentions forms and the latest local weather forecasts.

DOC / TREVOR JOHNSTON

Dramatic scenery from the Kerr Bay jetty

MARLBOROUGH

ALEXANDERS HOLIDAY PARK
Canterbury Street, Picton

Contact: 03 573 6378
alexanders.picton@xtra.co.nz
www.alexanderspicton.co.nz

Tariff: $20–60

BLENHEIM TOP 10 HOLIDAY PARK
78 Grove Road, Blenheim

Contact: 03 578 3667
blenheimtop10@xtra.co.nz
www.blenheimtop10.co.nz

Tariff: $34–120

MOMORANGI BAY CAMP GROUND
Queen Charlotte Drive, RD 1, Picton

Contact: 03 573 7865
momorangi.camp@xtra.co.nz

Tariff: $24–40

OKIWI BAY HOLIDAY PARK AND LODGE
Okiwi Bay, Croisilles Harbour, on French Pass Road, Marlborough Sounds

Contact: 03 576 5006
info@okiwi.co.nz
www.okiwi.co.nz

Tariff: Please enquire for tariff

PARKLANDS MARINA HOLIDAY PARK
10 Beach Road, Waikawa Marina, Picton

Contact: 03 573 6343
parktostay@xtra.co.nz
www.parktostay.co.nz

Tariff: $26–88

PICTON CAMPERVAN PARK
42 Kent Street, Picton

Contact: 03 573 8875
picton.cvpark@xtra.co.nz
www.pictoncampervanpark.co.nz

Tariff: $28–45

PICTON TOP 10 HOLIDAY PARK
70–78 Waikawa Road, Picton

Contact: 03 573 7212
www.pictontop10.co.nz

Tariff: $30–140

PINEDALE MOTOR CAMP
820 Wakamarina Road, RD 1, Canvastown, Havelock

Contact: 03 574 2349
pinedale.motor.camp@xtra.co.nz

Tariff: $22–55

SMITHS FARM HOLIDAY PARK
1419 Queen Charlotte Drive, Linkwater, RD 1, Picton

Contact: 03 574 2806
www.smithsfarm.co.nz

Tariff: $26–110

SPRING CREEK HOLIDAY PARK
Rapaura Road, Spring Creek, Blenheim

Contact: 03 570 5893
springcreek@springcreekhp.co.nz
www.springcreekhp.co.nz

Tariff: $26–65

NELSON

BROOK VALLEY HOLIDAY PARK
600 Brook Street (off Tasman Street), Nelson

Contact: 03 548 0399
brook01@clear.net.nz,
www.brookholidaypark.co.nz

Tariff: $35–56

CABLE BAY HOLIDAY PARK
800 Cable Bay Road, off SH 6, Nelson

Contact: 03 545 0003
cablebayfarm@tasman.net
www.cablebayfarm.co.nz

Tariff: $30–55

CLUB WAIMEA
345 Queen Street, Richmond, Nelson

Contact: 03 543 9179
clubwaimea@t.s.co.nz
www.clubwaimea.co.nz

Tariff: $17.50–22

MAITAI VALLEY MOTOR CAMP
Maitai Valley Road, Nelson

Contact: 03 548 7729
maitaivalleymc@xtra.co.nz
www.mvmc.co.nz

Tariff: $8–30

NELSON CITY HOLIDAY PARK
230 Vanguard Street, Nelson
Contact: 03 548 1445
www.nelsonholidaypark.co.nz
Tariff: $26–79

TAHUNA BEACH HOLIDAY PARK
70 Beach Road, Tahunanui, Nelson
Contact: 03 548 5159
tahuna@tahunabeach.co.nz
www.tahunabeach.co.nz
Tariff: $30–105

TASMAN BAY, GOLDEN BAY AND INLAND NELSON

COLLINGWOOD MOTOR CAMP
6 William Street, Collingwood, Golden Bay
Contact: 03 524 8149
manager@collingwoodcampingground.co.nz
Tariff: $25–75

FERNWOOD HOLIDAY PARK, MOTELS AND CABINS
519 High Street South, Motueka
Contact: 03 528 7488
fernwoodholidaypark@clear.net.nz
www.fernwoodholidaypark.co.nz
Tariff: $24–105

KAITERITERI BEACH CAMP
Sandy Bay Road, Kaiteriteri
Contact: 03 527 8010
kaiteritericamp@xtra.co.nz
www.kaiteriteribeach.co.nz
Tariff: $22–55

LAKE ROTOITI AND LAKE ROTOROA DOC CAMPS
SH 63, St Arnaud
Contact: 03 521 1806
nelsonlakesao@doc.govt.nz
Tariff: $20–24

MOTUEKA TOP 10 HOLIDAY PARK
10 Fearon Street, Motueka
Contact: 03 528 7189
info@motuekatop10.co.nz
www.motuekatop10.co.nz
Tariff: $36–150

MURCHISON MOTOR HOME PARK
SH 6 (8 km north of Murchison), Murchison
Contact: 03 523 9666
murchmotor.park@xtra.co.nz
Tariff: $20–28

OLD MACDONALDS FARM AND HOLIDAY PARK
Harveys Road, Marahau, RD 2, Motueka
Contact: 03 527 8288
oldmacs@xtra.co.nz
www.oldmacs.co.nz
Tariff: $24–140

POHARA BEACH TOP 10 HOLIDAY PARK
Abel Tasman Drive, Pohara, Golden Bay
Contact: 03 525 9500
pohara@xtra.co.nz
www.poharabeach.com
Tariff: $34–155

QUINNEY'S BUSH CAMP
SH 6, Motupiko, RD 2, Nelson
Contact: 03 522 4249
quinneys-bush@xtra.co.nz
www.quinneys-bush.co.nz
Tariff: $24–46

RIVERVIEW HOLIDAY PARK
Riverview Tce, Murchison
Contact: 03 523 9591
riverview.hp@xtra.co.nz
Tariff: $24–100

TAKAKA CAMPING GROUND
56 Motupipi Street, Takaka
Contact: 03 525 7300
Tariff: $24–50

TAPAWERA SETTLE MOTELS AND CAMPGROUND
19 Tadmor Valley Road, Tapawera, Nelson
Contact: 03 522 4334
camping@settle.co.nz
www.settle.co.nz
Tariff: $20–90

THE BARN
Abel Tasman National Park, Harvey Road, Marahau, RD 2, Motueka
Contact: 03 527 8043
info@barn.co.nz
www.barn.co.nz
Tariff: $54–62

FOLLOWING PAGE:
Picton Harbour

→ LET'S GO CAMPING ON

THE WEST COAST

Kohaihai River, Kahurangi National Park, 15 km north of Karamea (at the end of the Karamea–Kohaihai Rd)

Contact
DOC Karamea Information and Resource Centre
03 782 6652
www.doc.govt.nz

Capacity
50 unpowered

Open
all year
(max. 2 nights consecutive stay)

Bookings
not required

Price
$6 adult / $1.50 child

North of the Buller River mouth at Westport begins nearly 100 km of coastal road that leads to the end of the line, Kohaihai, the nikau-covered finale of the spectacular Heaphy Track. The Karamea Highway is a tourer's treat, wending around the base of the ranges. Often the mountains tower dramatically overhead; at other points they stand in handsome profile in the distance, foregrounded by lush, fertile dairy flats. Along the way, the road passes Karamea, a tiny town (population 680) with a museum, dairy, post office and visitor information office. It also has Saracens Café, an honest country kitchen serving up yummy homemade pies, toasted sammies and cakes. Their rustic Bush Bar cranks up from time to time, too. The local pub — the Karamea Village Hotel — has beer by the jug and the ubiquitous whitebait sandwich.

Heading off from Westport there is plenty of pasture, but as you travel north the paddocks dwindle and eventually surrender entirely to the rugged wilderness of Kahurangi National Park, one of New Zealand's most diverse and important landscapes (gazetted only in 1996). Kohaihai is the magical spot where the road stops. It serves as trailhead, campground and daytrippers' retreat.

Considering its location, this is a well-visited place, with many making use of its tidy grounds and basic facilities. The beach out front — a definite no-swim zone — is an eyeful of dramatic, crashing breakers, often veiled in an ethereal salt spray. Flowing out to meet them is the Kohaihai River, bound by lush rainforest, which slips quietly under a picture-postcard swing bridge before reaching the intertidal zone where it swirls around, cuts through the sands and is released into the turgid waters.

Kohaihai offers a haven for campers in a rugged environment, its grassy pitches nestled among groomed hillocks which afford a degree of shelter from the onshore breeze. Along the beachfront, a stand of stunted and gnarled pines shelter those wishing to pitch closer to the ocean and enjoy every last sliver of sunset.

Kohaihai is an electricity-free zone. Facilities are confined to well-maintained flush toilets, small sinks, potable water and a telephone (located in the day shelter). The river will serve you for bathing, but remember: no soap. Be prepared to take your rubbish out with you, and don't feed the weka, no matter how plaintively they look at you.

Weka won't be the only ones eyeing you up: the sandflies will, too. So be glad of that breeze — it'll blow at least a few away — and remember to take your longs, your hat and your bandana. Clothes are your best defence against the particularly voracious West Coast sandfly.

MOSEY THROUGH THE NIKAU

With its instantly recognisable profile — a smooth, straight trunk, bulbous leaf sheaths and giant geometric fronds — the nikau is one of New Zealand's most iconic trees. Starting from the campsite, the Nikau Walk (40 minutes) offers an easy opportunity to get right into the thick of them. Once over the swing bridge, the path follows a flat track through a dense grove of nikau with glimpses through to the river alongside. Another good short walk is the 20-minute zigzag path up to the small knoll behind the campsite, from where you can enjoy a bird's-eye view of the reserve and river mouth — a good place to get your bearings.

GET A TASTE OF THE HEAPHY TRACK

The Heaphy is the longest and arguably most diverse of DOC's Great Walks — a 78 km, four- to six-day epic linking Golden Bay to the West Coast. For a bit of a leg stretch, take the track signposted for Scott's Beach: either stop at Scott's Lookout and take a few snaps from the picnic bench (one hour return) or, better still, continue on to Scott's Beach (two hours return) — the view from the saddle may well make this option impossible to resist. Should this whet your appetite, you can always keep going to the Heaphy River mouth (16 km, five hours one way from Kohaihai). You can either pitch your tent for the night or stay in the DOC hut (bookings essential).

EXPLORE THE OPARARA BASIN

Of course the West Coast has no shortage of astounding natural wonders, but one of the most incredible along this stretch of coast is the limestone arch at Oparara. Those who have seen it will regale you with tales of its grandeur — 219 m from end to end, its ceiling 43 m above the river. Even if they exaggerate, it's largely all true. It's only about a 20-minute walk to the main arch, so that should leave you with time to explore the spooky Box Canyon Cave, sit and reflect by Mirror Tarn, or keep an eye out for the rare blue duck (whio) on the river. An old forestry road — approximately 6 km south of Kohaihai — provides access to the Oparara Basin. From there it's 12 km to the arch car park and another 3 km to the cave car park.

PREVIOUS PAGE:
Moria Gate Arch in the Oparara Basin, Kahurangi National Park, Karamea
FAR LEFT: Kohaihai
LEFT: **The striking form of the nikau palm — an icon of the South Island's West Coast**

DOC / SONIA FRIMMEL

Owen Street (off State Highway 6), Punakaiki, 44 km north of Greymouth, 57 km south of Westport

Contact
03 731 1894

Capacity
30 unpowered / 21 powered

Open
all year

Bookings
recommended during peak season

Price
$15 adult / $6 child

PHOTONEWZEALAND / LLOYD PARK

The stretch of State Highway 6 between Westport and Greymouth is the most dramatic along the West Coast. Bounded on the inland side by dense rainforest with its stunning, almost architectural forms of flax, ferns and nikau, the road sweeps through lush farmland and winds along the tops of limestone bluffs, affording incredible views along the shoreline and out to sea. Below, white-capped rollers surge up shingly beaches and pound against rocky outcrops. A fine spray lends a misty-eyed soft-focus to the scene.

Eye-popping vistas abound in this area, many of them found in Paparoa National Park, which lies inland around Punakaiki, a must-see wonder in itself. The Pancake Rocks, as they are known, are the highlight for many a West Coast tourer, and account entirely for its township, a veritable Piccadilly Circus in the summer, when the car park is crammed, the cafés churn out coffee and sammies and the gift shop cranks through the postcards and possum-wool socks. Bus loads of walkshort-wearing tourists file along the rocks' walkway, right across the road from the rumpus.

The campground, however, is like another world, even though it's just a short walk away — about a kilometre or so back along the highway, tucked behind the pub. In an enviable spot, this fairly large campground faces onto both the beach and an estuary. Set among bushy shelterbelts, the sites are neatly grassed and sport unfathomably good drainage, which on the West Coast can only be a bonus.

Another plus is the drying room, which may well also come in handy, located in the amenities block along with a decent kitchen. It has hotplates (some gas), as well as the usual appliances and fridges. A small lounge offers homely comfort, while right outside is a covered picnic area. There are also 10 cabins for those desperate days. Having stopped here many times over many years, we've never found the facilities anything less than clean and in good order.

This camp attracts all types — the campervan convoy, nana and granddad in their 1960s caravan, the Christmas-holiday family and the pup-tenting trampers. For many, it's their first time here — and they'll be just as wowed by this wild and wooliness as you are. It's a little bit of magic in a magical spot.

Set among bushy shelterbelts, the sites are neatly grassed and sport unfathomably good drainage, which on the West Coast can only be a bonus.

TOURISM WEST COAST

SEE NEW ZEALAND'S FAMOUS STACK OF PANCAKES

A memorable short walk takes you through a flaxy bush reserve before reaching the *pièce de résistance*, the Pancake Rocks. Formed more than 30 million years ago, they're made up of fragments of dead plants and marine creatures, which settled on the seabed and solidified under the sea's immense pressure into hard and soft layers. Earthquakes have thrust them up above sea level, where the wind, sea and rain have sculpted them into the curiously shaped limestone towers you see today. The best time to visit is at high tide when the chambers will be wildly sloshing pools and the blowholes will be booming, amplifying the impact of the waves crashing below.

GO TO BLACKBALL

Founded by gold prospectors in 1864, Blackball had turned into a coal town by 1900. In 1908, the mines were the focus of the 'Crib Time Strike', a protest that secured longer lunch breaks for miners (increased from 15 minutes to half an hour) and led to the formation of the Federation of Labour, known as the Red Feds, several of whose members went on to become prominent in the first Labour government. So the UN can thank Blackball for Helen. However, with the coalmine long since closed, the town has largely lost its political plot — and most of its population to boot. It does have excellent smallgoods though, made by the Blackball Salami Company (tel 03 732 4111, www.blackballsalami.co.nz). It also has the historic Blackball Hilton or, rather, Formerly The Blackball Hilton, a character-filled pub and hotel, crammed to the gunwales with local memorabilia. If you've never been to Blackball, this is your chance. It's 61 km from Punakaiki, and 22 km from Greymouth.

TAKE THE PORORARI PATH IN PAPAROA

This easy three-hour walk offers up a taste of what the national park is all about — sparkling rivers, limestone gorges and lush bush. Starting right beside the campground, the track meanders alongside the Pororari River through broadleaf coastal forest dotted with impressive tracts of nikau palms, limestone cliffs and towering bluffs. The river itself is stunning — crystal clear and refreshingly cool — with many spots conducive to a dip. Beyond the gorge, the path meets up with the Inland Pack Track (25 km, two to three days); if you take the north fork and walk about 50 m, you'll reach a ford — the perfect place for your picnic lunch. To make a loop of the walk, however, head south along the Inland Pack Track where you will meet up with the shingly Punakaiki River. Cross the river at its broadest point and it's a short walk back to the highway south of the township.

FAR LEFT: **Kayaking on the crystal-clear Pororari River**
LEFT: **Blowhole in action at the Pancake Rocks**

State Highway 7, 6.5 km east of Springs Junction, 88 km northwest of Hanmer Springs

Contact
DOC Punakaiki
03 731 1895
www.doc.govt.nz

Capacity
12 unpowered

Open
all year

Bookings
not required

Price
$6 adult / $1.50 child

Evison's Wall was built along an unusual exposed terrace of the Alpine Fault, to investigate whether the fault is 'creeping'. There's been no movement as yet, which should help you sleep at night . . .

One of the best meadow-camping spots in the country, Marble Hill is located in the Maruia Valley, within the Lewis Pass National Reserve. This reserve represents a landmark moment in the New Zealand conservation story, triggered by the decision of the Forest Service to fell nigh-on 90 percent of the forest's lowland beech in the 1970s. It was saved from the chop by the now legendary conservation collective the Native Forest Action Council, which in 1975 delivered to Parliament a petition of 341,159 signatures — the 'Maruia Declaration' — which saved the forest in its entirety. This victory was to spark off a chain of positive decisions on New Zealand's remnant wilderness, including the eventual establishment of the Department of Conservation in 1987.

Lying in this neck of the woods, upon the flats at the confluence of the Maruia and Alfred Rivers, is Marble Hill, a quiet place to break a journey through Lewis Pass. It offers simple, back-to-nature camping: a row of sites nestled against the beech forest, overlooking an expanse of grassy field, encircled by forested mountains. Spacious pitches are set into bushy nooks, dotted along the access road which concludes at the trailhead for the Lake Daniells track. There are picnic benches, fire pits and long-drop toilets. The tap water must be treated before drinking.

The sheltered pitches command a magnificent view down the valley, and in the foreground is the curiosity known as Evison's Wall. Built in 1964, this 24 m long concrete wall was built along an unusual exposed terrace of the Alpine Fault, to investigate whether the fault is 'creeping'. There's been no movement as yet, which should help you sleep at night . . . after all, you are camping on New Zealand's largest faultline.

If that — or perhaps the 'quor-quo' of the morepork — keeps you up at night, you can always star-gaze. With zero light pollution, this is a perfect place to rug up, lie down and cast your eyes up to the inky, unreachable ceiling.

THINGS TO SEE AND DO NEAR MARBLE HILL

TAKE AN AMBLE ALONG THE LAKE DANIELLS TRACK

Climbing slowly along the Alfred River flat and the Frazer Stream to the lake, this easy, well-graded but often muddy walk is about four to six hours return. The mature beech forest is a botanist's delight, with plants such as matagouri (New Zealand's only thorny native plant) and pretty mistletoe. The latter is easy to spot during December and January when its scarlet flowers colour up the trunks of the beech trees. The lake itself is well worth the journey — a tranquil spot with views of the surrounding hills. The hut alongside is an ideal place to stop for lunch or, better still, sit on the end of the jetty. Anglers can hook brown or rainbow trout in season (November to April) — don't forget your licence.

HAVE A HOT SOAK AT MARUIA SPRINGS THERMAL RESORT

Just 9 km from Marble Hill on State Highway 7 (and a one-and-a-half-hour drive from Hanmer Springs, see page 158), Maruia is the more back-to-nature of the Lewis Pass's two steam baths. This Japanese-inspired resort offers great value soaking — just $15 for unlimited day-access to both the alfresco stone-lined pools and the Japanese bathhouse alongside (sex-segregated, so you can soak in the buff). Private spa rooms are also available, but we prefer the public pools with their more open feel and grand views of the Freyberg Range across the valley. The geothermally heated water has a high mineral content and is believed to have many healing properties. It's certainly good for the soul (tel 03 523 8840, www.maruia.co.nz).

BRUSH UP ON YOUR WEST COAST GOLDMINING HISTORY AT REEFTON

Originally built 'on the promise of gold and lasting prosperity', Reefton has endured many hard times, numerous storms and two major earthquakes, which makes it all the more surprising that so many of its original buildings remain. There is so much heritage here, if it were anywhere else in New Zealand it'd be overrun with trendy cafés and no-expense-spared renovations. But Reefton is just Reefton: unassumingly real, genuinely rustic and looking after its history as well as it can. It was the first town in New Zealand to have electric streetlights, don't you know! The visitor centre has everything you need, including a barely legible heritage trail guide. It's about 50 minutes' drive from Marble Hill.

DANIEL MURRAY

Lake Daniells

**State Highway 6,
10 km south of Hokitika**

Contact
DOC Punakaiki
03 731 1895
www.doc.govt.nz

Capacity
100 unpowered

Open
all year

Bookings
not required

Price
$6 adult / $1.50 child

If you're looking for a roadside stop between Greymouth and the glaciers, Lake Mahinapua may well fit the bill, being handily located between the gold rush towns of Hokitika and Ross. The lake is just 700 m off the main road, signposted opposite the Mahinapua Hotel on State Highway 6.

A short, tree-lined drive leads to the picturesque lake and surrounding reserve, a pleasant surprise after the seemingly never-ending farmland along the highway. Maori believe the lake was created by chief Rakaihautu with his digging stick as he travelled through the South Island, and the area was once a popular food-gathering place for Kati Wairaki iwi as they travelled the coast gathering pounamu (greenstone). When Ngai Tahu came to claim the precious resource for themselves, a battle occurred in which the invaders were defeated. This event is remembered in the name of the lake, meaning 'early morning haze', the conditions in which the battle took place.

After European arrival, as the gold rush gathered momentum, Lake Mahinapua made up part of an inland waterway, transporting people and goods to Ross on a variety of vessels, including paddle steamers. The boat traffic brought many more people to the lake, and around the turn of the twentieth century it was a popular tourist spot.

Transport on the waterway ceased in 1905 when the railway came through (the historic Mahinapua Creek railway bridge can be visited 5 km north on State Highway 6; trains ceased running in 1980), and over the last century the lake has returned to a quiet and more natural state. There is now an abundance of bird life including black swans, grey and mallard ducks, the rare bittern and seasonal white heron.

The lake itself is densely bordered by podocarp and hardwood forest, giving it a secret hideaway feel. A large recreation area is welcoming for both day-users and campers alike — it makes a great place to stop for a picnic lunch, and a convenient and quiet spot to stop for the night. As evident by the new plantings and spruced-up facilities, the campground has recently undergone improvements. Facilities are confined to flush toilets, washing-up sinks, a water supply and rubbish disposal. Soapless bathing (and indeed swimming) can be enjoyed in the lake (a short track to Swimmer's Beach leads to a good spot). The camp is self-registration, so don't forget to bring cash.

A couple of short bush walks start right next to the camp, and the pub is just down the road. And that combination gets our vote.

ABOVE: **Kahikatea stand tall along the banks of Mahinapua Creek**
RIGHT: **Lake Kaniere**

DID SOMEONE MENTION WATER?

Not far away is yet another beautiful West Coast lake, Kaniere, best appreciated on foot via the Lake Kaniere Walkway, which starts at the Sunny Bight picnic area (17 km southeast of Hokitika). The track is three to four hours one way, so your best bet is to try to organise a pick-up at the southern end. Thick forest surrounding the lake provides an ideal habitat for our feathered friends. If luck is on your side and your eyesight's good you may even spot New Zealand's smallest bird, the tiny rifleman, (titipounamu) recognised by its short tail, spiralling flight and high pitched 'zit-zit' song.

DOC JOHN MAZEY

TAKE A WETLAND WALK

Three pleasant short walks start from the campground — up to half an hour each — allowing you to explore the western side of the lake. A longer but still undemanding stroll amid this moist and verdant landscape can be had on the Mahinapua Walkway (two hours one way), starting 2 km north of the campground on State Highway 6. This old logging tramline traverses the northern side of the lake, passing through wetlands, swamp (on boardwalks) and rimu forest. A good side-trip is the walk to the aptly named Picnic Point (40 minutes return).

GET OUT ON THE LAKE

Lake Mahinapua has been a popular spot for boaties for more than 150 years — the interpretive display by the lake has some intriguing photographs of dapper sailors cruising the waters back in the day. It's BYO kayak or, if you pass by on Sunday, pop into the Aquatic Club (tel 03 755 7397), right on the lakeshore: they sail every Sunday and welcome visitors.

Thick forest surrounding Lake Kaniere provides an ideal habitat for our feathered friends.

OKARITO COMMUNITY CAMPGROUND

Russell Street, Okarito, 14 km from the turn-off on State Highway 6 (18 km north of Franz Josef Glacier)

Contact
Okarito Community Association, via Paula and Swade at Okarito Boat Tours: 03 753 4223

Capacity
30 unpowered

Open
all year

Bookings
not required

Price
$10 adult (children free)

Okarito is a tight-knit community offering homespun hospitality, the sort of place where you can buy whitebait from the back door.

This is one of the West Coast's best-kept secrets and one we are reluctant to share. However, campgrounds like this one are the cornerstones of the New Zealand camping experience, and to omit it would be selfish — especially as we reckon there's a good weather thing going on here, too. There seems to be a hole in the clouds over Okarito, for every time we visit, the clag sits grey over the alps, but by the time we get out to the coast the sky is clear. Maybe we've just been lucky, or maybe this really is a special spot.

The turn-off to Okarito on State Highway 6 is at The Forks, between the small inland town of Whataroa and Franz Josef Glacier. From there a 13 km long sealed road leads through the lowland forest of the Okarito Forks Ecological Area, before reaching the township and lagoon.

With a population of around 30, sleepy Okarito has a couple of gold-rush buildings including Donovan's Store (circa 1865, said to be the oldest surviving building on the West Coast) and the School House (1867, now the sweetest youth hostel you've ever seen), along with a clutch of modest houses and board-and-batten baches. It's a tight-knit community offering homespun hospitality, the sort of place where you can buy whitebait from the back door.

It is, however, the lagoon which defines Okarito. New Zealand's largest unmodified coastal wetland, covering more than 3200 ha, its shallow waters are a feeding ground for white heron (kotuku) and royal spoonbill, along with many other birds. Fortunately the locals are well set up to help you get you amongst it, while for landlubbers an excellent walking track leads south to the smaller Three Mile Lagoon.

Okarito's laid-back, self-registration campground — on a DOC reserve, run by the local community association — is well-tended and monitored. It lies close to the beach, separated only by a seldom-used grass airstrip. The beach is too treacherous for swimming, but you can light a fire when there isn't a ban. Gather some driftwood and coax your fire into life in the face of the onshore breeze, then rug up in your blanket and watch the sun disappear . . . this simple act is one of life's great pleasures and a wondrous way to commune with this untamed environment.

The grounds are well hedged, and dotted with fire pits and picnic tables. The kitchen shelter is basic but comfortable (with fridge / freezer), as are the showers ($1 coin) and flush toilets. A laundry sink outside features an old-school wringer — that'll buy you a carbon credit, as will the full recycling facilities.

THINGS TO SEE AND DO AROUND OKARITO

KAYAK THE LAGOON

If you've a mind to get those shoulders working, kayaking is the most peaceful way of exploring this stunning wetland — we consider it the not-to-be-missed activity in the area. It couldn't be easier either, with Okarito Nature Tours (tel 03 753 4014, www.okarito.co.nz) right opposite the historic wharf and boat ramp. Richard and Edwina offer guided trips — their two-hour and half-day adventures will take you to the best spots while they tell you the inside story. Their freedom rentals can be just as much fun though — paddle into the middle and watch the birdlife go by, or make it more of a mission and set off for those inlets. Spectacular.

CHECK OUT THE BIRDS

Okarito is a twitcher's paradise with up to 70 species visiting the area. Several operators can help you get your eye in, one of whom is Swade of Okarito Boat Tours (tel 03 753 4223, www.okaritoboattours.co.nz). His two-hour nature tour is a great way to see the birdlife and learn about the area's ecology. Those keen to see kiwi can set off on a two- to four-hour sunset walk with Okarito Kiwi Tours (tel 03 753 4330, www.okaritokiwitours.co.nz), who proclaim a 90 per cent chance of spotting a kiwi in its natural environment. There's also a rare chance to see kotuku on their nests (October to March), escorted by White Heron Sanctuary Tours (tel 03 753 4120, www.whiteherontours.co.nz) who will guide you through the Waitangiroto Nature Reserve.

POP INTO WESTLAND NATIONAL PARK

Five minutes' walk along The Strand from the campground is the trailhead for walks to the Okarito Trig and Three Mile Lagoon, just within the boundary of Westland National Park. The trig track (one and a half hours return) includes a short, sharp shock of gutbusting steps, but its stupendous views of the lagoon and alps make the climb well worthwhile. The much less arduous inland route to Three Mile Lagoon follows an old pack track through dense lowland. If you time it right, you can make a loop by returning to Okarito along the dramatic beach — but only within two hours of low tide, so check the times.

The view from Okarito Trig

**Gillespies Beach Road,
off Cook Flat Road,
22 km west of Fox Glacier**

Contact
DOC Fox Glacier
03 751 0807
www.doc.govt.nz

Capacity
8 unpowered

Open
all year

Bookings
not required

Price
$6 adult / $1.50 child

For those who don't mind driving down a winding gravel road with lots of blind bends, Gillespies Beach is an invigorating stop while exploring the southern segment of the West Coast. The beach is wild and the campground is back to basics, but for its sunset views and proximity to the area's attractions, including the Haast Pass, this is our pick, particularly in good weather.

So who built this road to nowhere, ending at an empty black-sand beach? Well, it's the sand that holds the secret, for when James Gillespie found gold glinting in the grains back in 1865, there was the usual rush to claim the spoils. A town sprang up like a rabbit from a hat; at one time there were 700 miners here, plus three hotels, butchers, bakers and presumably the odd lady of the night. And guess what happened next?

The campground sits where the town once stood, the miners long gone except the souls in the cemetery. Other testaments lie here and there, their stories whispering on the salt-laden breeze. To visit is one thing, to live here another . . . especially when the rain hangs about, the west wind blows across the sea, and the waves pound hard against the shingly shore. This is a tough environment.

Nestled in behind the dunes of this classic West Coast beach, Gillespies camp is perfectly pleasant in fair weather, even better when it's fine, affording spectacular views of the alps. Although one of the smallest DOC campsites we've stayed at, its eight intimate pitches have recently been landscaped, their elevation offering relief from the sog. Regenerative plantings, once they've taken off, will further improve the aesthetic — this looks like a camp on the up.

There's no public shelter or rubbish bins, although next to the new car park is the new uber-loo (certainly smart by unplumbed standards). These facilities serve not just the campers but day-users, for there are lots of good walks from the trailhead here.

There's not much more to it, folks . . . except to say that you can drink the water, but you can't light a fire. Of course, if it's raining you can't light a fire anyway, right? Good luck!

ABOVE: **Gillespies Beach**
RIGHT: **Exploring the Franz Josef Glacier**

THINGS TO SEE AND DO NEAR GILLESPIES BEACH

WALK THE COAST

With its windswept beaches, wetlands and wildlife, the area around Gillespies Beach offers all sorts of adventure. A good place to start is the path north to Galway Bay. After about 90 minutes you'll pass over the lagoon estuary on a trestle bridge and connect with a well-graded pack track — once the main route along the coast, believe it or not. Keep going to the old miner's tunnel (cut through in the 1890s) and lookout. From this point it's just half an hour down to Galway Beach and its fur seal colony. During the winter months, the rocks are chock-a-block with well over a thousand seals, but come summer the numbers dwindle to 30 to 40 immature bulls, mainly lazing around with the occasional neck-waving display of hierarchical competitiveness. Do them a favour and leave them to it.

BREAK THE ICE

The Fox and Franz Josef glaciers are the New Zealand's most famous icicles, marvelled at by legions of visitors each year. You can, of course, take a guided tour onto the ice, but you can also get a reasonably good gander at them from their official lookout points, clearly signposted from the main road. Arguably as intriguing are the overseas tourists, dallying along the highway in their motorhomes and thronging the streets of the Fox and Franz townships in their flash outdoorsy duds. Love it or loathe it, this is an undeniably good place to make a friend from a foreign land.

ISTOCK

REFLECT AT LAKE MATHESON

A depression left behind when Fox Glacier retreated around 14,000 years ago, Lake Matheson is now fringed with ancient forest and filled with brown water, 'reminiscent of dark ale, and with the same froth in places', according to DOC. Beer-like or not, these mirror-like waters are famous for reflecting the prominent peaks of Mount Tasman and Aoraki / Mount Cook — a scene snapped ceaselessly by amateur and professional photographers alike. Think you've seen this vista on a postcard somewhere? You most certainly have. To view it for yourself, early morning is best — oh, and you might want to wait for the mountains to emerge. Failing that, just go for a wander: the lake circuit takes just over an hour. The Lake Matheson turn-off on Cook Flat Rd is 17 km from Gillespies Beach and 5 km from Fox Glacier township.

> With its windswept beaches, wetlands and wildlife, the area around Gillespies Beach offers all sorts of adventure.

OTHER CAMPGROUNDS ON THE WEST COAST

BEACH WALK HOLIDAY PARK
SH 6, Hokitika
Contact: after hours 03 755 6550
kiwi.house@xtra.co.nz
www.jacquiegrantsplace.com
Tariff: $10–60

CENTRAL MOTOR HOME PARK
117 Tainui Street, Greymouth
Contact: 03 768 4924
after hours 03 768 5837
coastautos@xtra.co.nz
Tariff: $20

CHARLESTON MOTOR CAMP
SH 6, Westport
Contact: 03 789 6773
cmcamp@xtra.co.nz
Tariff: $20–50

FOX GLACIER CAMPERVAN PARK
Sullivan Road, Fox Glacier
Contact: 03 751 0888
foxglacierlodge@xtra.co.nz
Tariff: $30

FOX GLACIER HOLIDAY PARK
Kerrs Road, Fox Glacier
Contact: 03 751 0821
info@fghp.co.nz
www.fghp.co.nz
Tariff: $26–160

GREYMOUTH SEASIDE TOP 10 HOLIDAY PARK
2 Chesterfield Street, Greymouth
Contact: 03 768 6618
www.top10greymouth.co.nz
Tariff: $34–135

HAAST BEACH HOLIDAY PARK
1438 Jackson Bay Road, Haast
Contact: 03 750 0860
haastpark@xtra.co.nz
www.accommodationhaastpark.co.nz
Tariff: $28–140

HAAST LODGE AND MOTOR PARK
Marks Road, Haast
Contact: 03 750 0703
www.haastlodge.com
Tariff: $85–140

JACKSONS CAMPERVAN RETREAT
SH 73, Jacksons, West Coast
Contact: 03 738 0474
jacksonsretreat@xtra.co.nz
Tariff: $20–39

KARAMEA HOLIDAY PARK
Maori Point Road, RD 3, Karamea
Contact: 03 782 6758
info@karamea.com
www.karamea.com
Tariff: $22–75

MOKIHINUI MOTOR CAMP
Lewis Street, Mokihinui, Westport
Contact: 03 782 1832
Tariff: $12–55

OCEANSIDE HOLIDAY PARK
137 Revell Street, Hokitika
Contact: 0800 44 56 56
patrick@oceansideholidaypark.co.nz
www.oceansideholidaypark.co.nz
Tariff: $10–85

RAINFOREST HOLIDAY PARK
46 Cron Street, Franz Josef
Contact: 0800 897 246
comestay@rainforestretreat.co.nz
www.rainforestholidaypark.co.nz
Tariff: $22–209

RAPAHOE BEACH CAMP
10 Hawken Street, Rapahoe
Contact: 03 762 7025
rapahoebeach@actrix.co.nz
Tariff: $16–30

SEAL COLONY TOP 10 HOLIDAY PARK
57 Marine Parade, Carters Beach, Westport
Contact: 03 789 8002
holiday@top10westport.co.nz
www.top10westport.co.nz
Tariff: $28–130

SHINING STAR BEACHFRONT HOLIDAY PARK
16 Richards Drive, Hokitika

Contact: 03 755 8921
shining@xtra.co.nz
www.shiningstar.co.nz

Tariff: $99–159

SOUTH BEACH MOTEL AND MOTOR PARK
318 Main South Road, SH 6, Greymouth

Contact: 03 762 6768
stay@southbeach.co.nz
www.southbeach.co.nz

Tariff: $79–135

ISTOCK

Lake Matheson

→ LET'S GO CAMPING IN
CANTERBURY

200 Jacks Pass Road, 2.5 km northwest of Hanmer Springs

Contact
03 315 7112
www.hanmerspringsaccommodation.
co.nz

Capacity
40 unpowered / 48 powered

Open
all year

Bookings
required peak summer only

Price
$15 adult / $5 child
($20 for two adults) unpowered;
$20 adult / $6 child
($26 for two adults) powered

ALPINE PACIFIC TOURISM

Hanmer Springs is New Zealand's only alpine thermal resort. Its legendary hot springs have been a year-round drawcard for nearly 130 years, and during that time it's evolved into a spa town, its permanent population of 750 swollen with out-of-towners. A spectacular natural setting has jollied things along, with its legions of visitors enjoying all sorts of energetic activities such as tramping, skiing, rafting and kayaking so everyone's well and truly ready for their soak in the springs.

The hot pools are the hub of the town, situated in the leafy town centre which boasts a disproportionate number of cafés, restaurants and bars. Beyond the business precinct, the streets branch out into a typical resortscape of holiday homes, the odd chalet and an increasing number of flash retirement retreats. Thanks to an excellent campground — with cabins and flats — you too can partake in this great escape without breaking the bank.

Alpine Adventure Holiday Park is about 2.5 km from the centre of town, along Jacks Pass Road. Don't be put off by the big-box hardware store and unsightly gravel pit as you approach it, for at the end of this road you will find a little gem, a park-like campground nestled up against a hillside, screened by attractive trees all achirp with birdsong.

This is a proud and attractive holiday park, the legacy of excellent planning and smart planting back in its early days. Mature trees abound — mostly graceful exotics such as willow and silver birch — which provide ample shade and privacy. There is, nonetheless, still plenty of lawn for larking around on or playing ball. Other child-friendly diversions are dotted around the grounds, such as tyre-swings and a blind rope trail. There's a brand-new swimming pool, too. All of this makes the park ideal for families.

Only marginally outnumbered by powered sites, the unpowered contingent is allocated its own spacious areas. The larger of these is the most appealing, its lawn-like pitches well away from the amenities blocks and campervan area.

The facilities are as well maintained as the grounds. The kitchen is immaculate, and has plenty of hotplates, fridge space and a water boiler. The television room has an internet terminal as well as Wi-Fi. The bathrooms and laundry are both up to scratch and there's a full recycling station. Various cabins and flats are available should you need a (proper) roof over your head.

To get into town, take a walk, pedal a bike (cheap bike hire is available from the camp office), or hop on the holiday park's free courtesy coach.

HAVE A LONG, HOT SOAK

Hanmer Springs Thermal Pools and Spa is undoubtedly the town's most popular attraction, and no visit would be complete without a therapeutic soak. Choose from 11 pools of varying temperatures — just flit from one to the next until you're hot and tender, like a perfectly boiled new potato. The on-site café has decent food and a pleasant alfresco area good for people-watching. Those looking for major bodily restoration might like to visit the health and beauty spa, which offers a variety of luxurious treatments. Hydrostorm infusion, anyone? (Tel 03 315-7511, www.hanmersprings.co.nz.)

ALPINE PACIFIC TOURISM

FIND A THRILL ON CONICAL HILL

A good old uphill zig-zag track (signposted from town) climbs to a charming old-school lookout (550 m) where you can enjoy splendiferous views of Hanmer Basin and the mountainous horizon. And if you've made it this far, you may as well make a loop of it: just take the Majuba and Woodland walks on the way down. The whole loop will take about an hour and a half.

HANG OUT IN HANMER

Ever since the first baths opened in 1883, enterprising Hanmerites have been looking for ways to stall you in their town. They have certainly succeeded, for Hanmer is a pleasant place to linger. For instant gratification, try its collection of shops, cafés, restaurants and bars. Beyond that, head to the bustling i-SITE which can line you up with all manner of fun activities such as mountain biking in Hanmer Forest Park, crazy golf, jet boating and horse trekking. One of our favourite things to do is to sit in the shade of the leafy town square, licking an ice cream and watching all the squeaky clean people go by.

LEFT: **Just a snapshot of the expansive views from Conical Hill**
ABOVE: **Hanmer Springs, arguably New Zealand's best thermal resort**
PREVIOUS PAGE: **Looking out to the coast from Waipara**

Molesworth Cob Cottage: 122 km southwest of Blenheim; Acheron Accommodation House: 26 km northeast of Hanmer Springs

Contact

DOC South Marlborough
03 572 9100
www.doc.govt.nz

Capacity

Cob: 20 unpowered;
Acheron: 20 unpowered

Open

28 Dec–1 April

Bookings

not required

Price

$6 adult / $1.50 child

Growing up in Blenheim,
Sarah would often hear
of locals 'going up the
Molesworth'. It lay in
some mystical valley,
and definitely involved
Swanndris, stock whips
and horses.

Molesworth Station is New Zealand's biggest farm — 180,476 ha of high country lying between the Wairau Valley and the Inland Kaikoura Range — a glacial landscape of wide open grasslands flanked by scree-covered slopes. Two passable roads run through it: the Rainbow Road (Hanmer Springs to St Arnaud) and the Acheron Road (Hanmer Springs to Blenheim via the Awatere Valley). The Rainbow Road requires a four-wheel-drive vehicle, but the Acheron Road is entirely manageable in a regular car.

Manageable it may be, but short it is not: Hanmer to Blenheim is 207 km, almost all of it unsealed. There's 59 km of gravel from gate to gate, with another 110-odd km unsealed at either end — the only sealed part of the drive is the portion of State Highway 1 from Blenheim to the Awatere Valley turn-off, and another 10 or so km from there. The rest is dusty, skiddy and slow (a 50 kph speed limit applies within the Molesworth, although you'd hardly want to go any faster). The drive can be done in a day, but you may enjoy it even more if you stop overnight at one of two campgrounds at either end of the station.

First travelled by Maori on their way to gather food and access the West Coast, the route through the Molesworth was bedded down by drovers, who funnelled stock through the Acheron from around 1850 until well into the twentieth century. 'The Canterbury Track', as it was known, was dotted with bunkhouses. Very few of these remain, but you can camp right next to two of them on this journey.

Molesworth Cob Cottage, at the northern entrance of the station, was the farm's first homestead, built in 1866. Basic camping can be found alongside it, in a grassy area set in a thin stand of bush. There are toilets, a water supply and interpretive displays.

At the southern gate is the Acheron Accommodation House, another cob cottage, this one built in 1862 — the oldest building in the Molesworth. Don't be fooled by the name — there is no accommodation here anymore. The setting and facilities are similar to those at Cob Cottage: a grassy paddock, some bush, water, toilets and information displays. There are no rubbish bins at either camp, so you'll need to take your rubbish out with you. Dogs are not permitted.

The Acheron Road is open from the end of December to early April, 7am–7pm. It may also be closed at other times due to adverse weather conditions or fire danger. To check the road status, ring DOC on the number above. Oh, and another thing: once you reach the Molesworth, there's no cellphone coverage, and the AA breakdown service won't come. Make sure you're oiled and watered up, and carry a good spare tyre.

Seek out DOC's brochure, *Molesworth Station*, before you go — $2 from DOC offices or download it from their website.

EXPERIENCE A NATURAL HIGH

Toiled upon by a succession of hardy run-holders, the Molesworth passed into the care of DOC in 2005. As a conservation project, they have much work to do, the land having been left eroded and barren — overgrazed, overrun with rabbits, and invaded by weeds including the pretty pink briar that looks blooming lovely but doesn't belong here. Restoration work has long since begun, however, including rabbit culls, swapping sheep for cattle, and revegetation. Of significant ecological importance, the Molesworth is well worth preserving. It is home to more than 70 threatened plant species, including native mistletoe and daisy, and the oddly named hairy mountain cress. In dry, elevated areas, matagouri, hebe and mountain flax can be seen, while wetter spots are dominated by red tussock. Where there used to be beech (long since burnt), manuka and kanuka shrubland is now beginning to flourish. There are also all sorts of lizards and native fish in the lakes and tarns. Your efforts to commune with this natural wonderland will be hampered by a lack of walking tracks, but DOC is considering its options.

TAKE A STEP BACK IN TIME

Molesworth's cob cottages are time capsules . . . time capsules made of tussock, clay and cowpats. Around 150 years ago, Acheron Accommodation House would have seen you right for a meal, bed and stabling for horses for just two shillings and sixpence a night. By the turn of the twentieth century, it was the centre of much enterprise, housing a store and unofficial post office and hosting race meetings, pigeon shoots, dog trials and the rifle club. There was always room for one more traveller at the inn, if not on the billiard table then on the floor underneath it. In 1932 the accommodation licence lapsed and the building was subsequently used by musterers and other station hands. It was finally abandoned in 1954, and has been restored and maintained over recent years by DOC and a team of volunteers. Molesworth Cob Cottage, at the northern entrance of the station, was the farm's first homestead, built in 1866 and restored in the 1980s and '90s. These two cobb buildings are rare, fascinating and fine examples of their kind — do stop and look around, even if you don't intend to camp next to them.

CHRISTCHURCH PHOTOGRAPHIC SOCIETY

The Molesworth — classic New Zealand high country

State Highway 73

Contact

DOC Arthur's Pass, 03 318 9211
www.doc.govt.nz

Capacity

Craigieburn: 20 unpowered;
Hawdon shelter: 20 unpowered but
room for more
Klondyke Corner: 30 unpowered
Waimakariri River: unlimited

Open

year round

Bookings

not required

Price

$6 adult / $3 child; Waimakariri River:
free

The nine campsites
along this drive provide
a place to break your
journey or a base from
which to explore this
alpine wonderland.

Linking Canterbury and the West Coast, the road through Arthur's Pass is the South Island's most popular crossing. As it cuts through the Main Divide it passes through Arthur's Pass National Park, a rugged reserve of craggy peaks, scree slopes, steep gorges and wide, braided rivers. It's a wonder the road builders ever found a way through.

Built way back in 1865, the Arthur's Pass road took just over a year to complete — half the time it took to build the Otira Viaduct, the 440 m engineering marvel that now spans the Otira Gorge. The viaduct was built in 1999 to bypass a particularly treacherous stretch of road appositely known as the Zig-Zag.

There is plenty to divert you on this incredibly scenic road, within the national park either side of it. There are also plenty of places to camp. However, no one campsite will likely tick all your boxes — none are comprehensively serviced or even particularly stunning (which is a bit of a surprise). Rather, the nine campsites along this drive provide a place to break your journey or a base from which to explore this alpine wonderland. Here are our picks of the bunch, starting from the Canterbury side.

Craigieburn Shelter (116 km from Christchurch) is located at the entrance to Craigieburn Forest Park, which has much to offer in the way of recreation including walks, mountain biking and skiing in winter. It is also the closest campsite to the amazing limestone outcrops of Castle Hill (11 km away — see page 165). Craigieburn is a small, shady campground set alongside a stream, with sites dotted under a canopy of beech forest, among tussock and on a small grassy flat. As the name suggests, there is indeed a shelter which has a washing-up sink and fireplace, and there are long-drop toilets at your disposal. Water can be drawn from the stream.

Twenty kilometres further on (about 24 km shy of Arthur's Pass township) is the turn-off to Hawdon Shelter. From here a gravel road leads over the Waimakariri River and across the river plain to a grassy flat in the lower reaches of the Hawdon Valley. On the drive in, while you're out in the open, get out of your car and take a look around — the head-swivelling panorama of angular greywacke peaks is a site to behold. The campground lies just within the boundary of the national park and offers what feels like a genuine and remote wilderness experience (with the benefit of living out of the car boot). Essentially a big meadow butted up against Woolshed Hill (1429 m) and sheltered on all sides by beech trees, there are acres of wide open space and the odd shady nook. A basic shelter has tables and a fireplace. The long-drops are ancient, and water can be sourced from the stream. Klondyke Corner is 8 km south of Arthur's Pass village (There is also a campground in the village — Avalanche Creek Shelter — but we don't recommend it.)

Klondyke is a pretty spot, with terrific views of the Waimakariri Valley and the Black Range. As the name suggests it is also, however, on a corner and right next to the road, which gets quite busy, especially in summer. There are toilets and the stream is your water supply.

Opposite Klondyke Corner is a gravel road signposted 'Waimakariri Valley'. You can camp pretty much anywhere on the north side of the Waimakariri River for approximately 2 km. While this is a designated DOC reserve, it's definitely back to basics (and we mean *basic*), so be prepared to clonk your car's diff on the rocky road, work hard to scope out a flat spot and stagger across boulders to fetch your water. The long-drop loo's a bit dicey, too. However, this area does provide some stunning views and — considering you're not far from the highway — a real back-country feel.

Otira Viaduct, built in 1999, a welcome improvement to the Arthur's Pass road

FEAST YOUR EYES — AND YOUR STOMACH — ON NEW ZEALAND'S BEST PIES

The Original Sheffield Pie Shop is the winner of six awards and counting. Try the Supreme pie (steak, bacon and onion), which we thought was aptly named, although all of them look pretty darn good. The roasted vegetable pie was a triumph: tasty enough to satisfy both vegetarian and carnivore — a rare feat indeed. The bakers here also turn out some fine loaves and plenty of sweet baking too, so it's a good place to stock up before your alpine excursions. The pie shop (tel 03 318 3876) is right on the main road in Sheffield (95 km from Arthur's Pass village), so you can't really miss it, whichever way you're travelling.

CLAMBER AROUND KURA TAWHITI

Named by Maori 'treasure from a distant land', early European travellers thought these remarkable limestone boulders resembled vast battlements and christened the site Castle Hill. Either way, you can't fail to notice them sitting alongside the highway, their soft curves alien against the brutal and angular backdrop of the surrounding mountains. They're only a short walk from the roadside car park. You thought they looked amazing from down there? Wait until you see them up close! Kura Tawhiti is 11 km from Craigieburn Shelter, and 55 km from Darfield.

WALK IN THE PARK

Arthur's Pass is a mecca for trampers, with numerous expeditions starting from (or very close to) the township itself. The 131 m high Devil's Punchbowl Falls (one hour return) is a must-do, but for something a bit longer try the relatively easy Bealey Valley track (three hours return) to the base of Mount Rolleston. To escape the closeness of the township and river valley, however, you'll need to head uphill. Rewarding options for a full day include Avalanche Peak (1833 m) and Mount Bealey (1836 m), both of which offer outstanding views. Reaching the summit of either peak involves a hard day's slog (six to eight hours return) and should only be attempted by fit and experienced folk, in good weather. Track conditions and maps are available at the DOC Visitor Centre, as is a wealth of information on the area's geology, ecology and history.

ABOVE: The Devil's Punchbowl, just a short walk from Arthur's Pass township
RIGHT: Kura Tawhiti, also known as Castle Hill

State Highway 72 (Rakaia Gorge Road), 75 km west of Christchurch, 11 km north of Methven

Contact
03 302 9353

Capacity
59 unpowered

Open
all year; May–Sept: toilet facilities only

Bookings
recommended 1 Oct–30 April

Price
$7.50 per person (under 12s free)

Cutting fast and deep through the gorge in a brilliant, almost surreal azure (unless muddied by rain), the Rakaia untangles over the wide gravel bed downstream before disappearing way, way off into the distance.

The Rakaia is not only one of New Zealand's largest braided rivers, but also said to be one of the finest rivers of this kind on Earth. Fed by the melting snows of the Southern Alps, it flows nearly 150 km before meeting the coast south of Christchurch. Starting out deep and swift in the mountains, it gradually widens and separates into strands over a gravel bed. As it reaches the Rakaia Gorge, the waters are confined to a narrow chasm, and it is here that the 'twin bridges' cross it (one of only two crossing places its entire length). Also at this dramatic location is a terrific little campground.

The Rakaia Gorge Camping Ground is located on the Inland Scenic Route, from Amberley in the north to Geraldine in the south, with its fine vistas of mountains and farmed plains. At just over 2 ha, this is a fairly small, simple campsite on the south terrace overlooking the river — the short Leonie's Walk leads down to the water. There are plenty of activities to be enjoyed from here, including rafting, canoeing, jet boating, fishing, picnics and walks.

The campsite is run by an incorporated society, members of which you are bound to meet during your stay — their annual fees secure them their own allocated sites. Communing together over wine and petanque or chewing the fat under an awning, they're a convivial bunch — making the most of the little piece of paradise they help to maintain. No doubt about it: there's a friendly, community-spirited feel to this place.

Casual visitors are allocated an unoccupied site or can pitch on the sites dotted along the terrace edge, from where there's a grandstand view of that world-famous river. Cutting fast and deep through the gorge in a brilliant, almost surreal azure (unless muddied by rain), it untangles over the wide gravel bed downstream before disappearing way, way off into the distance. It's a truly amazing spot to pitch your tent, but be prepared for a bit of wind — it is rather exposed.

The rest of the sites are laid out over a grassy flat with plenty of hedging, trees and picnic tables. There is no power at all. The kitchen shelter has sinks with hot water but no cooking equipment. There's no fridge either, so bring your chillybin; ice is 10 minutes away in Methven. Barbecues are provided — just hook up your own gas bottle. Laundry facilities are confined to a tub. The new ablution block is excellent and sports hot showers (hooray!), and a fish-cleaning sink is available for those who get lucky on the river.

A camp supervisor is likely to be on site over the summer holidays; the rest of the time you need to self-register at the booth.

ESCAPE TO LAKE COLERIDGE

A hidden high-country gem off the beaten track, this is a place to make your own fun, whether it's swimming, walking or boating the lake. Coleridge is about 25 minutes' drive from Rakaia Gorge: from the campground, take the unsealed road signposted for the Terrace Downs resort; at the junction, turn left back onto tarseal. From here, it's about another 20 km to the settlement. You can get your bearings by picking up pamphlets from Lake Coleridge Lodge on Hummocks Road (where you can get a cup of tea) or look at the boards that tell the story of the lake's history and geography, plus the area's various walks ranging from a 30 minute stroll to the three-hour return lake walk. www.lakecoleridgenz.info

The Rakaia River

SALMON SANDWICH, ANYONE?

The Raikaia is widely considered one of the best salmon rivers in New Zealand, a claim supported by the landing of 10 kg monsters on a regular basis. Now that's a good dinner. Fishing in the upper river is best between January and March, where you will likely see dozens of anglers lining the banks. If you want to join them, you might like to go out with a guide. The Methven i-SITE (tel 03 302 8955, www.methveninfo.co.nz) can hook you up — literally.

WALK THE GORGE

The well-graded Rakaia Gorge Walkway makes for a relatively easy and interesting outing that can be enjoyed by the whole family. It'll take you about two hours each way, along which interpretive displays afford insights into the area's rich natural and human history. Following the river terraces into the upper gorge, the path passes through forest and past the historic ferryman's cottage and old coalmines; there are plenty of good picnic spots along the way. The highlight of the walk is the lookout at the end, which offers a view of the mountains and river. An easier and more thrilling alternative is to take a jet boat up the river with Rakaia Gorge Scenic Jets (tel 03 318 6515) and walk back down the track. The start of the walkway is clearly signposted on the north bank of the river, close to the twin bridges.

96 Morgans Road (off Old Coach Road), 500 m from Akaroa centre

Contact
03 304 7471
www.akaroa-holidaypark.co.nz

Capacity
38 unpowered / 121 powered

Open
all year

Bookings
recommended peak season

Price
$32 two adults / $8 per child unpowered; $34–38 two adults / $8 per child powered

The views alone — from almost every site — are worth a million dollars.

Originally settled by the French in 1838 after Captain Jean Langlois negotiated with Ngai Tahu chiefs to purchase much of Banks Peninsula, Akaroa was seen as a great base from which to service whaling operations off the New Zealand and Australian coasts. However, when Langlois returned home to hatch plans to annexe the entire South Island, the British pipped him to the post. The advance party of French settlers, arriving in New Zealand in August 1840, discovered that they would now be settling in a British colony. *Sacré bleu!* Despite this, two small towns of around 60 French inhabitants were indeed established, and their influence is very much in evidence on the peninsula today, especially in and around Akaroa.

The considerable delights of historic Akaroa township can be easily explored from the Akaroa Top 10 Holiday Park, an uncommonly excellent facility. Set up high on the hill, with just a five-minute bush walk down to town, this is a hugely popular campground, catering to hordes of ice-cream-licking Kiwi families and convoys of campervans — anywhere near peak season and holiday weekends you will likely find this place close to capacity.

However, such is the outstanding location, intelligent layout and excellent management that this holiday park offers a surprisingly peaceful experience. There's sufficient room to move, and a comprehensive range of facilities make for an affordable yet luxurious experience — or at least as luxurious as camping can get. The views alone — from almost every site — are worth a million dollars.

Set within a delightfully landscaped park with plenty of mature trees and shrubbery, sites are grassy and generously spaced. Tenters enjoy their own terraced areas with some privacy hedges — those close to the bottom of the hill are undoubtedly the best seats in the house. The harbour lies gloriously below, the town sitting pretty in its French Bay nook.

The amenities are first rate. The kitchen has hotplates, fridge / freezers, water boiler and toasters, and there's a dining table for sit-ins. Just outside is an attractive barbecue area along with a few picnic tables. The laundry has washers, dryers and a washing line. There's a playground and trampoline for the children, as well as a swimming pool — a pretty outstanding one at that. More amusement may be found in the comfortable television and internet lounge (adults only).

The Akaroa Top 10 proves that the best of New Zealand camping isn't always found in forest parks or along the sandy shore.

WANDER THE STREETS OF AKAROA

Akaroa is one of the prettiest towns in New Zealand, dotted with historic cottages and gardens overflowing with a profusion of form, colour and scent. The legacy of the French is unmissable, with many of the town's streets sporting Gallic names, and the Tricolour flying here and there on the breeze. Our suggested walking tour is along Rue Lavaud, up Rue Balguerie, onto Muter Street and then back down to town via Rue Benoit. The tridenominational cemeteries (up Onuku Road) are also worth contemplation. To learn more about the town's fascinating past, visit the Akaroa Museum (71 Rue Lavaud, tel 03 304 1013).

CRUISE THE HARBOUR

The scenic waters around Akaroa are home to the world's smallest and rarest dolphin, Hector's. A flotilla of boats will take you out to spot these inquisitive creatures, most offering that once-in-a-lifetime experience — the chance to swim with them. A dolphin sighting is *almost* guaranteed, but there's also a good chance that you'll catch a glimpse of the pint-sized, white-flippered little blue penguin. Too cute! If you're *really* unlucky and don't spot either, don't despair — this is still a great day out and the best way to explore the scenic bays, sea caves and volcanic cliffs of Akaroa Harbour. For detailed information on tours, contact Akaroa Visitor Information, tel 03 304 8600, www.akaroa.com.

STOP AND SMELL THE ROSES AT THE GIANT'S HOUSE

When you're wandering up Rue Balguerie, we highly recommend a detour up the steep drive of number 68, Akaroa's most colourful and quirky attraction. Artist Josie Martin has transformed the grounds of Linton, an elegant totara and kauri house, into a psychedelic garden bejewelled with playful sculptures and mosaic. A-maz-ing! Lounge on the grass or under a tree with coffee and cake from the Artist's Palate café, listening to the strains of Edith Piaf flowing from the ceramic, succulent-planted piano. The house is also the venue for regular musical soirees and art workshops hosted by Josie. The Giant's House, 68 Rue Balguerie (open 12pm–5pm daily, December to April, tel 03 304 7501, www.linton.co.nz).

Akaroa is one of the prettiest towns in New Zealand, dotted with historic cottages and gardens overflowing with a profusion of form, colour and scent.

The view of Akaroa Harbour from Lighthouse Road

PHOTO NEWZEALAND / TONY BRUN

Rangitata Gorge Road,
22 km north of Geraldine

Contact
Peel Forest Café and General Store
03 696 3567
www.doc.govt.nz

Capacity
23 unpowered / 24 powered

Open
all year

Bookings
recommended peak season

Price
$9 adult / $5 child unpowered;
$13 adult / $9 child powered

The pitching is perfectly flat and covered in enviable, spongy grass — this is a great place for running around in bare feet.

Remnants of native forest are like hen's teeth on the farmed plains of Canterbury, and those that remain are often strangled in old man's beard or chomped bare by possums. This makes Peel Forest something of a rarity, particularly as it was once part of an extensive forest long since logged out and cleared for pasture. Established in 1909, the park conserves a meagre but precious 773 ha on the south bank of the Rangitata River — a little bush oasis at the base of the mountains.

The main peaks of the Peel Range stand beyond the park boundary, but Little Mount Peel (1311 m) lies within. On its slopes and foothills is a thick canopy of podocarps (kahikatea, totara and matai), with bush-encircled clearings on the flat. A sawmilling village was situated around here at the turn of the twentieth century, and the remains of several sawpits can still been seen.

On Clarke's Flat, the DOC-concession campground is a peach. The grounds are well established, with a dreamy combination of attractive native plantings and open lawn. And we mean *lawn*. The pitching is perfectly flat and covered in enviable, spongy grass — this is a great place for running around in bare feet.

Fire pits are dotted here and there. The fairly old amenities block is in tip-top condition, although planning for a new one is underway. The kitchen has all the necessary electricals and the bonus of an open fire and dining area. At our last visit, the water needed to be treated before drinking. There's a coin phone and four enticing little cabins.

Ten minutes' walk from the campground is Te Wanahu Flat, a large grassy picnic area (good for ball sports) and a picnic shelter. Another 30 minutes' walk away is the general store (which you will have passed on your way in to the park). This is the home of the camp managers and where you pay your fees. Basic groceries and takeaways are available, and Musterer's Café and Bar is during the open peak season. Mountain bikes are available for hire here, too.

RIDE RAPIDLY DOWN THE RANGITATA

No banjos around here. No siree. Just white water, mountains, gorgeous scenery and some of New Zealand's most exciting rafting. A memorable two-and-a-half-hour trip with Rangitata Rafts begins on relatively sedate water (grade 1), giving you the chance to learn the basics and gain a modicum of confidence. Things crank up rapidly after that, eventually reaching the thundering maelstrom of the grade 4 and 5 sections. If you've any adrenalin left in the tank, then there's also the (optional) 10 m leap into the river off Jump Rock. If you're too chicken for such an escapade, you can opt to float down the river instead along the calmer sections. Rangitata Rafts (tel 0800 251 251, www.rafts.co.nz; September to May) is based 10 km north of the campground.

KNOCK OFF LITTLE MOUNT PEEL

This full-day walk (five to seven hours return) takes you above the bushline where, on a fine day, views extend to Mount Somers and Mount Hutt to the north, and all the way across the chequerboard Canterbury plains to the coast. From Blandswood car park, the Deer Spur track passes through fuchsia and fern forest, then southern rata, before thinning and arriving at a small alpine tarn. Above this point, the landscape changes dramatically to open alpine grasslands, then it's onwards and upwards along the spur and boardwalk to the summit. Care is required near the top as the last 100 m or so are steep indeed. Atop this rocky pinnacle you can marvel at the expansive views, with the Tristram Harper Memorial Shelter clinging precariously to the mountain just below the summit.

HUG A TREE

Peel Forest boasts a dozen walks of varying lengths, half of them starting at Te Wanahu Flat, 10 minutes' walk from the campground. The remainder can be accessed from the end of Blandswood Road, approximately 4 km from the camp. From Te Wanahu, an enjoyable two- to three-hour loop climbs through tall podocarp forest on Allans Track before dipping down steeply on the Deer Spur track to Fern Walk. Peel Forest's mild and moist climate provides ideal growing conditions for ferns, and on this appropriately named track you'll see many of the 68 species that grow here. Also starting at Te Wanahu is Big Tree Walk (30 minutes return), on which you'll see massive totara, one of which is almost 3 m in diameter and thought to be over 1000 years old. The DOC booklet *Peel Forest Park Tracks* (available from the general store) has information on all of the walks in the area.

A tranquil raft ride down the Rangitata

CHRISTCHURCH AND CANTERBURY TOURISM

Lake Alexandrina Road, off Godley Peaks Road, 11 km north of Lake Tekapo township

Capacity
60 unpowered

Open
all year

Bookings
not required

Price
$5 per person

FRASER GUNN

The big-sky country of the Mackenzie Basin is named after the legendary rustler Jock Mackenzie, who ranged his stolen stock across its undulating plains. What a legacy that is — especially for an outlaw — to have one of New Zealand's best-loved landscapes named in his honour.

The Mackenzie Country is like a postcard, printed sharply in focus but with the colours gone awry. The snowy peaks cut into the clear air in a crisp profile, curtaining a seemingly endless expanse of golden tussock. In incredible contrast, in the middle of the picture, lies the vivid, turquoise pool of Lake Tekapo. It's all quite surreal, especially so in the summer when the lupins explode into yellow, pink and purple. If you haven't been here yet, we predict eyes like saucers and some shaking of the head in disbelief. (And just wait until you see it from on high.)

Lake Tekapo is undoubtedly the star attraction of the area, and fortunately a decent commercial campground can be found on its shores. However, if you're a quiet type, into your birds, and happy to take your turn at cleaning the loo, you might like to consider trekking a little bit further on to lakes Alexandrina and McGregor, which sit side by side to the west of Lake Tekapo.

Turn off State Highway 8 about 1.5 km west of Tekapo and head up Godley Peaks Road (signposted to the Mount John Observatory). As indicated by a sign, there is camping down the first road to the left — that's the 'southern settlement' — but there's not much room for casuals here. We recommend you continue on to the 'outlet settlement', around 10 km from the State Highway 8 turn-off. There are two camping areas at the outlet: the first on the edge of Lake McGregor (the smaller of the two lakes, and the smaller campground), the other a short walk away on Alexandrina — 'a lovely splotch of inky blue, dabbed and spread onto a tawny dry landscape' (as poetically described by travel writer Derek Grzelewski).

The campgrounds are looked after by the Lake Alexandrina and Lake McGregor Camping Committee, a group comprised largely of local 'hut-holders' (whose 'huts' are mostly well established baches) who keep an eye on the place. Whether you opt for the larger Lake Alex campground, or the quieter spot at Lake McGregor, be prepared to park up or pitch around the regular caravanners — this is very much a locals' spot, but casual visitors are welcome. Just make sure you close the gate, tidy up after yourself and follow any other instructions — this is communal, not commercial camping.

Facilities are basic, which is what you get for five bucks. There's running water (boiling required), long-drop toilets and shower stalls (BYO solar shower). Pitches are a bit rocky and there is no power.

GET LUCKY ON THE LAKES

Lying amid tussocky hills with a backdrop of snow-capped peaks, the pristine waters of Lake Alexandrina are a sublime place to have a little row or hook yourself a trout or two. The birdlife is a highlight. The two lakes form the DOC-managed Lake Alexandrina Wildlife Refuge, frequented by almost 50 bird species, 14 of which breed here. With a bit of luck you'll see the endangered southern crested grebe (cute little bird that it is) and may also spot scaup, grey teal, shoveller and paradise duck, among others. Motorboats are forbidden, ensuring a particular tranquillity you may not encounter on many other southern lakes. Along with the excellent water quality, this makes Alex one of the south's best known fishing areas — hats off to the award-winning weed-busting locals, the Lake Alexandrina Conservation Trust.

SEE A SKY FULL OF DIAMONDS

The sky over the Mackenzie Country is of such clarity and intensity that it may soon be gazetted as the inaugural World Heritage Starlight Reserve — the first ever world heritage site that is part of the ether rather than terra firma. So things are certainly looking up for the Mount John Observatory, the visitor-friendly twinkle-tracker on top of Tekapo's big hill. Unsurprisingly, the best time to visit is at night, when you can have a two-hour stargazing tour — bookings are essential (tel 03 680 6960, www.earthandsky.co.nz). However, a visit during the day is also compulsory: the views are staggering, and the conservatory-like Astro Café serves excellent coffee and cake. The Mount John walking track takes you up and down from Tekapo and around the hill, offering maximum views.

INHALE THE BIG SMOKE OF LAKE TEKAPO VILLAGE

This tiny township turns into a bustling tourist stop during the summer season, and as such offers hot food, cold beer, lots of tourist activities and racks of merino wear.

A good place to pause and reflect is the Church of the Good Shepherd on the lakefront, a photogenic little building built of stone in 1935. Head there early morning to avoid the flock, and be sure to get your snap with Tekapo's luminous waters in the background.

The Mackenzie Country is like a postcard, printed sharply in focus but with the colours gone awry. The snowy peaks cut into the clear air in a crisp profile, curtaining a seemingly endless expanse of golden tussock.

FRASER GUNN

FAR LEFT: Big skies reflected in Lake Alexandrina
LEFT: Mount John Observatory, with Lake Tekapo in the background

Hooker Valley Road, off State Highway 80, 2 km from Mount Cook village, 66 km north of Twizel

Contact
DOC Mount Cook Visitor Centre
03 435 1186
www.doc.govt.nz

Capacity
100 unpowered (50 tents, 50 vans)

Open
all year

Bookings
recommended peak season

Price
$6 adult / $3 child

In a spectacular alpine setting, White Horse Hill has an open aspect, with views of Mount Sefton (3158 m).

Mighty Aoraki / Mount Cook is of course New Zealand's highest mountain. Its Maori name, Aoraki, translates as 'cloud piercer', which it certainly does, at 3754 m above sea level. It is a somewhat elusive soul, however; we have met travellers who have spent a fortnight in Aoraki / Mount Cook National Park waiting for the maunga to reveal itself — to no avail. It pays to venture forth into this region expecting similar treatment . . . and the odd raindrop or two.

Irrespective of whether you see Aoraki or not, this is an awe-inspiring place to be, rain or shine. Walkers will be wowed, while those sitting tight are well provided for at Mount Cook village, which offers an array of diverting indoor activities. These warm, welcoming facilities will be particularly appealing to those who stay at DOC's White Horse Hill campground, about 2 km away (walked effortlessly in half an hour via the Kea Point Track).

In a spectacular alpine setting, White Horse Hill has an open aspect, with views of Mount Sefton (3158 m). Offering economical lodging in one of New Zealand's most visited spots, it's unsurprisingly busy in peak season. Fortunately it holds a lot of people — a couple of hundred at capacity.

Accordingly, DOC staff put considerable effort into its upkeep. In recent years some landscaping and planting has been done, and it boasts brand new facilities, including one of the country's flashest shelters. It's a cracker, with regularly serviced flush toilets and a large kitchen / dining area with acres of stainless steel benchtops, numerous sinks and dining tables where you can enjoy your dinner unmolested by sandflies.

Tent pitches are a bit on the rocky side, but there are easy drive-on spots for vans. The occasional picnic bench is dotted around. Drinking water allegedly requires boiling, and there are rubbish facilities, including recycling. A hot shower can be had at the DOC day shelter in the village. You'll need a dollar coin: that'll get you five heavenly minutes of hot water.

EXPLORE THE MOUNTAINS

. . . or at least get up close and gawp at them. There are plenty of walks that lead you amid the scenery, including the must-do Hooker Valley track (one hour return) — one of this country's most scenic short walks. The more adventurous might wish to consider the Sealy Tarns track (three to four hours return), a steep clamber worth every gut-busting step for its stupendous views of the peaks — including Aoraki / Mount Cook — and a profusion of alpine flowers in summer. If this is all new to you and you're keen to learn more about the area while you're walking (or climbing or scrambling . . .), you might like to consider going with a local guide. Their presence will greatly enhance your experience and assure your safety. The DOC visitor centre will help you find one.

CHOCKS AWAY!

To really appreciate the extent and grandeur of this vast alpine wilderness, you need to get up on high. The more courageous (and slightly crazy) of our outdoorsy ilk will strap on the crampons and head up into the tops to 'bag a peak' or two. For the rest of us, our best bet is to hop aboard an aeroplane or helicopter. A scenic flight over the Mount Cook region will be one you will never forget, buzzing around the peaks and over glaciers, and maybe even landing on the snow. You'll have no trouble finding someone to take you up: good one-stop shops for information and bookings are the DOC visitor centre or Twizel i-SITE (tel 03 435 3124, www.twizel.com).

WHILE AWAY THE HOURS IN THE NEW DOC VISITOR CENTRE

Opened in 2008, this excellent facility is a mine of information about Aoraki / Mount Cook National Park. Learn about the geology, flora and fauna; learn of Maori and Pakeha history in the area, and its mountaineering and recreational heritage. Behold the power and beauty of this wilderness through the eyes of writers, artists, photographers and filmmakers. Find out what it takes to survive in this rugged environment, and be amazed and moved by its stories of triumph and tragedy. Then get back to reality with a spot of retail therapy in the shop. Tel 03 435 1186.

The flash new Aoraki / Mount Cook Visitor Centre

DOC / SHIRLEY SLATTER

Lake Ohau Road, 57 km northwest of Twizel (turn-off on State Highway 8, 13 km from Twizel, signposted to Lake Ohau)

Contact
DOC Twizel
03 435 0802
www.doc.govt.nz

Capacity
30 unpowered

Open
all year

Bookings
not required

Price
free

If the grandeur of Aoraki / Mount Cook has whet your appetite for mountain wilderness and you fancy exploring this area further, then the Ruataniwha Conservation Park may be just what you're looking for.

If the grandeur of Aoraki / Mount Cook has whet your appetite for mountain wilderness and you fancy exploring this area further, then the Ruataniwha Conservation Park may be just what you're looking for. Less than an hour's drive from Twizel, and only around 45 km as the crow flies from Mount Cook village, Ruataniwha feels much more remote, separated from the tourist hordes by a couple of mountain ranges.

Butting up against the Southern Alps, this rugged 36,800 ha reserve borders both the Westland / Tai Poutini and Aoraki / Mount Cook national parks. Two major glacial river valleys bisect its ranges: the Dobson and Hopkins, which converge before emptying into Lake Ohau, which you pass on the drive in. Funnelling water from the many mountain tops within the park are numerous other rivers and streams, one of which is Temple Stream, where a secluded DOC campsite can be found.

It's a reasonably easy drive to Temple Valley from State Highway 8, but one which gets you quickly amid the grandeur. Not far from the turn-off the road meets Lake Ohau, a hydro lake lying in the glacial valley, flanked by the tussocky Ben Ohau and Barrier ranges. Flumes of scree avalanche to their feet while around their tops hang wisps of cloud. Beyond the lake head and the Lake Ohau Station, the entire valley floor is taken up by the stony bed of the Hopkins River; the Dobson can be seen bearing off in the direction of Aoraki.

In all, it's 44 km from State Highway 8 to the Temple campsite at the head of the lake, the last 16 of which are unsealed. Note that in heavy rain, the road is likely be impassable due to flooding, but you probably won't want to be camping then anyway! Lying at the convergence of the north and south branches of Temple Stream, the campground comprises a grassy flat beyond which beech forest begins. As indicated by the farm gates, there is livestock about.

The facilities are very basic. A small, three-sided shelter has a fireplace — so you can crank that up for comfort, at least. There are long-drop toilets and the odd picnic bench; water can be collected from the stream.

There are two other campsites along the Lake Ohau Road, both administered by the Waitaki Lakes District Council (tel 03 434 8060). Around 17 km from the State Highway 8 turn-off, the Lake Middleton campground is split into two, with part lying on the Middleton lake shore and part on Lake Ohau, which lies right next to it. A further 9 km north on Lake Ohau Road is Round Bush. Both of these camps are pretty basic, too: Round Bush has long-drop toilets and stream water only; Lake Middleton has flush toilets and tap water (treatment required). Both campgrounds cost $10 per site and you need to take your rubbish out with you.

Tramping along the south branch of the Temple Valley

EXPLORE A TRAMPERS' PARADISE

The Ruataniwha Conservation Park offers tramps of all shapes and sizes, three starting right from the campsite including the Temple Valley Circuit Track (one hour), and longer walks up the north and south streams (each around four to five hours return; there's a hut up the south branch if you want to overnight). To access tramps in the upper reaches of the Dobson and Hopkins Valleys you'll need a four-wheel-drive, while a few further down the valley require landowner permission. Detailed information and an overview map are in DOC's *Ruataniwha Conservation Park* track guide, although you'd be wise to adhere to the standard practice of taking a topographic map and leaving your intentions with someone before you set off. Mountain biking can also be had on the Parsons and Monument tracks (see DOC's pamphlet, *Mountain Biking in Canterbury*).

HOOK A TROUT FOR TEA

Lake Ohau provides ample opportunity for landing your dinner — should you have the gear, licence, time, patience . . . You can troll from your boat if you have one, or spin from the shore if you don't. The lake head is a popular spot, particularly where the Dobson River flows into it. Handy to the campground, the Temple Stream forks is also worth a shot, or venture up to where the Huxley River joins the Dobson. More information, including contacts for local guides, can be found at www.nzfishing.com.

SUP A PINT IN THE TWIZEL PUB

'Twizzel, rhymes with drizzle' say its detractors, but try saying that to the blokes who built this town — you may meet some of them at the Top Hut pub. Twizel sprang up in 1968 to service the building of the Waitaki hydroelectric project, the idea being that the town would be 'decommissioned' when construction was complete. Fast forward the 18 years it took to finish the job and no one wanted to leave: the trees had grown by then and everyone was no doubt in rude health from all that hard work and fresh mountain air. The Top Hut is a real locals' bar: slip in unobtrusively, play pool by local rules and take a ticket in the meat raffle. Heartland New Zealand. Top Hut, 13 Tasman Road, Twizel, tel 03 435 0832.

NORTH AND MID-CANTERBURY

ALPINE HOLIDAY APARTMENTS AND CAMPGROUND
9 Fowlers Lane, Hanmer Springs

Contact: 03 315 7478
alpineholidayapartments@xtra.co.nz
www.alpine-apartments.co.nz

Tariff: $20–120

GORE BAY AND BUXTON CAMPGROUNDS
Gore Bay Road
(off SH 1 at Cheviot),
Cheviot, North Canterbury

Contact: 03 319 8010

HANMER RIVER HOLIDAY PARK
26 Medway Road (6 km before Hanmer), Hanmer Springs

Contact: 03 315 7111
stayhanmerriver@xtra.co.nz
www.hanmerriverholidaypark.co.nz

Tariff: $24–85

HANMER SPRINGS FOREST CAMP
243 Jollies Pass Road,
Hanmer Springs

Contact: 03 315 7202
Hanmer.Forest.Camp@xtra.co.nz
www.hanmerforestcamp.co.nz

Tariff: $20–85

KAIKOURA COASTAL CAMPGROUNDS
Goose Bay, Boat Harbour,
Omihi, Paia Point, 15 km
south of Kaikoura on SH 1

Contact: 03 319 5348
goosebay@ihug.co.nz

Tariff: $14–40

KAIKOURA PEKETA BEACH HOLIDAY PARK
SH 1, 7 km south of Kaikoura

Contact: 03 319 6299
beachfront@kaikourapeketabeach.co.nz

Tariff: $26–50

LEITHFIELD BEACH MOTOR CAMP
Leithfield Beach,
North Canterbury

Contact: 03 314 8518

Tariff: $10

MOUNTAIN VIEW TOP 10 HOLIDAY PARK
Main Road, Hanmer Springs

Contact: 03 315 7113
www.mountainviewtop10.co.nz

Tariff: $26–130

RANGIORA HOLIDAY PARK
337 Lehmans Road, RD 1, Rangiora

Contact: 03 313 5759
rangioraholidaypark@hotmail.com

Tariff: $22–85

THE PINES HOLIDAY PARK
158 Argelins Road, Hanmer Springs

Contact: 03 315 7152
reservations@pinesholidaypark.co.nz
www.pinesholidaypark.co.nz

Tariff: $24–95

SPENCER BEACH HOLIDAY PARK
Heyders Road (off Lower
Styx Road), Spencerville

Contact: 03 329 8721
spencerpark@xtra.co.nz
www.spencerbeachholidaypark.co.nz

Tariff: $26–85

WAIKUKU BEACH HOLIDAY PARK
Domain Terrace, Waikuku
Beach, Rangiora

Contact: 03 312 7600
arkiwi@hotmail.com

Tariff: $20–50

WOODEND BEACH HOLIDAY PARK
14 Woodend Beach
Road, Woodend Beach,
RD 1, Kaiapoi

Contact: 03 312 7643
woodendbeachhp@xtra.co.nz
www.woodendbeachholidaypark.co.nz

Tariff: $20–78

CHRISTCHURCH

ADDINGTON ACCOMMODATION PARK
4751 Whiteleigh Ave,
Addington, Christchurch

Contact: 03 338 9770
addacc@xtra.co.nz

Tariff: $25–85

ALL SEASONS HOLIDAY PARK
5 Kidbrooke Street (off
Linwood Ave), Christchurch

Contact: 03 384 9490
rosslee@actrix.co.nz
www.allseasonsholidaypark.co.nz

Tariff: $30–110

AMBER PARK HOLIDAY PARK
308 Blenheim Road,
Christchurch 8041

Contact: 03 348 3327
info@amberpark.co.nz
www.amberpark.co.nz

Tariff: $18–125

**CHRISTCHURCH
TOP 10 HOLIDAY PARK**
Meadow Park, 39 Meadow Street,
Christchurch

Contact: 03 352 9176
stay@christchurchtop10.co.nz
www.christchurchtop10.co.nz

Tariff: $30–160

NORTH SOUTH HOLIDAY PARK
530 Sawyers Arms Road, Christchurch

Contact: 03 359 5993
info@northsouth.co.nz
www.northsouth.co.nz

Tariff: $10–135

RICCARTON PARK HOLIDAY PARK
19 Main South Road, Christchurch

Contact: 03 348 5690
riccartonholidaypark@hotmail.com
www.riccartonparkholidaycamp.co.nz

Tariff: $30–85

**SOUTH NEW BRIGHTON
MOTOR CAMP**
59 Halsey Street, Christchurch

Contact: 03 388 9844
relax@southbrightonmotorcamp.co.nz
www.southbrightonmotorcamp.co.nz

Tariff: $22–65

**MACKENZIE COUNTRY
AND SOUTH CANTERBURY**

**ABISKO LODGE APARTMENTS
AND CAMPGROUND**
74 Main Street, Methven

Contact: 03 302 8875
abisko@paradise.net.nz
www.abisko.co.nz

Tariff: $30–185

**ALPINE VIEWS FARMSTAY
AND B AND B**
28 Symes Road, Inland Scenic
Route 72, Staveley, Canterbury

Contact: 03 303 0800
anna@alpineviews.co.nz
www.alpineviews.co.nz

Tariff: $25–150

ASHBURTON HOLIDAY PARK
Tinwald Domain, Maronan
Road, Ashburton

Contact: 03 308 6805
pat.sue@xtra.co.nz

Tariff: $22–45

FAIRLIE TOP 10 HOLIDAY PARK
10 Allandale Road, Fairlie

Contact: 03 685 8375
relax@fairlietop10.co.nz
www.fairlietop10.co.nz

Tariff: $30–150

FARMYARD HOLIDAY PARK
Coach Road, RD 22, Geraldine

Contact: 03 693 9355
thefarmyard@xtra.co.nz

Tariff: $25–90

GERALDINE HOLIDAY PARK
39 Hislop Street, Geraldine

Contact: 03 693 8147
geraldineholidaypark@xtra.co.nz
www.geraldineholidaypark.co.nz

Tariff: $70–115

GLENMARK HOLIDAY PARK
Beaconsfield Road, Timaru

Contact: 03 684 3682
glenmarkmotorcamp@xtra.co.nz
www.timarumotorcamp.co.nz

Tariff: $24–65

GLENTANNER PARK CENTRE
SH 80, Mount Cook

Contact: 03 435 1855
www.glentanner.co.nz

Tariff: $28–110

GLENTUNNEL HOLIDAY PARK
Homebush Road,
Glentunnel, Christchurch

Contact: 03 318 2868
glentunnelholidaypark@xtra.co.nz

Tariff: $28–55

GRUMPY'S RETREAT 'N' HOLIDAY PARK
Cnr Keen and Main
North Roads, Orari Bridge,
Geraldine
Contact: 03 693 7453
reservations: 0800 247 8679
www.christchurch2mountcook.co.nz

Tariff: $26–95

KELCEYS BUSH FARMYARD HOLIDAY PARK
Mill Road, RD 8, Waimate

Contact: 03 689 8057
kelceysbush@xtra.co.nz
www.kiwicamps.com

Tariff: $26–80

KNOTTINGLEY PARK MOTOR CAMP
Waihao Back Road, Waimate

Contact: 03 689 8079
after hours 03 689 8954
graeme@waimatedc.govt.nz

Tariff: $16

LAKE TEKAPO MOTELS AND HOLIDAY PARK
Lakeside Drive, Lake Tekapo

Contact: 03 680 6825
www.laketekapo-accommodation.co.nz

Tariff: $26–150

METHVEN CAMPING GROUND AND HOLIDAY PARK
Barkers Road, Methven

Contact: 0800 122 685
methvennz@hotmail.com

Tariff: $22–34

MOUNT SOMERS HOLIDAY PARK
Hoods Road, Mount Somers,
RD 1, Ashburton

Contact: 03 303 9719
camp@mountsomers.co.nz
www.mountsomers.co.nz

Tariff: $22–69

PARKLANDS ALPINE TOURIST PARK
122 Mackenzie Drive, Twizel

Contact: 03 435 0507
parklands1@xtra.co.nz

Tariff: $28–100

RAKAIA RIVER HOLIDAY PARK
Main South Road, Rakaia

Contact: 03 302 7257
rrjackson@xtra.co.nz
www.rakaiariverholidaypark.co.nz

Tariff: $26–115

ST ANDREWS CAMPING GROUND
SH 1 (250 m south
of hotel), St Andrews (between
Timaru and Waimate

Contact: 03 612 6628

Tariff: $10–13

TEMUKA HOLIDAY PARK
1 Ferguson Drive, Temuka

Contact: 03 615 7241
temukaholiday@xtra.co.nz
www.temukaholidaypark.co.nz

Tariff: $26–50

TIMARU TOP 10 HOLIDAY PARK
154a Selwyn Street, Timaru

Contact: 03 684 7690
topten@timaruholidaypark.co.nz
www.timaruholidaypark.co.nz

Tariff: $30–110

VICTORIA PARK MOTOR CAMP
Naylor Street, Waimate

Contact: 03 689 8079
after hours 03 689 8954
graeme@waimatedc.govt.nz

Tariff: $20–55

Kaikoura coastline

→ LET'S GO CAMPING IN

OTAGO

**27 Hereweka Street,
Portobello, Otago Peninsula**

Contact
03 478 0359
www.portobello.co.nz

Capacity
14 unpowered / 25 powered

Open
all year

Bookings
recommended in peak season

Price
$14 adult / $7 child unpowered;
$15 adult / $7.50 child powered

The action-packed Otago Peninsula is right on Dunedin's doorstep, which makes it a very lucky town. For throughout these hills and along these shores are all sorts of interesting things to see and do — beaches, birdlife (including albatrosses and penguins), seals, fishing, walking tracks, historic homes and gardens . . . all within an hour's drive of downtown. It's not often that a large city has a line-up of such diverse natural attractions so close — although you could also argue that it's not often that an albatross gets to live so close to such a groovy city, right? Whichever way you look at it, the peninsula's a winner.

Portobello is one of many small settlements on the harbour side of the peninsula. It's home to the family-owned Portobello Village Tourist Park,

the only camping ground out this way. While pleasant enough, it won't blow your socks off with its beauty — it's just a small, friendly campground offering functional camping in a handy location. Just 25 minutes' drive from the city centre, it makes a good base from which to explore not only the peninsula itself, but also the delights of New Zealand's most Scottish city. Portobello itself has a shop, pub and a couple of cafés, at last count.

The campground is just off the main road, on the cusp of rural surroundings. It's relatively small, with just 25 powered sites and a tents-only grassed area with room for around 14 pitches. A central building houses a few motel rooms (upstairs), and the communal amenities at ground level. The kitchen is small and homely — we've always found it particularly social when we've stayed. A little room next door has an internet terminal. Some stylish cabin are the park's most recent addition.

A sheltered picnic area has a gas barbecue, while a recycling station sits alongside. Owners Sherryl and Kevin have recently built seven snazzy en suite cabins on an upper terrace, which could come in handy if it rains.

**PREVIOUS PAGE: Dunedin Railway Station
LEFT: View towards Taiaroa Heads from the Otago Peninsula
RIGHT: Albatrosses, Taiaroa Head**

TOURISM DUNEDIN

VISIT THE WORLD'S ONLY MAINLAND ALBATROSS COLONY

One of New Zealnd's most exciting birding experiences, this is a must-do for anyone remotely interested in our feathered friends. On Taiaroa Head, at the far end of the peninsula, is the Royal Albatross Centre (tel 03 478 0499, www.albatross.org.nz), operated by the Otago Peninsula Trust. The albatross colony here was established in 1938, and is currently populated by around 140 birds, including some rather outsize chicks. Admission to the excellent visitor centre (with interpretive displays, shop and café) is free, and you may be lucky enough to spot a bird or two soaring from the viewing area near the car park — so that's a good option if you're short on time or money. However, undoubtedly the best way to see these majestic creatures up close up is by taking the tour (90 minutes, $45 / 22 adult / child, and worth every penny). You will have to book in advance: these tours are popular.

HIDE OUT FOR THE HOIHO

With an estimated population of only 1700 breeding pairs, the yellow-eyed penguin (hoiho) is thought to be the world's rarest penguin. It's also the third largest, weighing in at a hefty 5–7 kg. Around 600 pairs nest on the south coast of the South Island, some of which may be spotted — if you're lucky — from the DOC hide at Sandfly Bay, around 15 minutes' drive from Portobello. Viewing them is a privilege: obey all signage and treat them and their habitat with respect. To both reduce your impact and increase your chances of seeing the birds, we recommend you go on a tour with the Yellow-eyed Penguin Conservation Reserve (tel 03 478 0286, www.penguinplace.co.nz).

SEE THE BRIGHT LIGHTS OF NEW ZEALAND'S FIFTH LARGEST CITY

With its elegant but under-insulated Victorian and Edwardian architecture, edgy arts scene and rampant student population, Dunedin is a hardy and slightly anarchic city. It's a satisfying place to visit, with heaps of activities packed into a small area: wander the streets, visit the museum or art galleries, see a band at one of many live music venues, eat and drink in the city's fine establishments . . . A great number of the city's attractions are within walking distance of The Octagon, Dunedin's town 'square', where you'll find the i-SITE visitor centre (tel 03 474 3300, www.dunedin.govt.nz). Portobello is only 25 minutes' drive from downtown, so you may as well make the most of it.

It's not often that a cruise country has a handful of such diverse natural attractions so close — although you could also argue that it's not often that an albatross got to live so close to such a groovy city, right?

114 Haven Street, Moeraki,
40 km south of Oamaru;
78 km north of Dunedin

Contact
03 439 4759
www.moerakivillageholidaypark.co.nz

Capacity
30 unpowered / 28 powered

Open
all year

Bookings
required for powered
sites in high summer

Price
$26 for 2 people

Moeraki is a pretty,
sleepy town . . .
It's rustic and utterly
unselfconscious —
an honest, quiet, salt-
encrusted corner of
civilisation.

Ever since the first human beings visited the Otago Coast, Moeraki's claim to fame has quite rightly been the big, round boulders scattered along its beach. But in recent times these geological wonders have been vying for attention with New Zealand's most famous out-of-the-way seafood restaurant, Fleur's Place.

But there's more to this place than boulders and a bowl of chowder, for Moeraki is a memorable place with a fascinating history. The area was a long-established food-gathering place of early Waitaha Maori who enjoyed a rich harvest from its shore — it was they who named it Moeraki, meaning 'a place to rest by day'. This bounty was soon sniffed out by Europeans, who established a whaling station here in 1836, although that lasted only the tragic decade it took for the whales to be exterminated. About the same time, a hapu of Ngai Tahu migrated south and settled here too. Inextricable Maori–Paheka links are a legacy of this era, largely through intermarriage and the church. (Do check out the stained glass image of Tiramorehu, a Maori leader, in the old village church, named Kotahitanga — 'unity'.)

Once the whales were gone, the townsfolk turned to farming, Moeraki remaining a busy port until usurped by Oamaru in the 1870s. By that time, the railway had come to town (or at least to Hillgrove, close by), bringing a tourist trade that has never (thankfully) reached full tilt. So it was fish and farm that kept the town afloat, at least until the fishery declined, by which time an influx of settlers — largely from Dunedin — was contributing both economic diversity and critical mass.

Today, Moeraki is a pretty, sleepy town. A small fleet of fishing boats bobs in the bay while against its hilly backdrop is a combination of ramshackle cribs and established homes, cobbled together with hard-bitten byways, pockets of bush and runaway reserves of noxious weeds. It's rustic and utterly unselfconscious — an honest, quiet, salt-encrusted corner of civilisation.

The Moeraki Village Holiday Park is the only campground in town, and fits right in with its surroundings, being homespun, independently owned and low key. Nestling up against the hill, the sheltered grounds ramble over several terraces from where you can get sneaky peaks of the bay below. Roomy, flat and well grassed, bordered by pine and the odd ngaio tree, this is just simple camping in a peaceful place.

The facilities blocks are modern and spotless, supplied with solar-heated water and offering all necessary amenities. They are, however, quite utilitarian, having no comfy or particularly welcoming communal areas for hanging about in. For that, you'll have to book into one of the holiday park's motel or cabin options, some of which have good views of the bay.

Moeraki Boulders

ROCK ON DOWN TO THE BOULDERS

These large spheres are amongst the most peculiar things you will ever see lying on the beach. Technically referred to as concretions, it is believed they were formed by the cementing of calcite around a particle (such as a bone fragment or shell), in a similar way to a pearl forming around a grain of sand in an oyster. It's estimated that large boulders like those at Moeraki took around four million years to form, although Maori have a much more romantic explanation for their presence: according to legend, the boulders are gourds and kumara that fell overboard from the ancestral canoe, Arai Te Uru, which was shipwrecked at Matakaea (Shag Point) further south. The boulders are about 2.5 km along the beach from Moeraki village, which can be walked at mid- to low tide in about 45 minutes.

GOOD COD! IT MUST BE FLEUR'S PLACE!

You'd have to be offering something pretty exceptional to keep a place like this cranking all year round. And that's exactly what Fleur Sullivan is famous for — fabulous food in a cracker location (the site of the old whaling station). Her fan club includes none other than Mr Fish himself, Rick Stein. Fleur's seafood platter, piled high with smoked, steamed and marinated kaimoana, remains unsurpassed from Cape Reinga to Bluff, although you'd be hard pressed to find anything on the menu that isn't just as fresh and delicious. It pays to book in advance — word is well and truly out. Fleur's Place, Moeraki, tel 03 439 4480, www.fleursplace.com.

TAKE YET ANOTHER CHANCE TO SEE PENGUINS

It's a 5 km drive from Moeraki's main road to the Lighthouse Reserve on Katiki Point, an old pa site. The lighthouse has held a torch for mariners since 1877; below it is a small reserve, home to some very special wildlife including blue and yellow-eyed penguin, the Stewart Island shag and a colony of New Zealand fur seals (October to March). A viewing hide (with binoculars considerately left inside) will help you spot them. You may also see the odd angler fishing from the rocks — this is considered one of the best shore-fishing spots along this part of the coast.

Yellow-eyed penguin

**State Highway 6 (Haast Pass),
14 km north of Makarora,
64 km southeast of Haast**

Contact

DOC Makarora
03 443 8365
www.doc.govt.nz

Capacity

40 unpowered

Open

all year

Bookings

not required

Price

$6 adult / $3.50 child

Julius von Haast, the German-born geologist, set out on numerous intrepid journeys around the South Island in his capacity as an official geological explorer. It was his party who was said to be the first Europeans to conquer the pass that now bears his name between Central Otago and the West Coast, in 1863. However, the facts of the matter are clouded in a Malloryesque mist for, in 1881, a surveyor by the name of Thomas Brodrick found on a cairn a flask belonging to Scottish prospector Charles Cameron. An inscription on the flask indicated that he got through the pass two weeks before Haast, alone. Good old Brodrick: he named a nearby mountain in Cameron's honour. The mist has yet to clear on this topic, but it was apparently clear for Maori, who favoured this route for transporting pounamu (greenstone) from the West Coast: they named it Tioripatea, meaning 'the way ahead is clear'.

Heading towards Central Otago from the West Coast, the road from Haast township follows the Haast River before reaching the Main Divide and the marginally passable Gates of Haast — a narrow, thunderous, cascading chasm which must be crossed before entering Otago and the Mount Aspiring National Park. There are three basic campsites between the West Coast and Makarora, and not one is named after Haast, no siree. It's the Scot who takes the honours here: Cameron Flat is the best out of the three.

An easy pull-over off the main road, this elevated campsite ranges over several terraces, an aspect that hushes any noise from the road below (although it's fair to say the traffic's not exactly gridlocked). From this commanding vantage point the views are quite enchanting, like the most beautiful postcard of nothing but nature (even the road is hidden if you're standing in the right spot). The picture-perfect Makarora River meanders off down the valley towards Mount Brewster, the area's highest peak and there are myriad other mountaintops reaching up left, right, and centre.

Needless to say, this campsite is best enjoyed in the sun, but this is not only mountain country but a place where weather systems wrestle. On a good day, misty cloud may push southwards, hang about and then recede — repelled by fine weather around lakes Wanaka and Hawea. It's a contest that's fascinating to observe, and one that often results in a sort of rain-sun-rain-sun stalemate. On a bad day, it's somewhat soggy and you'll be glad of that handsome DOC shelter.

The upside of all the precipitation is that the grass is super-spongy, so your bed will be comfy at least. The flush toilets are in good nick, and the water can be drunk from the tap. Motorhomers will find a dump station but remember to pack your plastic bags: you have to take your rubbish out with you.

SARAH BENNETT AND LEE SLATER

POP TO THE BLUE POOLS

This short nature walk is signposted from campsite. It's an hour-long loop from there to the pools, although you can make it an much shorter outing by parking at the Blue Pools car park, a little further south along the highway. Depending on river conditions, you will find the pools either deep blue or a rough-and-tumble grey. When the water's calm and glassy, keep an eye out for rainbow and brown trout. If you want to stretch your legs a bit more, take a walk up the Cameron Valley (starting from the campground), where a spectacular gorge and towering bluffs lie in wait. It's five hours one-way to the Cameron Hut, but a good tramp can be enjoyed by venturing as far as the large slip (about two hours) and back.

GET A LESSON IN PREDATION

If you're really lucky, you'll see a mohua (yellowhead), a sparrow-sized bird readily identified by its . . . purple beak (just kidding). If you're flush enough to have a $100 bill in your wallet, you'll find the cute little fella on there. Once one of Aotearoa's most abundant forest birds, the mohua is now seriously endangered. Habitat destruction and the introduction of predators such as stoats and rats decimated populations, and numbers are still in decline. If you spot one, you can thank DOC and Forest & Bird for the privilege; they've been trapping the invaders since 1998. For more information, take a look at the interpretive display at the campground or visit www.doc.govt.nz.

ENJOY THE JOURNEY, STOPPING OFTEN

Completed in 1965, the Haast Pass highway took a gruelling 36 years to build. Today, it's 140 km of pure driving pleasure between Haast and Wanaka, with plenty of lay-bys and short walks darting off along its length. On a fine day, you'll encounter jaw-dropping views of the mountains of the Main Divide. On rainy ones, you'll get swollen rivers and crashing waterfalls. It's a win-win situation. This is the road of a thousand photographs, so make sure you allow time to stop and look around. You might want to check your fuel gauge before you set off, too — it's a long way between petrol stations.

DOC / NICOLA VALLANCE

FAR LEFT: Cameron Flat
LEFT: The Blue Pools, reached on a one-hour loop walk from the campsite

**Mead Road (off State Highway 6),
40 km north of Wanaka**

Contact
DOC Wanaka
03 443 7660
www.doc.govt.nz

Capacity
40 unpowered

Open
all year (although water can
freeze in the pipes in winter)

Bookings
not required

Price
$6 per person

Occupying two large trenches gouged by long-gone glaciers, lakes Wanaka and Hawea are the watery centrepieces of a landscape boasting no shortage of remarkable landforms, including Mount Aspiring and its fellow Southern Alps, and the Matukituki and Clutha rivers, the latter of which is New Zealand's second-longest. Startling geological features, such as schist outcrops, moraines and river deltas, make it an enduring place for exploration. A kind summer climate and ample outdoor pursuits, including a wealth of good walks (it is, of course, the gateway to Mount Aspiring National Park), account for the relative hustle and bustle, particularly around Wanaka where many upmarket comforts are close at hand.

There are commercial campgrounds in both Wanaka and Lake Hawea townships. However, should you desire to pitch or park up in a quieter, more natural setting, we suggest you head north to The Neck. Situated along the Haast Pass Highway (State Highway 6), The Neck is a small land-bridge between the two lakes, around 23 km from Hawea township. Here a turn-off leads to Kidds Bush Reserve, but it isn't clearly signposted — look for the sign reading Hunter Valley Station and Mead Road. Six kilometres of gravel and you're there, a total of around 40 minutes' driving time from Wanaka.

The flats around Kidds Bush Reserve have been farmed since 1862, although much of the two large stations here were flooded in 1956 when the level of Lake Hawea was raised by 19 m to provide a reserve for the hydroelectric dams further downstream. The remnant forest here has been luckier in its escape, for when the sheep arrived much of the bush was felled and milled to make way for pasture. The reserve was established in 1891 — fairly early by New Zealand standards.

Running from the high hills down to the lake edge, the forest is dominated by mountain beech. There are plenty of mature specimens as well as a diverse array of understorey species; some regenerative planting was undertaken in the early 1990s. This thick greenery gives way to a clearing next to the lake's shingle beach. It's a picturesque setting with a grand outlook, shelter from the prevailing nor'wester making it an even more enticing spot to camp.

This basic but handsome campsite is shared with the daytrippers and boaties who come to use the ramp (Lake Hawea is a famously good fishery). The grassy terrain is dotted with exotic trees which signal a particularly attractive pitch or park for the van. The picnic shelter has interesting interpretive displays, and there are flush toilets alongside. The water is drinkable and you can stoke up a fire in the pits of an evening.

Kidds Bush campground

MAKE A BEELINE FOR THE BUSHLINE

The walk to Sawyer Burn Hut starts from the campground and takes about five hours return. It's a good old huff and puff up the zig-zags through mountain beech forest until you reach the bushline (about an hour and a half one way). Payback time! The views south over Lake Hawea are stupendous. The old station hut — about another hour up — is your turning point. Hardcore trampers, however, may carry on upwards along an unmarked route to Sentinel Peak (1814 m), a foot-bruising nine to twelve hours return from the campground. Meanwhile, back at the ranch, the less intrepid of us will be taking the flatter alternative, the eastward wander along the road through the lowland forest to Sawyer Burn. From the burn, follow the stream down to the lake at Bushy Point and head back to camp along the beach (one and a half hours return).

EXPERIENCE SIBERIA

At 355,543 ha, Mount Aspiring National Park is our third largest national park and forms part of Te Wahipounamu — the South West New Zealand World Heritage Area. Well deserving of its status as one of the world's places of 'outstanding universal value', its rugged beauty may well bring a tear to your eye. An action-packed way to get into the thick of things without having to embark on a multi-day tramp is on the Siberia Experience. This half-day adventure takes off with a 25-minute scenic flight over the mountains, landing in the remote Siberia Valley. From there it's a three-hour walk through river valleys and forest before meeting up with a jet boat for the homeward leg. Now that's a grand day out! Tel 03 443 4385, www.siberiaexperience.co.nz.

WISH YOU LIVED IN WANAKA

Sitting on the edge of a very pretty lake and surrounded by mountains, the township of Wanaka has an enviable setting. And it's been having a bit of a growth spurt: in the last eight years its population has more than doubled — from 3300 in 2001 to over 7000 in 2008 — and that's not counting the year-round influx of visitors (including a mountain of skiers in winter). But despite lots of new houses and associated urban development, Wanaka manages to retain a certain small-town charm, making it a decidedly pleasant place to hang out. To get it in your sights, take a walk up the rocky knoll of Mount Iron (240 m). From the summit you'll get 360-degree views of the Pisa Range, Clutha Basin, Lake Wanaka and the Alps. Who wouldn't want to live here?

Manuherikia Road (State Highway 85), Alexandra

Contact
03 448 8297
www.alexandraholidaypark.com

Capacity
100 unpowered / 400 powered

Open
all year

Bookings
recommended peak season

Price
from $27 two adults

ABOVE: The view from Flat Top Hill
RIGHT: The Otago Central Rail Trail

Not far from its source at Lake Wanaka, the mighty Clutha River is interrupted by the long, damn-flooded channel of Lake Dunstan, on the shores of which lie Cromwell and Clyde. A little further on, where the Clutha resumes, is Alexandra, which makes up this close trio of towns in the heart of Central Otago. Originally settled in the rush to find gold, this bountiful area is now better known for some mighty fine stone fruit, merino wool and pinot noir. It also has excellent weather — long, dry summers, entirely conducive to camping, but alas: good camping is surprisingly hard to find.

It is Alexandra which comes to the party. With by far the largest population of the three towns (at around 4600), Alex offers a wide range of services and a good concentration of attractions — including the remains of the old bridge over the Clutha, the Shaky Bridge, historic buildings and a museum. It also has the 'clock on the hill', the iconic (and practical) monument which landmarks the town in much the same fashion as the Hollywood sign over LA. (There ending any similarity, of course.)

The town sits at the junction of the Clutha and Manuherikia rivers, and it is just upriver on the latter where you will find the great, big Alexandra Holiday Park. Right on State Highway 85, the somewhat austere entranceway promises little, and once you've pulled up at the office you may well still be unsure. But don't be fooled: besides some satisfactory, shady rows for powered vans, there is a tenters' delight hidden in here.

The campsite is believed to be more than 60 years old, and this is evident in the mature trees and well-settled landscaping. The camp slopes down from the road to the river, rambling over numerous terraces. Well away from the caravan sites and amenities block at the top is a small, flat field with plenty of dry pitching and shade under a border of mature willow. The river runs enticingly by — clean and good for a dip, with rocky outcrops above for sunning yourself. And shine the sun does on this spot . . . late into the summer evening.

This is a family holiday park and the facilities are appropriately utilitarian. The amenities blocks are breeze block all over, but are clean, functional and full of useful appliances. There's internet access in the lounge. Owner Janice boasts of their famously good showers, which will be welcomed by those coated in a layer of sweat and Central Otago dust. There are cabins for when it rains (hardly ever) and the camp shop is open in peak season.

The centre of Alexandra can be reached by bicycle along the riverbank and those keen on a longer trip can cycle all the way to Clyde along one side of the river and back the other on the Centennial Walkway between the two towns. It's a lovely ride.

SARAH BENNETT AND LEE SLATER

CYCLE THE OTAGO CENTRAL RAIL TRAIL

This now-famous trail passes through Alexandra on its way between Clyde (8 km northwest) and Middlemarch — a total journey of 150 km, usually completed in three to five days (www.otagocentralrailtrail.co.nz). Some of the most spectacular scenery lies around the Alexandra end of the line, and a relatively easy day ride starts at Auripo (10 km east of Lauder) and finishes at Clyde, 55 km away. This section gives you a great taste of the whole journey, taking you through tunnels, over viaducts and past tiny little settlements boasting tearooms and pubs. You can cut it short at Alexandra (making it 47 km from Auripo) — although you'll miss the Clyde pub. This outing (and longer trips) can easily be organised with Altitude Adventures (www.altitudeadventures.co.nz, tel 03 448 8917), who offer freedom hire and drop-offs, as well as all sorts of guided rides around Central Otago, one of New Zealand's best mountain biking regions.

TASTE SOME WINE WITH ALTITUDE

Central Otago is New Zealand's highest and the world's most southerly winemaking region. Recognised as a potentially stellar grape-growing area by Italian viticulturalist Romeo Bragato, who visited in the late nineteenth century, it wasn't until around the new millennium that the region's winemaking reputation went stratospheric. The star is pinot noir, although there is some excellent chardonnay and riesling, too. Around 40 wineries are spread from Wanaka down to Alexandra and through to Lake Hayes, just shy of Queenstown, with most around Bannockburn and Cromwell, and the Gibbston Valley. Pick up a wine map from the Alexandra i-SITE, then draw straws to see who's designated driver. Bottoms up!

WALK FLAT TOP HILL

Flat Top is a major landmark of a conservation reserve set aside in 1992 to protect one of New Zealand's most threatened ecosystems: the dry, tussocky grasslands with their rare plant species. A two-hour loop ambles around this interesting landscape, with good displays on the area's natural and goldmining history. The walk begins by crossing Butcher's Dam, then heads up onto the mesa — the isolated flat-top hill formed by the uplift of horizontal layers of metamorphic schist. From the top there are wide-ranging views of the surrounding area: the Alexandra basin, down the gorge and serpentine Lake Roxburgh towards Alexandra and out west to the Old Man Range. To get there from Alexandra, take State Highway 8 south across the bridge and then drive south for about 8 km. Turn left onto the gravel road when you see the dam.

Skippers Road, off Coronet Peak Road, north of Queenstown

Contact
DOC Visitor Centre
Queenstown
03 442 7935
www.doc.govt.nz

Capacity
36 unpowered

Open
all year, road often impassable in winter

Bookings
not required

Price
$7 adult / $3.50 child

SARAH BENNETT AND LEE SLATER

Heaven forbid that any visitor to Queenstown should get so caught up in its honeytrap of ski fields, gondola, shops, restaurants and the like that they fail to find what the town's really about. The flashy jewel in the tourist crown it may well be, but it's the back-of-beyond attractions that make the Wakatipu area so special. An area of significant historical interest and monumental beauty, there is much to be discovered by the inquisitive traveller.

One of the most exciting and intrepid journeys that can be made in these parts is the drive into Skippers Canyon. A drive, you say? How intrepid can that be? Well, the answer is *very*. The Skippers Road is the stuff of legends, most of them probably true.

Located within the 9100 ha Mount Aurum Recreation Reserve, Skippers Canyon campground is 26 km from Queenstown, of which 17 are unsealed, most cut into the steep schist cliffs high above the tumbling Shotover River. It's a dramatic drive, windy and steep with precipitous drop-offs around many a corner, and particularly challenging in the wet. It should be attempted only by experienced drivers; as DOC says, 'this is not a road on which to learn gravel-driving techniques'. From Queenstown, the drive to Mount Aurum Recreation Reserve will take a good hour and a half in ideal conditions.

Back in 1862, the rugged and remote Shotover River was the scene of a feverish gold rush after Irishman Malcolm 'Skipper' Duncan struck some colour. Within weeks some lucky souls had made their fortune, including two Taranaki Maori who panned 300 ounces in one afternoon — worth around $460,000 today. However, the gold soon dwindled, and just one year later the get-rich-quick population of up to 700 was already starting its inevitable decline. By the late 1860s it was down to a few hundred stayers; the last few left in the 1940s. The miners were outlasted by a succession of Mount Aurum Station runholders, who had settled in the area about the same time as the gold rush. The station eventually became a reserve, in 1985.

Within the reserve are the ghostly remains of the major Shotover settlement, Skippers Township, situated on several terraces cut improbably into the steep-sided gorge. Here DOC and volunteer groups have done an admirable job of restoring both the Skippers School (built 1879, restored 1992, peak roll 35) and, next door, the Mount Aurum Homestead (built circa 1860, restored 1995). You can camp right next to these two historic buildings, upon the lush grassy glade that surrounds them. Across the valley, the Harris Mountains and the twin peaks of Vanguard (1780 m) and Advance (1749 m) make for an awe-inspiring outlook.

The facilities are reasonably new and include flush toilets, a washing-up basin, a day shelter and refreshing drinking water.

WEAR DOWN YOUR BATTERIES
ON THE DYNAMO FLAT TRACK

This day-walk starts five minutes from the campground, just past the ruins of the old hotel. Built in 1863, the machinery of the Phoenix mine at Bullendale (north of Skippers Township) was originally powered by water. However, 22 years later it was converted to electric power with the installation of two dynamos — the very first industrial use of hydroelectric power in New Zealand. It's a five- to six-hour return walk to Bullendale along Skippers Creek, which you must cross on numerous occasions, so be prepared to get your feet wet. Remains of the power plant's machinery can be seen on a two-hour side trip up the left branch of the creek. Interpretive displays will leave you in no doubt as to the significance of this important industrial archaeology site.

GO FOR GOLD IN THE ARROW RIVER

The era of the pioneering gold miners is one of the most colourful in this country's short history, and one that left an indelible mark on both the landscape and people. Go to Arrowtown to rediscover these stories and even try your hand at panning (hire pans from the visitor centre — good luck!). The town has a fine collection of heritage buildings, while along the riverbank is the partially restored Chinese diggers settlement with its humble dwellings and evocative information displays. The Lakes District Museum (tel 03 442 1824, www.museumqueenstown.com) retells the stories of the area, from Maori exploration to today.

EXPLORE THE HISTORY
OF SKIPPERS

Many fascinating relics from Skippers' gold-rush era are dotted around within walking distance of the camp. Next to the campground, the schoolhouse and homestead are excellent places to start your explorations. Full of artefacts and information displays, they provide a vivid insight into the lives of those who lived and worked around here. Back along the road is Skippers Point cemetery, where worn headstones and to-the-point epitaphs keep their own silent record. Further along the road you'll find the ruins of Johnston's Otago Hotel, the town's only pub. Finally, no trip to Skippers would be complete without a walk across the magnificent suspension bridge. Built in 1901 and considered one of this country's most important heritage bridges, it spans almost 100 m across the river. And it's a long, long way down to the water . . . although you might not want to look.

FAR LEFT: Skippers campsite
LEFT: Skippers Canyon

DOC

Kinloch Road,
26 km from Glenorchy,
71 km from Queenstown

Contact
DOC Visitor Centre
Queenstown
03 442 7935
www.doc.govt.nz

Capacity
20 unpowered

Open
all year

Bookings
not required

Price
$7 adult / $3.50 child

The defining
feature of this small
campground is its
humbling mountain
views. Peaks tower
above you in every
direction.

If you keep driving through Queenstown and out the other side, you'll find yourself on the road to Glenorchy — the so-called 'Gateway to Paradise'. The drive there ain't bad either, sidling along the edge of Lake Wakatipu, with gob-smacking views all the way.

Glenorchy is the larger of two small settlements at the north end of the lake, nestled into a rugged high-country landscape of mountain ranges, ancient beech forest and two glacier-fed rivers: the Rees and the Dart. Paradise itself is 20 km away, a historic property with a dilapidated guesthouse. Built in 1883, the guesthouse is lined up for restoration by a group of locals under the supervision of the Historic Places Trust.

Dilapidated guesthouses notwithstanding, Glenorchy and Kinloch, on the other side of the Rees–Dart delta, are undoubtedly the gateway to paradise in the literal sense of the word. Located less than 20 km from the boundaries of both the Fiordland and Mount Aspiring national parks, they serve many of the travellers venturing into this great wilderness. Indeed, three of New Zealand's most famous tramps can be accessed from here (see page 197).

There is a pleasant commercial camp at Glenorchy, which has powered-up amenities and family-friendly activities close by. However, if you're after that 'end of the line' feel, keep going to Kinloch — only a few kilometres away as the crow flies, but 26 km by road, across both the rivers. There is little at the settlement save for the welcoming Kinloch Lodge (tel 03 442 4900, www. kinlochlodge.co.nz), which has a range of comfortable rooms, homely communal areas and a restaurant-cum-bar. There is also a simple DOC campground right across the road on the lakeshore.

The defining feature of this small campground is its humbling mountain views. Peaks tower above you in every direction — the Humbolts to the west, the Richardsons to the east, and to the north the solitary mass of Mount Alfred standing sentinel over the Dart Valley. Laid out in front is an expanse of lake, in which swimming and fishing can be enjoyed (although pay attention to the conditions: the waters may look pretty serene but strong currents from the river can be dangerous).

Camping ranges along the lakeside strip, on fairly uneven but grassy terrain. There are plenty of picnic tables, fire pits, long-drop toilets and a water spigot. And that's where the facilities stop . . . at least if it weren't for the camp's proximity to Kinloch Lodge. Not only is their restaurant open to non-residents, for $5 you can partake of a hot shower. And for $10 you can have a hot-tub, if they're not too busy.

A hot-tub, a beer and a home-cooked meal, followed by a warming fire under the stars: the best of both worlds.

EXPERIENCE THE MAGIC OF MIDDLE EARTH

The dramatic scenery around the head of Lake Wakatipu has caught many a filmmaker's eye, the area's film credits including *The Lord of the Rings trilogy*, The *Chronicles of Narnia*, *The Lovely Bones* and *X-Men*. Based in Glenorchy, Dart Stables (tel 03 442 5688, www.dartstables.com) offers guided horse treks across the Dart and Rees delta flats and past *LOTR* set locations such as Lothlórien, Amon Hen and the Golden Mile. Treks range from a one-and-a-half-hour Ride of the Rings tour to a two-day ride where you get to stay overnight in wood cabins among the untouched beech forest of Paradise. Riders of all abilities are welcome. Don't forget to bring your camera!

DART UP THE VALLEY

Dart River Jet Safaris runs a mind-blowing trip up the beautiful braided Dart River, deep into Mount Aspiring National Park. The scenery is unforgettable, particularly once you get into the thick of the glacial mountain terrain: the impressive peak of Mount Earnslaw / Pikirakatahi (2830 m) is a high-light. Their three-hour trip is the longest jet boat ride in the region, but while you're at it you may as well opt for one of their multi-tours: combine your boat ride with a guided walk and a scenic four-wheel-drive trip, or a float down the river in an inflatable kayak. Pick-ups are available from Kinloch or Glenorchy (tel 03 442 9992, www.dartriver.co.nz).

DART RIVER JET SAFARIS

WALK IN SPLENDOUR

Kinloch makes for easy access to the Routeburn, Caples and Greenstone tracks, three deservedly popular routes that link Lake Wakatipu with Fiordland National Park. The Routeburn (32 km, two to three days), starting 18 km north of the campground, is synonymous with dramatic alpine scenery and accordingly involves some serious uphill work. However, a fine day walk — without *excessive* elevation change — can be had by walking in as far as the Routeburn Falls Hut (six to seven hours return), where you'll be rewarded with fine views back down the valley. More sedate walking can be had on the flatter and less travelled Greenstone (36 km, two to three days) and Caples (27 km, two days) tracks, beginning 12 km south of Kinloch at the end of the Greenstone Station Road. Following river valleys, the views are less expansive but impressive nonetheless. A good daytrip option is to walk in as far as the gorge just shy of the Mid Caples Hut (five to six hours return).

Powering up the Dart River

NORTH AND CENTRAL OTAGO

ALEXANDRA TOURIST PARK
31 Ngapara Street, Alexandra

Contact: 03 448 8861
alex.touristpark@xtra.co.nz

Tariff: $24–95

CLYDE HOLIDAY AND SPORTING COMPLEX
Whitby Street, Clyde

Contact: 03 449 2713
crrc@ihug.co.nz

Tariff: $26–40

CROMWELL TOP 10 HOLIDAY PARK
1 Alpha Street, Cromwell

Contact: 03 445 0164
www.cromwellholidaypark.co.nz

Tariff: $34–115

DANSEY'S PASS HOLIDAY PARK
Dansey's Pass Road, 45 km west of Oamaru, 15 km south of Duntroon (Waitaki Valley)

Contact: 03 431 2564
office@danseyspass.com
www.danseyspassholidaypark.co.nz

Tariff: $28–90

ETTRICK HOLIDAY PARK
7 James Street, off SH 8, Central Otago

Contact: 03 446 6600

Tariff: $20–30

KUROW HOLIDAY PARK
76 Bledisloe Street, Kurow, North Otago

Contact: 03 436 0725
kurowholidaypark@clear.net.nz
www.nz-holiday.co.nz/kurow

Tariff: $26–70

LARCHVIEW HOLIDAY PARK
8 Swimming Dam Road, Naseby

Contact: 03 444 9904
bookings@larchviewholidaypark.co.nz
www.larchviewholidaypark.co.nz

Tariff: $23–70

MILLERS FLAT HOLIDAY PARK
Teviot Road, Millers Flat, Central Otago

Contact: 03 446 6877
millers_flat_holiday_park@xtra.co.nz,
www.millersflat.co.nz

Tariff: $20–75

OAMARU TOP 10 HOLIDAY PARK
Chelmer Street, Oamaru

Contact: 03 434 7666
oamarutop10@xtra.co.nz
www.top10.co.nz/parks/oamaru-holiday-park

Tariff: $30–130

OMARAMA TOP 10 HOLIDAY PARK
Junction SH 8 and SH 83, Omarama

Contact: 03 438 9875
omarama.holiday@xtra.co.nz
www.omaramatop10.co.nz

Tariff: $30–125

OTEMATATA HOLIDAY PARK
East Road, Otematata, Waitaki Valley

Contact: 03 438 7826
otem.camp@xtra.co.nz

Tariff: $30–44

ROXBURGH'S TEVIOT COUNTRY MOTELS AND BACKPACKERS
141 Roxburgh East Road (over Clutha River bridge, turn left), Roxburgh, Otago

Contact: 03 446 8364
teviotmotels@xtra.co.nz

THE CHALETS HOLIDAY PARK
102 Barry Ave, Cromwell

Contact: 03 445 1260
thechalets@xtra.co.nz
www.thechalets.co.nz

Tariff: $28–110

SOUTHERN LAKES

ARROWTOWN BORN OF GOLD HOLIDAY PARK
12 Centennial Avenue, Arrowtown

Contact: 03 442 1876
arrowtownpark@qldc.govt.nz
www.arrowtownholidaypark.co.nz

Tariff: $16–130

ASPIRING CAMPERVAN PARK
263 Studholme Road North, Wanaka

Contact: 03 443 6603
www.campervanpark.co.nz

Tariff: enquire for tariff

FRANKTON MOTOR CAMP
Yewlett Crescent, Frankton, Queenstown

Conact: 03 442 2079

Tariff: $20–80

GLENDHU BAY MOTOR CAMP
Wanaka–Mount Aspiring Road, Glendhu Bay, Wanaka

Contact: 03 443 7243
glendhucamp@xtra.co.nz
www.glendhubaymotorcamp.co.nz

Tariff: $26–40

GLENORCHY HOLIDAY PARK AND INFORMATION CENTRE
Oban Street, Glenorchy

Contact: 03 441 0303

KINGSTON MOTELS AND HOLIDAY PARK
Kent Street, Kingston

Contact: 03 248 8501
stay@kingstonmotels.co.nz
www.kingstonmotels.co.nz

Tariff: $24–129

LAKE HAWEA HOLIDAY PARK
SH 6, Lake Hawea

Contact: 03 443 1767
office@haweaholidaypark.co.nz
www.haweaholidaypark.co.nz

Tariff: $28–110

LAKE OUTLET HOLIDAY PARK
Lake Outlet Road, Lake Wanaka

Contact: 03 443 7478
info@lakeoutlet.co.nz
www.lakeoutlet.co.nz

Tariff: $24–45

QUEENSTOWN LAKEVIEW HOLIDAY PARK
Upper Brecon Street, Queenstown

Contact: 03 442 7252
holidaypark@qldc.govt.nz
www.holidaypark.net.nz

Tariff: $18–160

SHOTOVER TOP 10 HOLIDAY PARK
70 Arthurs Point Road, Queenstown

Contact: 03 442 9306
stay@shotoverholidaypark.co.nz
www.shotoverholidaypark.co.nz

Tariff: $32–125

WANAKA LAKEVIEW HOLIDAY PARK
212 Brownston Street, Wanaka

Contact: 03 443 7883
wanakalakeview@xtra.co.nz
www.wanakalakeview.co.nz

Tariff: $30–89

WANAKA TOP 10 HOLIDAY PARK
217 Mount Aspiring Road, Wanaka

Contact: 03 443 7360
www.wanakatop10.co.nz

Tariff: $40–110

DUNEDIN, SOUTH AND COASTAL OTAGO

BALCLUTHA MOTOR CAMP
56 Charlotte Street, Naish Park, Balclutha

Contact: 03 418 0088
balcluthacamp@xtra.co.nz

Tariff: Please enquire for tariff

DUNEDIN HOLIDAY PARK
41 Victoria Road, St Kilda, Dunedin

Contact: 03 455 4690
www.dunedinholidaypark.co.nz

Tariff: $21–110

**KAITANGATA RIVERSIDE
MOTOR CAMP**
20 Water Street, Kaitangata
9210, South Otago

Contact: 03 413 9219
ithaca11@hotmail.com

Tariff: $22–25

**KAKA POINT
CAMPING GROUND**
39 Tarata Street,
Kaka Point

Contact: 03 412 8801
kakapoint@hotmail.com

Tariff: $25–44

LAKE WAIHOLA HOLIDAY PARK
Waihola Domain (off SH 1),
Waihola, Otago

Contact: 03 417 8908
lakewaiholaholidaypark@xtra.co.nz
www.holidayparknz.co.nz

Tariff: $20–50

LEITH VALLEY TOURING PARK
103 Malvern Street, Dunedin

Contact: 03 467 9936
lvtpdun@xtra.co.nz
www.leithvalleytouringpark.co.nz

Tariff: $32–109

POHUTUKAWA MOTORPARK
10 Albion Street, Lumsden

Contact: 03 248 7090

Tariff: $26–70

SINCLAIR WETLANDS
Clarendon/Berwick Road, SH 1,
Waihola (south of Dunedin)

Contact: 03 486 2654

Tariff: $16–30

PENGUIN PLACE LODGE
Harington Point Road,
RD 2, Dunedin

Contact: 03 478 0286

Tariff: $25

**WAIKOUAITI BEACH
MOTOR CAMP**
186 Beach Street,
Waikouaiti

Contact: 03 465 7432

Tariff: $18–40

→ LET'S GO CAMPING IN
FIORDLAND AND SOUTHLAND

**52 km from Mossburn
(via Centre Hill Road);
66 km from Te Anau
(via Mavora Lakes Road)**

Contact
DOC Te Anau
03 249 7924
www.doc.govt.nz.

Capacity
60 unpowered

Open
all year

Bookings
not required

Price
$5 adult / $2.50 child

Cloaked in beech, the valley walls pitch steeply skyward, terminating in a range of rocky peaks which contrast starkly against the gently undulating blanket of golden grassland on the valley floor. This is a truly magnificent landscape, one in which it feels a privilege to park up.

Is this the Holy Grail of accessible wilderness camping in New Zealand? We think it may be. It's certainly one our favourites — and one of DOC's finest.

The Mavora Lakes Park lies within Te Wahipounamu South West New Zealand World Heritage Area. It feels remote, but a look at the map will reveal that, as the crow flies, it's in the thick of the action, being reasonably close to the tourist magnets of Queenstown, Te Anau and the Milford Road. But a combination of a slow, gravelled access road (the last 35 km or so are unsealed) and sparse facilities mean that only the eager venture in — those woolly types, content just to go for a bit of a tramp or simply fold out the camping chair and sit and contemplate nature in all its glory.

The park is centered around two lakes, South Mavora and North Mavora, which lie in a narrow, glacial valley. A beautiful sight to behold, the lakes are bounded by wetland and connected by the Mararoa River. Cloaked in beech, the valley walls pitch steeply skyward, terminating in a range of rocky peaks which contrast starkly against the gently undulating blanket of golden grassland on the valley floor. This is a truly magnificent landscape, one in which it feels a privilege to park up.

Mavora's large, grassy meadow offers countless options for a winning site, whether out in the open or along the edges of the forest, river or lake. On the access road skirting South Mavora are several pull-over nooks offering absolute lakeside camping with trees for shelter and privacy. Although this is a popular camping area in the summer, you shouldn't have any trouble finding space to yourself.

Long-drop toilets are dotted all over, and there are plenty of water spigots and picnic benches. Don't forget cash for your self-registration envelope and bags for your rubbish. Equally important is your insect repellent: the Mavora sandflies rate eight out of ten on the nibble-ometer.

The *Mavora Lakes Park* pamphlet can be downloaded from DOC's website or picked up at one of their local offices, and you'll find a ranger in residence during busy periods.

WALK, OF COURSE

Day-walkers will find enough track here to keep them busy for several days. The obligatory trip is an easy, three-hour circuit of South Mavora Lake. On the western edge of the lake the track passes through mature beech forest, while on the eastern side it traverses largely grassy flats and the well-graded Mavora Road. There are two springy swing bridges to cross, views galore and all sorts of birds — from honking flocks of waterbirds amid the marsh to forest flitters with their sweet, warbling songs. Another opportunity to soak up the grandeur is the Mavora–Greenstone Walkway. Finishing four days (and 50 km) away at Lake Wakatipu, you can walk in just as far as you like and come back out again — a good day's walk is to Boundary Hut and back. From the campground, it'll take you about two hours to reach the top of Hikurangi (North Mavora Lake), where the track splits. The right fork marks the start of the Mavora–Greenstone Walkway: follow this along the Mararoa River to DOC's Boundary Hut, about two hours away.

INDULGE IN OUTDOOR PURSUITS

Here you can do things you're not allowed to do in the national parks and many other reserves. For a starter, Mavora's track network allows mountain biking, motor biking and four-wheel-driving, as indicated on signage and in DOC's *Mavora Lakes Park* brochure. (Mountain bikers and four-wheel-drivers can use the walkway as far as Boundary Hut.) Horses are also welcome, and can be tethered in a paddock by North Mavora Lake. Boats are permitted on both lakes and in the Mararoa River — small motorised craft on North Mavora, unpowered only on South. Trout will no doubt be awaiting your attention. You can bring your dog too, if you keep the fella under control at all times.

PARK UP AND RELAX

This is an area of such hypnotic beauty that you may find the hours just float quietly by, punctuated only by the flappety fly-over of some waterbird, or the need to boil the billy for a cup of tea. Lie on a blanket and get your book out. Lift your eyes now and then to take in the view. At dusk approaches, crack open a bottle and watch the last of the sun's rays illuminate the Thomson Mountains in an ever-changing mellow wash of colour. Oh, wondrous Mother Nature. (Obviously this suggestion applies only in good weather . . .)

SARAH BENNETT AND LEE SLATER

PREVIOUS PAGE: Luxmore Hut on the Kepler Track, looking out over Lake Te Anau
ABOVE: Looking north up South Mavora Lake, with the Thomson Mountains in the distance beyond North Mavora

Milford Road, Te Anau to Milford Sound (119 km)

Contact
DOC Te Anau
03 249 7924
www.doc.govt.nz

Capacity
Deer Flat: 20 unpowered;
Totara: 10 unpowered;
Mackay Creek: 6 unpowered

Open
all year

Bookings
not required

Price
$7 adult / $3.50 child

ABOVE: View from Mackay Creek campground
RIGHT: Mount Christina from Key Summit, Routeburn Track

Designated a World Heritage Area in 1990, Fiordland National Park is not only the largest park in New Zealand, but one of the largest in the world.

Such a vast and remote wilderness, almost completely uninhabited, it is hardly surprising that Fiordland is so ecologically important. A diversity of habitats allows a profusion of different plants to flourish here — more than 700 of them endemic to the area. It's also home to some of our rarest birds, including the takahe. Thought to be extinct from the late 1800s, a small colony holed up in the Murchison Mountains managed to evade detection for the next 50 years until found by Dr Geoffrey Orbell and his companions. The colony remains there still: at one time it reached a peak of 150 birds, but suffered a steep decline to around 100 after a particularly savage stoat raid in 2007.

The furrowed topography of Fiordland National Park means that the average camper will only be able to skirt around its edges, largely in the east where access roads grant some degree of penetration into the wilds. The most well-beaten paths are the park's renowned tracks — the Milford, Kepler, Routeburn, Hollyford, Dusky and the newer Hump Ridge Track, accessed further south.

The road from Te Anau to Milford Sound is the most popular route into the park, skirting first along the side of Lake Te Anau (the South Island's largest lake), before following the Eglinton River Valley as far as The Divide, where the road forks. Most travellers carry on to Milford Sound itself after squeezing through the improbable Homer Tunnel, while others head down the Hollyford Valley (see page 207).

Along the Milford Road's 119 km length are dotted 11 DOC campsites, all of which are virtually on the roadside. In terms of facilities they are all much of a muchness — long-drop toilets, stream water supply, the odd picnic table and some fire pits.

Lying auspiciously at precisely 45 degrees south latitude, our pick of this bunch is Deer Flat — 62 km from Te Anau, about halfway to Milford Sound. This is the largest and most open campsite, and also the furthest from the road. Pitching can be had either on the open, grassy flat or alongside the shelter of riverside beech trees. The river snakes its way through the valley, flanked by the Earl Mountains to the west and the Livingtones to the east. It's an enchanting scene indeed, sandflies notwithstanding, and the lupin bloom in high summer is nigh-on psychedelic.

Of the other campgrounds, we would opt for one of two lying close together: Totara or Mackay Creek. The latter is more open, with expansive views up the valley, while Totara has spectacular bluff views and offers more shelter.

DRIVE THE WORLD HERITAGE HIGHWAY

The journey between Te Anau and Milford Sound will mesmerise you with its profound beauty, from epic lake to valley low, mountain high and beyond to the magical sound itself. Start your adventure at Te Anau DOC visitor centre where you can learn about the national park's unique flora, fauna, natural and human history, and pick up any maps and guides (and leave your intentions, if you're off for a tramp). Covering 1.26 million hectares — nearly five per cent of New Zealand's land area — this massive, mostly untouched wilderness is marked by deep fiords and lakes, rugged and often snow-dusted mountains, sheer cliffs, tussock grasslands and thick forest.

Once you're on your way you'll pass many worthy stopping points, all well signposted and some with trailheads. Te Anau Downs, Mirror Lakes and Lake Gunn are recommended places to pull over: short walks can be taken at all of them. Once you've passed through the 1200 m Homer Tunnel, be sure to visit The Chasm, an impressive series of cascades and water-sculpted basins. While you're there keep an eye out for Mount Tutoko — Fiordland's highest mountain at 2723 m — peeking from behind the clouds. Impressed? Just wait until you get round the corner . . . the sound awaits.

PHOTONEWZEALAND / COLIN MONTEATH, HEDGEHOG HOUSE

SEE IT FROM ON HIGH

From The Divide (at one end of the Routeburn Track), the path to Key Summit is a gentle but steady 90-minute climb through interesting flora to a remarkable lookout. Starting off in typical silver beech forest, the trees give way at the bushline to mountain flax, snow totara and the prehistoric-looking *Dracophyllum* (Latin for 'dragon-leaf'), while at the top is a strange forest of stunted beech. From the summit, the 360-degree views rival those of Milford: on a good day you'll see the Hollyford Valley to the north, the Eglington to the south, Greenstone to the east and to the west the impressive Lake Marian basin with pyramidal Mount Christina (2474 m) behind. DOC has kindly established an informative interpretive walk around the rocky tops, alpine tarns and sphagnum bogs so you can find out for yourself why this place is so amazing and how it became so.

77 Manapouri–Te Anau Highway, 1 km south of Te Anau town centre

Contact
03 249 7457
www.teanauholidaypark.co.nz

Capacity
100 unpowered / 150 powered

Open
all year

Bookings
recommended peak season

Price
$15 adult / $10 child unpowered;
$17.50 adult / $10 child powered

TE ANAU LAKEVIEW HOLIDAY PARK / CLINT TAURI

Lake Te Anau is the South Island's largest lake, up to 400 m deep in some places. It is surrounded by mountain ranges: to the north and west the rugged mountains of Fiordland, to the south the Takitimus, and to the east the Livingstone Mountains, on the other side of which lie the Mavora Lakes (see page 204). The township on its shore is both pretty and practical, well set up for the visitors who flock to Fiordland to see and experience its natural wonders, including Milford and Doubtful sounds, and the myriad marvels of its walking tracks (the Milford, Kepler, Routeburn, Hollyford, Dusky and Hump Ridge).

No doubt about it: Te Anau is an excellent base from which to explore Fiordland, placing you right in the thick of the action. And with the comforts of hot showers, excellent communal areas and close proximity to the town's hospitality, Te Anau Holiday Park is an absolute winner — the best of the town's campgrounds and a top-notch holiday park full stop.

A 10-minute lakeside stroll from the township, the campground occupies extensive, park-like grounds, much of which command inspiring views of the lake and the Jackson Peaks beyond. It is heavily visited by campervanners, who will enjoy the sites at both the front (lake views) and the back of the park. However, as tempting as it may be for tenters and unpowered vanners to park up near the front in one of several allocated areas, we suggest you opt for a pitch out the back. The road between Te Anau and Manapouri is very busy in summer, and unless you want to bring your earplugs, you may find the views aren't worth the vroom-vroom-vroom.

There are several amenities blocks, the biggest and best of which is more or less in the middle of the park. It's fresh, flash and genius. The stylish building features two spacious kitchen wings which fly off in either direction, while in the centre front — with floor-to-ceiling windows taking in the lake views — is a comfortable dining room and lounge. Warm, bright, clean and cheerful, it has a big-screen television down one end, computer terminals down the other and Wi-Fi for those with their own computer.

Besides all the other usual facilities (which include, we must add, divine power showers), there are many bonuses including barbecues, a sauna and a range of wet-weather accommodation options, including a backpackers' lodge, cabins and motel rooms.

Staff will not only arrange transport and tour options via the affiliated Tracknet bus service (www.tracknet.net), but can also store your car while you're away. So, you've got no excuse: get out there. Go hard and get wet, sweaty, dirty and tired . . . because when you get back, the shower is going to be blissful, and that hot meal and a beer are only 10 minutes' walk away.

REAL JOURNEYS

HEAD UNDERGROUND
TO SEE THE GLOW WORMS

The name Te Anau is probably a shortened form of Te Ana-au, the Maori name which translates as 'caves with a current of swirling water'. The caves in question were lost in the mists of time until 1948 when, after an epic three-year search, they were rediscovered by local explorer Lawson Burrows. Under the Murchison Mountains, on the isolated western shore of the lake, Burrows found a stream emerging from under a rock. He swam through the watery entrance and surfaced into a cavern twinkling with a city of glow worms. Imagine that! Well, you can do better than that by taking a tour with Real Journeys (tel 03 249 7416, www.realjourneys.co.nz) — they'll take you into this mysterious subterranean land of whirlpools, waterfalls, fossils, crazy rock formations and glow worms, of course. Tours depart from the Te Anau wharf on a fancy catamaran called *Luminosa*.

TREK A LITTLE KEPLER

Opened in 1988 to relieve pressure on the crowded Milford Track, the Kepler Track soon became a classic in its own right. Its appeal lies in its diversity: in the three to four days it takes to complete the 67 km circuit, the track passes through lowland beech forest, along the edge of two mighty lakes, through alpine meadows and across high mountain tops. You can get a taste of the Kepler from the Lake Te Anau control gates, from where it's a three-hour-return walk to Brod Bay: an ideal spot for a picnic or a brisk dip in the lake. The energetic may wish to continue onwards and upwards to Luxmore Hut, which offers amazing views down the lake and across to the multifarious peaks of the Livingstone, Eyre and Takitimu mountains (eight to ten hours return).

CRUISE DOUBTFUL SOUND

When Captain Cook eyed up this waterway in 1770 he decided not to venture in as he was 'doubtful' that the winds in the sound would be sufficient to blow the *Endeavour* back out again. (Boy, did he miss out.) Doubtful it may have been, but what we now know for sure is that it's three times as long and ten times larger than the better known Milford Sound, and arguably the more impressive of the two. Accessible only on a boat tour, its remoteness makes it all the more alluring. The sound is reached by first boating across Lake Manapouri — around 20 minutes' drive from Te Anau — then jumping on a bus for a scenic 22 km drive along the Wilmot Pass road. Your tour proper starts at Deep Cove, 32 km from the Tasman Sea. Stunning vistas of towering peaks chiselled by ice, hanging valleys, dense forest and lofty waterfalls await you. Keep an eye out for bottlenose dolphins and penguins too. There are several operators based around Manapouri or Te Anau; you can't really miss them, but if you do, the visitor centre will be only too pleased to help.

FAR LEFT: Te Anau Lakeview Holiday Park
ABOVE: Te Anau glow-worm caves

**Te Waewae Bay,
25 km west of Riverton**

Contact
For infomation call Tuatapere
Information Centre 03 226 6739

Open
all year

Bookings
not required

Price
free

Let's just get this straight: you won't actually be camping on the island and the nearest monkey is probably at the Orana Wildlife Park in Christchurch.

Beautiful and sheltered campgrounds along the mainland's southernmost coast are few and far between. Considerate locals appear to have realised this, their generous response being to allow visitors to camp on private land at Monkey Island, just off State Highway 99, almost right at the bottom of New Zealand. But let's just get this straight: you won't actually be camping *on* the island and the nearest monkey is probably at the Orana Wildlife Park in Christchurch.

Just off the beach and accessible only at low tide (if you want to keep your feet dry, at least), Monkey Island is little more than a rocky outcrop. Maori legend accounts for it as the anchor stone of the great voyaging waka Takitimu, which was said to have been wrecked on the bar of the Waiau River. Te Puka o Takitimu, as it was therefore known, was frequented by a small, hardy iwi who used it as a lookout for whales and a launching place for their fishing waka.

Although there's little evidence of it today, a European settlement existed here too, in the late 1800s. In the days before the road from Riverton reached here, supplies came in by boat, unloaded via a slipway on the island. The name Monkey Island is thought to originate from the monkey-winch that was used to haul the boats ashore.

The beach is a beaut: long and sandy, offering good swimming (safe shallows for children) and other salty activities such as rockpooling, fishing and windsurfing. Beyond the beach are views west to Te Waewae Bay and the peaks of Fiordland beyond. If you're particularly lucky, you may see the Hector's dolphins which are known to pass by.

Tucked behind the dunes, the camp area is confined to a narrow strip of grass, garnering a small degree of protection from the prevailing winds. There's a spring water spigot, two long-drop toilets and rubbish bins. No shelter, no power, no playground, no phone. This is a fair-weather camping spot with raw, natural appeal.

It's also free and on private land. Please return the owner's kindness by treating it with respect.

THINGS TO SEE AND DO AROUND TE WAEWAE BAY

HUNT FOR TREASURE ON OREPUKI'S GEMSTONE BEACH

Once a thriving goldmining settlement, Orepuki today sports little more than a wild and woolly beach (with excellent surf, but bring a *thick* wetsuit), sandstone cliffs and trees bent at right angles by the relentless, salt-laden winds. The gold may be long gone, but the beach may yet yield some booty. Storms and tides keep the beach in constant flux — one day sand, the next stones — replenishing stocks of semi-precious gemstones. 'Jewels' to be found here include the splendidly named hydrogrossular, orbicular jasper, garnet sands, rodingite quartz, epidote, idocrase and even the odd sapphire. Get fossicking! Orepuki is approximately 2 km north of Monkey Island on State Highway 99.

VISIT SOUTHLAND'S 'RIVIERA'

As suggested by this somewhat exaggerated moniker, Riverton is indeed worth a visit and makes a good stopping point between Invercargill and Monkey Island. Sitting astride the Jacobs River estuary, it's a pretty wee town, one of the oldest in New Zealand. Mores Reserve (follow the signs along Bay Road to Riverton Rocks) overlooking the town has some cracker views, particularly from the lookout towards Colac Bay, and on the coastal loop track to Howells Point. Back in town, take a wander down Palmerston Street and poke your nose into a couple of galleries, before heading to Te Hikoi museum to learn about the area's history. Oh, and don't forget to get a picture of yourself with the town's giant paua shell . . . it's right up there with Ohakune's carrot.

HAUL YOURSELF OVER THE HUMP RIDGE TRACK

Opened in 2001, this 53 km, three-day walk has already established a reputation as one of the best in the land. It's not difficult to see why, with its unique combination of beach, bush and alpine scenery. The second day's walk along the Hump Ridge itself provides eye-popping panoramas over Te Waewae Bay, the wilderness of Fiordland National Park and out to Stewart Island. Along the way, you'll stay at a couple of rather salubrious lodges — well, at least compared to your tent or the average DOC hut. The track was conceived and built by the local community and is run by a charitable trust. A maximum of 5000 people are allowed on the track each year, which is a lot less than the Great Walks. Bookings are, therefore, essential. Visit www.humpridgetrack.co.nz for more details.

LEFT: Te Waewae Bay and Monkey Island

601 Waikawa–Curio Bay Road, Catins Coast, 89 km east of Invercargill, 6 km south of Waikawa

Contact
03 246 8897
valwhyte@hotmail.com

Capacity
75 unpowered / 23 powered

Open
all year

Bookings
not required

Price
$15 for two people unpowered;
$25 for two people powered

This holiday park shares its home with not only one of the best examples of a petrified forest in the world, but also the endangered Hector's dolphin and one of the world's rarest penguins, the yellow-eyed penguin or hoiho.

Stretching from Waipapa Point in the south to just beyond Kaka Point in the north, on the coastal route between Invercargill and Dunedin, is the enchanting southeast corner of Southland known as the Catlins. It was named after the whaling captain Edward Cattlin, who was alleged to have bought more than five million acres of land from local Maori for £30 and some muskets in 1840 (a sale that was later challenged by the Land Claims Commission). It's a sleepy part of New Zealand, with low population and spartan services, but between its beautiful forest remnants, stunning coastal scenery and abundant wildlife, the Catlins is a unique and special place to visit.

Towards the south of the region, the aptly named Curio Bay just begs to be visited, particularly by campers who get to stay in the bay's best spot. Indeed, very seldom does a campsite offer such wonders on its doorstep, for this holiday park shares its home with not only one of the best examples of a petrified forest in the world, but also the endangered Hector's dolphin and one of the world's rarest penguins, the yellow-eyed penguin or hoiho.

The campsite is situated at the end of Porpoise Bay, lying back to back with Curio Bay (the much smaller of the two), on a strip of land which halts abruptly at a high, rocky promontory. Among a maze of house-high flax are secluded cul de sacs where tents and vans can be secreted, sheltered from the ever-present breeze. There are nearly 100 sites, but you'd never know it.

When we last visited, the amenities remained very basic: a tiny kitchen and laundry, flush toilets and couple of rough showers. However, moves are afoot to upgrade the facilities. In the meantime, the place to assemble your picnic dinner is the shelter overlooking Porpoise Bay. Recycling facilities are available.

Friendly hosts Steve and Val run the camp and the shop, which sells absolute essentials such as hot pies and Deep South ice cream. A small selection of groceries is also available, most useful in these parts. Steve and Val will happily provide you with local information, too.

VISIT A JURASSIC PARK

Curio Bay is justifiably famous for its 160-million-year-old petrified forest — one of the world's best examples. Buried by volcanic activity and river sediment, this ancient forest was then uplifted and now lies conveniently in view at the tidal boundary (best viewed at low tide). Wave action has eroded away the layers of sandstone and clay exposing solidified tree stumps and logs, and fossilised fern fronds and leaves in the mudstone rocks. It's forest, Jim, but not as we know it. And if this doesn't rock your socks off, what about that incredible swirling kelp?

WATCH THE WORLD'S SMALLEST DOLPHINS SURF

One the world's most endangered dolphin species, Hector's dolphins are believed to number just over 7000. As the name suggests, Porpoise Bay is one of their favourite hangouts, and with luck on your side you may see them close to shore — they are very fond of a frolic in the bay's breakers. If you're in the water, please don't hassle the dolphins or approach them — they'll come to you if they want to. Signing up to surf school (Catlins Surf, tel 03 246 8552 www.catlins-surf.co.nz) may make you irresistible to them: they're quite fond of checking out surfers' techniques. That's if there are no sharks around . . .

PHOTONEWZEALAND / HARLEY BETTS, HEDGEHOG HOUSE

SPOT THE WORLD'S CUTEST PENGUIN

The yellow-eyed penguin certainly is one beguiling creature. What is it that makes it so irresistible even to the most casual twitcher as it waddles ashore from a day's fishing? Travel writer Derek Grzelewski sums it up pretty well, citing their 'humanoid posture, the Chaplinesque gait, the immaculate dress code contrasted with a peroxide coiffure.' Several nest in Curio Bay, so arm yourself with some patience and commence viewing two hours before dusk: it's hard for these little fellas to schedule their arrival home precisely when they've been as far as 40 km out to sea. Please follow a few rules to avoid spooking these extremely timid birds: keep quiet and out of site, stay out of their nesting areas, never get between them and the sea, and definitely no dogs.

Curio Bay, the Catlins

**Purakaunui Bay Scenic
Reserve, Catlins Coast,
130 km east of Invercargill,
16 km south of Owaka**

Contact
DOC Owaka
03 419 1000
www.doc.govt.nz

Capacity
40 unpowered

Open
all year

Bookings
not required

Price
$6 adult / $3 child

On a tour of the Catlins you may notice a lot of up and down action — a alternation of ridges and valleys inland, and cliffs and sandy bays on the coast. There's a reason for this, and it's all to do with Mesozoic sediment — some of it's hard sandstone and some of it's soft mudstone. They erode at different rates, resulting in extreme landforms such as the craggy Nuggets and the expanse of sand at Surat Bay (see page 217). Purakaunui Bay is a great place to see both landforms toe to toe.

The turn-off to Purakaunui Bay is off State Highway 92 between Papatowai and Owaka (signposted for Ratanui). Follow Purakaunui Falls Road to Long Point Road, then turn left onto Purakaunui Bay Road and follow it to the end. It's 16 km from Owaka, which is the closest place to get fuel and groceries. The last 6 km to the bay were unsealed as we went to print.

One of the Catlins' hidden gems, this bay boasts a delightful white sandy beach flanked to the north by impressive 200 m high cliffs. Being the highest in the Catlins is one of the cliffs' claims to fame; the other is that the computer-generated castle in *The Chronicles of Narnia: The Lion, the Witch and the Wardrobe* was projected upon their tops.

A pretty, grassy flat lies at the centre of the bay, a large part of wich is occupied by the DOC campground, surrounded by lush, sheepy pasture and pockets of native bush. There's little to do here, although you can swim when the surf's off and surf when it's on. Although very popular in the summer holidays, the rest of the year you'll just about get Purakaunui Bay to yourself — a tranquil little piece of paradise.

The campsite has just had a makeover, part of the grounds relandscaped thanks to a fresh dump of topsoil care of the road builders next door (the road and land to the south are private property). By the time you read this book, this will all have bedded down. New composting toilets are as fresh as a daisy, and the water is largely safe to drink (but, as ever, DOC recommends boiling it). There's no shelter, and fees are payable via self-registration envelope.

**LEFT: Jacks Bay, the Catlins
RIGHT: The three-tiered
Purakaunui Falls**

THINGS TO SEE AND DO NEAR PURAKAUNUI BAY

DOC

SNAP THE PURAKAUNUI FALLS

One of the most photogenic of the Catlins' cascades, these falls are reached by a pleasant 10-minute walk on a well-graded track through mature beech forest. The 20 m falls are a lovely sight, pouring over three distinct tiers into their slippery pool. A frame of native bush will set that photo off nicely, and you'll be thankful for the rains if they come — the falls are much more dramatic when they're roaring. If you come back after dark you'll see glow worms here too. To get to the falls from the campground, head back up Purakaunui Bay Road; at the junction turn left into Purakaunui Falls Road and drive for about 5 km. Other falls in the area worth a look include McLean Falls and Matai Falls.

RIDE THE WAVE

Purakaunui is well known for its surf, with pretty reliable left- and right-hand waves to be ridden on the beach break to the south of the bay. (The best wind direction is northwest.) Even on good days there are relatively few surfers and you may even have the sea to yourself. In the winter 'big wave' season, the bay is known to dish up some of the largest and coldest waves in the country. Watch out for rips and dorsal fins.

WALK TO JACK'S BLOWHOLE

This hole was discovered, so the story goes, in 1875 by a local farmer who stumbled across (and nearly into) it when looking for stray stock. Yikes! At over 200 m long and 55 m deep, this bellowing chasm is a true testament to the power of the sea. Over thousands of years, the relentless waves exploited a weakness in the cliff, carving an underground chamber. Eventually the overlying rock collapsed, leaving the gaping rent you see today. Native vegetation grows around the blowhole, which makes a pleasant change in an area dominated by farmland. From the car park, it's a 30-minute walk across private land to get to the blowhole; please respect the farmer's property. The most exciting time to view it is at high tide on a good blowy day — pretty much par for the course in the Catlins. Follow signposts to Jack's Bay from Ratanui or State Highway 92.

One of the Catlins' hidden gems, this bay boasts a delightful white sandy beach flanked to the north by impressive 200 m high cliffs.

**1 Park Lane, Pounawea, Catlins
Coast, 131 km east of Invercargill,
2.5 km southeast of Owaka**

Contact

03 415 8483

pounawea.motor.camp@xtra.co.nz

Capacity

15 unpowered / 37 powered

Open

all year

Bookings

recommended peak season

Price

$11 adult / $5 child (under 5s free) ;
$15 per person / $26 for two

STEPHEN JAQUIERY

The campground at Pounawea is indisputably one of the authors' favourites, both for its setting, grounds and facilities and for the number of adventures that can be embarked upon in its near surrounds. Translating as 'where waters meet', the tiny settlement of Pounawea lies in the midst of the striking and diverse natural area where the Owaka River flows into the Catlins River estuary before reaching the sea beyond the heads. Pounawea Motor Camp lies on the estuary's edge, from where you can see and hear the waves crashing in, but far enough away to be protected from the full force of the coastal breeze.

This small, family-run campground is almost completely encircled by the Pounawea Scenic Reserve. The grounds are dotted with tall, mature native trees such as kahikatea and miro, while its well-groomed grass is lawn-like underfoot. Some shady nooks may be found — including a couple of choice spots along the estuary edge — as well as plenty of sunny, open area for the heat-seekers.

Bird lovers will be beside themselves here, for proximity to the scenic reserve and estuary means that there are non-stop opportunities to see (and hear) a remarkable variety of birdlife — bellbird, tui, native wood pigeon (or kukupa, as they're known in these parts), kea, spoonbill, grey heron, kingfisher, plover, sandpiper, morepork, tomtit, grey warbler, blackbird and maybe even a godwit. There is also a family of mischievous thrushes, standing by to hoover up your biscuit crumbs in a flash. For this pleasure we have to thank the visionaries who set aside this piece of virgin bush back in the late 1800s — a time when most were twitching for their axes or box of matches rather than the binoculars.

The communal facilities are excellent. The kitchen supplies not only the usual appliances but cupboards full of cutlery, crockery, pots and pans. The toilets are inexplicably stylish and the showers are hot and forceful. The laundry has washers, dryers and a proper washing line. There are also 15 cabins, four of which sit right along the estuary enjoying enviable views.

Commercial campground heaven? This is it.

**LEFT: The settlement of Pounawea, where
the Owaka and Catlins rivers meet
RIGHT: The spectacular Nuggets**

SPOT A BIRD AND HUG A TREE

Go for a walk on one of several short tracks from the edge of the campground — from a 15-minute nature trail to a 45-minute stroll through virgin bush (complete with tree identification displays) and out to the salt marsh (low tide only), where you can look out over the estuary and see if there are any herons or spoonbills noodling about. You can add another half an hour or so to this walk by continuing along to the other end of Park Lane where you can pick up a short bush walk along the Catlins River — another good place to spot birds — before looping back to the campsite via the main drag. A particularly memorable walk early in the morning or late afternoon.

STAND ON ONE OF NEW ZEALAND'S MOST SPECTACULAR HEADLANDS

The Nuggets can be seen up close via a short and easy walk from car park to lighthouse. Here you get a grandstand view out to these rocky islets, dressed in thick, rubbery kelp and adorned with fur seals and the occasional sea lion or elephant seal — bring your binoculars. And if you haven't seen the yellow-eyed penguins yet, you can give it another go at Roaring Bay, accessible from the Nugget Point car park (just follow the signs down to the hide). Your best chance of spotting them is from two hours before dusk. Keep an ear out for their shrill and trumpeting calls: Maori didn't call them hoiho ('noise shouter') for nothing. It will take you about 20 minutes to drive to the Nuggets (and the seaside settlement of Kaka Point) from Pounawea.

SEE A LION

Oops . . . we mean see a sea lion. Not to be confused with the svelte and pointy-nosed fur seal, Hooker's (or New Zealand) sea lions are much bigger, with females weighing in at 100–160 kg, and the big boys topping the scales at almost half a tonne. They've been protected in New Zealand since 1893, after being hunted very nearly to extinction by both Maori and Europeans. They started breeding again on the mainland only in the 1990s. Around 30 or so of their number call the Catlins Coast home, and Surat Bay is a reliable place to spot them — just a five-minute drive from Pounawea (clearly signposted). It will take up to an hour and a half to walk the length of Surat Bay, and another 15 minutes or so to reach Cannibal Bay across the lupin- and flax-covered dunes. Obey all signs — those sea lions sure can get tetchy.

OTHER CAMPGROUNDS IN FIORDLAND AND SOUTHLAND

CATLINS

CATLINS MCLEAN FALLS MOTELS AND HOLIDAY PARK
29 Rewcastle Road (off Chaslands Highway), Catlins
Contact: 03 415 8338
info@catlinsnz.com
www.catlinsnz.com
Tariff: $35–175

KESWICK PARK CAMPING GROUND
Pounawea Road, RD 1, Owaka
Contact: 03 419 1110
pounawea@ihug.co.nz
Tariff: $20–90

NEWHAVEN HOLIDAY PARK
Surat Bay, Newhaven Road, RD 1, Owaka
Contact: 03 415 8834
newhaven@ihug.co.nz
www.newhavenholiday.com
Tariff: $25–95

THOMAS'S CATLINS LODGE AND HOLIDAY PARK
Cnr Clark and Ryley Streets, Owaka, Catlins Coast
Contact: 03 415 8333
stay@thomascatlins.co.nz
www.thomascatlins.co.nz
Tariff: $50–145

FIORDLAND

FIORDLAND GREAT VIEWS HOLIDAY PARK
Milford Road, Te Anau
Contact: 03 249 7059
fiordland.holiday.park@xtra.co.nz
www.fiordlandgreatviewsholidaypark.co.nz
Tariff: $13–120

MANAPOURI MOTELS AND HOLIDAY PARK
86 Cathedral Drive, Manapouri
Contact: 03 249 6624
manapourimotels@clear.net.nz
www.manapourimotels.co.nz
Tariff: $28–115

POSSUM LODGE MOTELS AND HOLIDAY PARK
Murrell Ave, Manapouri
Contact: 03 249 6623
possumlodge@xtra.co.nz
www.possumlodge.co.nz
Tariff: $30–95

TE ANAU GREAT LAKES HOLIDAY PARK
Cnr Luxmore Dr and Milford Road, Te Anau
Contact: 03 249 8538
www.teanaugreatlakes.co.nz
Tariff: $15–105

TE ANAU TOP 10 HOLIDAY PARK
128 Te Anau Tce, Te Anau
Contact: 03 249 7462
fivestar@teanautop10.co.nz
www.TeAnauTop10.co.nz
Tariff: $36–170

SOUTHLAND

AMBLE ON INN HOLIDAY PARK
145 Chesney Street, Invercargill
Contact: 03 216 5214
ambleoninn@xtra.co.nz
www.ambleoninn.co.nz
Tariff: $30–120

BEACH ROAD HOLIDAY PARK
375 Dunns Road (5 km past airport), Otatara, Invercargill
Contact: 03 213 0400
beach-road@paradise.net.nz
www.beachroadholidaypark.co.nz
Tariff: $20–65

BLUFF MOTOR CAMP
Gregory Street (off Marine Pde), Bluff
Contact: 027 626 2018
Tariff: $20–32

DOLAMORE PARK CAMP
Croydon Bush Road, off Kingdon Road, 10km off SH 94, Southland
Contact: 03 208 6896
Tariff: $6

GORE MOTOR CAMP
35 Broughton Street (off SH 1), Gore
Contact: 03 208 4919
gorecamp@xtra.co.nz
Tariff: $28–85

INVERCARGILL TOP 10 HOLIDAY PARK
77 McIvor Road
Contact: 03 215 9032
info@invercargilltop10.co.nz
www.invercargilltop10.co.nz
Tariff: $30–105

LONGWOOD HOLIDAY PARK
43 Richard Street, Riverton

Contact: 03 234 8132
lex.wylie@xtra.co.nz

Tariff: $25–75

LORNEVILLE HOLIDAY PARK
352 Lorneville–Dacre Road
(SH 98), RD 6, Invercargill

Contact: 03 235 8031
lornepark@xtra.co.nz
www.lornevilleholidaypark.co.nz

Tariff: $28–95

MOSSBURN COUNTRY PARK
333 Mossburn–Five Rivers Road,
Mossburn

Contact: 03 248 6444
info@mossburncountrypark.co.nz

Tariff: $13–50

TIMBER TOPS MOTOR PARK
209 Tweed Street, Invercargill

Contact: 03 214 2226
mikeheywood@xtra.co.nz

Tariff: $25–30

WAIKAIA MOTOR CAMP
Scotswood Street, Waikaia

Contact: 03 202 7817

Tariff: $8–20

North Island

Travelling Times and Distances

To find the distance and time needed to travel between, for example, Thames and Hicks Bay, put one finger on the name Thames and the other on the name Hicks Bay. Move sideways along the chart from Thames and upwards from Hicks Bay. Where they meet you'll see the distance between them is 414km and the travelling time is 7 hours 50 minutes. This time is for a driver travelling at 80-100 km/h on open stretches, with a small allowance for traffic delays, petrol stops and refreshments.

Times courtesy of the Ministry of Transport.

South Island

Travelling Times and Distances

To find the distance and time needed to travel between, for example, Haast and Timaru, put one finger on the name Haast and the other on the name Timaru. Move down the chart from Haast and across from Timaru. Where they meet you'll see the distance between them is 418km and the travelling time is 8 hours 10 minutes. This time is for a driver travelling at 80-100 km/h on open stretches, with a small allowance for traffic delays, petrol stops and refreshments.

Times courtesy of the Ministry of Transport.

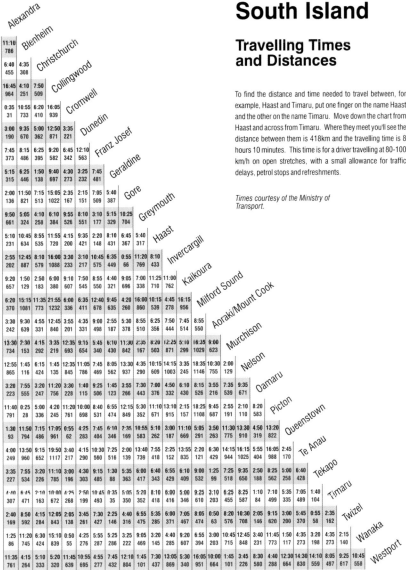

	Alexandra	Blenheim	Christchurch	Collingwood	Cromwell	Dunedin	Franz Josef	Geraldine	Gore	Greymouth	Haast	Invercargill	Kaikoura	Milford Sound	Aoraki/Mount Cook	Murchison	Nelson	Oamaru	Picton	Queenstown	Te Anau	Tekapo	Timaru	Twizel	Wanaka
Blenheim	11:10 / 786																								
Christchurch	6:40 / 455	4:35 / 308																							
Collingwood	16:45 / 964	4:10 / 251	7:50 / 509																						
Cromwell	0:35 / 31	10:55 / 733	6:20 / 410	16:05 / 939																					
Dunedin	3:00 / 190	9:35 / 670	5:00 / 362	12:50 / 871	3:35 / 221																				
Franz Josef	7:45 / 373	8:15 / 486	6:25 / 395	9:20 / 582	6:45 / 342	12:10 / 563																			
Geraldine	5:15 / 315	6:25 / 446	1:50 / 138	9:40 / 697	4:30 / 273	3:25 / 232	7:45 / 481																		
Gore	2:00 / 136	11:50 / 821	7:15 / 513	15:05 / 1022	2:35 / 167	2:15 / 151	7:05 / 509	5:40 / 387																	
Greymouth	9:50 / 661	5:05 / 324	4:10 / 258	6:10 / 384	9:55 / 526	8:10 / 551	3:10 / 177	5:15 / 329	10:25 / 704																
Haast	5:10 / 231	10:45 / 634	8:55 / 535	11:55 / 720	4:15 / 200	9:35 / 421	2:20 / 148	8:10 / 431	6:45 / 367	5:40 / 317															
Invercargill	2:55 / 202	12:45 / 887	8:10 / 579	16:00 / 1088	3:30 / 233	3:10 / 217	10:45 / 575	6:35 / 449	0:55 / 66	11:20 / 769	8:10 / 433														
Kaikoura	9:20 / 657	1:50 / 129	2:50 / 183	6:00 / 380	9:10 / 607	7:50 / 545	8:55 / 550	4:40 / 321	9:05 / 696	7:00 / 338	11:25 / 710	11:00 / 762													
Milford Sound	6:20 / 370	15:15 / 1081	11:35 / 773	21:55 / 1232	6:00 / 336	6:35 / 411	12:40 / 678	9:45 / 635	4:20 / 260	16:00 / 860	10:15 / 539	4:45 / 278	16:15 / 956												
Aoraki/Mount Cook	3:30 / 242	9:30 / 639	4:55 / 331	12:45 / 840	3:55 / 201	4:35 / 331	9:00 / 498	2:55 / 187	5:30 / 378	8:55 / 510	6:25 / 356	7:50 / 444	7:45 / 514	8:55 / 550											
Murchison	13:30 / 734	2:30 / 153	4:15 / 292	3:35 / 219	12:35 / 693	9:15 / 654	5:45 / 340	6:10 / 430	11:30 / 842	2:35 / 167	8:20 / 503	12:25 / 871	5:10 / 299	16:35 / 1029	9:00 / 623										
Nelson	12:55 / 865	1:45 / 116	6:15 / 424	1:45 / 135	12:35 / 845	11:05 / 786	7:45 / 469	8:05 / 562	13:30 / 937	4:35 / 290	10:15 / 609	14:15 / 1003	3:35 / 245	18:35 / 1146	10:30 / 755	2:00 / 129									
Oamaru	3:20 / 223	7:55 / 555	3:20 / 247	11:20 / 756	3:30 / 228	1:40 / 115	9:25 / 506	1:45 / 123	3:55 / 266	7:30 / 443	7:00 / 376	4:50 / 332	6:10 / 430	8:15 / 526	3:55 / 216	7:35 / 539	9:35 / 671								
Picton	11:40 / 791	0:25 / 28	5:00 / 336	4:20 / 245	11:20 / 761	10:00 / 698	8:40 / 531	6:55 / 474	12:15 / 849	5:30 / 352	11:10 / 671	13:10 / 915	2:15 / 157	18:25 / 1108	9:45 / 687	2:55 / 191	2:10 / 110	8:20 / 583							
Queenstown	1:30 / 93	11:50 / 794	7:15 / 486	17:05 / 961	0:55 / 62	4:25 / 283	7:45 / 404	6:10 / 346	2:35 / 169	10:55 / 583	5:10 / 262	3:00 / 187	11:10 / 669	5:05 / 291	3:50 / 263	11:30 / 775	13:30 / 910	4:50 / 319	13:20 / 822						
Te Anau	4:00 / 249	13:50 / 960	9:15 / 652	19:50 / 1117	3:40 / 217	4:15 / 290	10:30 / 560	7:25 / 516	2:00 / 139	13:40 / 739	7:55 / 418	2:25 / 152	13:55 / 835	2:20 / 121	6:30 / 429	14:15 / 944	16:15 / 1025	5:55 / 404	16:05 / 988	2:45 / 170					
Tekapo	3:35 / 227	7:55 / 534	3:20 / 226	11:10 / 785	3:00 / 196	4:30 / 303	9:15 / 485	1:30 / 88	5:35 / 363	6:00 / 417	6:40 / 343	6:55 / 429	6:10 / 409	9:00 / 532	1:25 / 99	7:25 / 518	9:35 / 650	5:00 / 188	8:25 / 562	5:00 / 258	6:40 / 428				
Timaru	4:40 / 307	6:45 / 471	2:10 / 163	10:00 / 672	4:25 / 268	2:50 / 199	10:45 / 493	0:35 / 35	5:05 / 350	5:20 / 352	8:10 / 418	6:00 / 416	5:00 / 346	9:25 / 610	3:10 / 203	6:25 / 455	8:25 / 587	1:10 / 84	7:10 / 499	5:35 / 335	7:05 / 489	1:40 / 104			
Twizel	2:40 / 169	8:50 / 592	4:15 / 284	12:05 / 843	2:05 / 138	3:45 / 261	7:30 / 427	2:25 / 146	4:40 / 316	6:55 / 475	5:35 / 285	6:00 / 371	7:00 / 467	8:20 / 474	0:50 / 63	8:20 / 576	10:30 / 708	2:00 / 146	8:20 / 620	3:00 / 200	5:45 / 370	0:55 / 58	2:35 / 162		
Wanaka	1:25 / 86	11:20 / 745	6:30 / 424	15:10 / 839	0:50 / 55	4:25 / 276	5:55 / 287	5:25 / 286	3:25 / 222	9:05 / 469	3:20 / 145	4:40 / 285	9:20 / 607	6:55 / 394	3:00 / 203	10:45 / 715	12:45 / 848	3:40 / 231	11:45 / 773	1:50 / 117	4:35 / 273	3:20 / 198	4:35 / 273	2:15 / 140	
Westport	11:35 / 761	4:15 / 264	5:10 / 333	5:20 / 320	11:45 / 639	10:55 / 695	4:55 / 277	7:45 / 432	12:10 / 804	1:45 / 101	7:30 / 437	13:05 / 869	10:00 / 340	/ 951	/ 664	1:45 / 101	3:45 / 226	8:30 / 580	4:40 / 288	12:30 / 664	14:30 / 830	14:10 / 559	8:05 / 497	9:25 / 617	10:45 / 558

ACKNOWLEDGEMENTS

The authors would like to thank all the i-SITE and DOC staff, and community organisations who have helped them on their New Zealand travels over the last 10 years. They also acknowledge the kind assistance of Jenny Allan and Reece Miller, Natacha Anthoni and Jason Hobman, the Bennett family, Robert Chisholm, Edwina Clarke and Richard Saunders, Mez Cooper, Grant Dyson, Paddy and Janine Niccol, the Parsons and Paul families, Barry Payne, Betty Ruffell, Joe and Daphne Slater, the Parklands' Smiths, Roger Smith and Mary Varnham.

Thanks also to the team at Random House, particularly Rebecca Lal, Sue Lewis and Sarah Ell.

ABOUT THE AUTHORS

Sarah Bennett and Lee Slater are co-authors of *The Best of Wellington* and *Don't Forget Your Scroggin: A How-to Handbook for New Zealand Tramping*. Sarah is also co-author of Lonely Planet's New Zealand guide.

Lee Slater and Sarah Bennett have camped from Orkney to Cornwall in the UK, from Shenandoah to Joshua Tree in the United States, and through the back-country and road-ends in Aotearoa. During these adventures their trusty Vaude tent has been pawed at by a black bear, sprayed by a skunk and torn to shreds by a Haumoana moggy (thank goodness for duct tape).

WEBSITES

AA Travel
(www.aatravel.co.nz)

A great one-stop online travel resource, covering accommodation, travel times and distances, activities and attractions, dining, shopping, and travel insurance. The AA has an extensive network of local area offices offering guidebooks, maps and local and national advice.

Department of Conservation
(www.doc.govt.nz)

The government organisation charged with conserving New Zealand's natural and historic heritage. Its website provides extensive information on our national parks, conservation areas, tracks and walks, campgrounds and huts, the country's flora, fauna and cultural heritage, and environmental management.

New Zealand Motor
Caravan Association
(www.nzmca.org.nz)

An association fostering and advancing the motorhome movement, promoting fellowship, vehicle safety, road courtesy and protection of the environment. Membership provides discounts, custom insurance schemes, a bi-monthly magazine and a useful travel directory.

Holiday Parks Association
of New Zealand
(www.holidayparks.co.nz)

The industry association for commercial holiday parks. Its website includes a downloadable directory of member holiday parks.

New Zealand Freedom Camping
Forum (www.camping.org.nz)

The 'Camping Our Way, Love NZ' website launched by the New Zealand Freedom Camping Forum to develop and encourage best practices for those pitching tents or parking campervans and caravans outside designated campgrounds.

BOOKS

Don't Forget Your Scroggin. A How-to Handbook for New Zealand Tramping, Sarah Bennett and Lee Slater (Craig Potton Publishing, 2007)

AA Great Kiwi Road Trips, Donna Blaber (The New Zealand Automobile Association Incorporated, 2007)

I Love You New Zealand: 101 Must-Do's for Kiwis, edited by John McCrystal (Random House New Zealand, 2007)

Landforms: The Shaping of New Zealand, Les Molloy and Roger Smith (Craig Potton Publishing, 2002)

Lonely Planet New Zealand (Lonely Planet Publications)

New Zealand's Wilderness Heritage, Les Molloy and Craig Potton (Craig Potton Publishing, 2007)

Reed Day Walks series (Reed Publishing)

The Geographic Atlas of New Zealand, GeographX (Craig Potton Publishing, revised edition 2009)

The Reed Field Guide to New Zealand Birds, Geoff Moon (Reed Publishing, 1998)

INDEX